C000125697

Once upon a Time

Once upon a Time
Myth, Fairy Tales and Legends in Margaret Atwood's Writings

Edited by

Sarah A. Appleton

Cambridge Scholars Publishing

Once upon a Time: Myth, Fairy Tales and Legends in Margaret Atwood's Writings,
Edited by Sarah A. Appleton

This book first published 2008

Cambridge Scholars Publishing

12 Back Chapman Street, Newcastle upon Tyne, NE6 2XX, UK

British Library Cataloguing in Publication Data
A catalogue record for this book is available from the British Library

Copyright © 2008 by Sarah A. Appleton and contributors

All rights for this book reserved. No part of this book may be reproduced, stored in a retrieval system,
or transmitted, in any form or by any means, electronic, mechanical, photocopying, recording or
otherwise, without the prior permission of the copyright owner.

ISBN (10): 1-84718-684-X, ISBN (13): 9781847188643

TABLE OF CONTENTS

ACKNOWLEDGMENTS

I am grateful for the encouragement given to me by my institution, Old Dominion University, and especially to the former chair of the English Department, David Metzger. My gratitude is also given to the Women's Studies Department at William & Mary College for granting me a visiting scholar's appointment. Others who deserve recognition include Timothy Bostic, Tracy Jewett, Jacqueline Sweeton, my children Sam and Jill, Evan Aguiar, and, as ever, my husband Mitchell Bonnett. Most of all, my warm regards and appreciation go to the extraordinary contributors to this volume whose warmth, wit, and wisdom made this a very enjoyable project indeed.

INTRODUCTION

SARAH A. APPLETON

While it is often acknowledged that Margaret Atwood's novels are rife with allusions from the oral tradition of myth, legends, fables, and fairy tales, the implications of her liberal usage bear study. From the figure of Little Red Riding Hood in *The Handmaid's Tale*, to the retelling of the *Odyssey* in *The Penelopiad*, Atwood's novels re-scrutinize the common assumptions behind the tales and re-conceptualize the feminine and masculine archetypes derived from these narratives. From—in particular —a Jungian perspective, the archetypes no longer hold power; in fact, the traditional figures —i.e., the virginal maiden, the wicked stepmother, the heroic champion, the wise old woman —come unbound from their rigid restrictions, gaining depth and dimension in Atwood's portrayals.

In his work, *The Uses of Enchantment: The Meaning and Importance of Fairy Tales*, Bruno Bettelheim contends, "nothing can be as enriching and satisfying to child *and adult alike* as the folk fairy tale" (5, my emphasis). He further allows that

> myths and fairy tales were derived from, or give symbolic interpretation to, initiation rites or other rites de passage—such as a metaphoric death of an old, inadequate self in order to be reborn on a higher plane of existence. (35)

These rites of passage, while often equated with the maturation process of a child, also invigorate passages in adulthood, providing models of continuing development on levels ranging from spirituality to psychology. The prevalence of myths, legends, and fairy tales in contemporary women's fiction, then, signals familiar territory for readers as remembrances from childhood reading are re-infused with adult challenges and choices, as well as old wisdom for a new world. As Sharon Rose Wilson contends, "A re-visioned fairy-tale sexual politics underlies Atwood's aesthetics and is evident from her earliest to her most recent work, including her fiction, poetry, essays, and visual art" (*"Fairy-Tale"*

6). Indeed, Margaret Atwood's writings contain a stunning array of references from these archetypal tales and legends.

Jack Zipes notes that for the original literary, that is, written, versions of the fairy tales, the readers were adults: "In most European countries it was not until the end of the eighteenth and early part of the twentieth centuries that fairy tales were published for children" (14). He states that the children's versions were "sanitized and expurgated versions of the fairy tales for adults" (14). In Atwood's use of fairy tales, legends, and myths, she restores the context of the stories to adulthood, relying on the juxtaposition of childhood reading expectations against the realities of complex maturity. That is, the heroine is not likely to be rescued by a dashing prince or benevolent god; the crone's "evil curse" may actually be masked munificence.

In an interview, Atwood stated,

> Myths mean stories, and traditional myths mean traditional stories that have been repeated frequently. The term doesn't pertain to Greek myths alone. Grimm's Fairy Tales are just as much myth or story as anything else" (Hammond 114).

It is these oft-repeated tales from throughout the ages that bring recognition to readers, whether the tales maintain their original trapping or they have been re-visioned with old lessons in new clothing. In addition, as Wilson so aptly notes,

> In deconstructing her fairy-tale and mythic intertexts, allowing the muted or silenced subtext to speak, Atwood's metanarratives consist of more than two narrative strands interwoven in dialectic with one another: the frame narrative (always more than a revised version of the traditional fairy-tale) and the 'embroidered' intertexts usually heightened, exaggerated, or parodied. ("Fairy-Tale" 31)

Thus, Atwood's writings are never simple revisions of its intertexts; as Wilson recognizes, the tales are enmeshed with other intertexts, inverted, enhanced and undermined, doubled, interrogated, and often confirmed in surprising fashion.

Atwood, as she relates in her essay, "Grimm's' Remembered," preferred the "unexpurgated" versions of the tales —the adult versions — when she was a child, convincing her parents to allow her to read the book they were concerned about. She relates, "I expect my parents gnawed their nails while their adored children read about pieces of bodies falling down the chimney, Godfather Death, and other horrors" (291). Yet, Atwood confessed that the book she read most frequently in her lifetime was indeed Grimm's' Fairy Tales (Atwood "Most" 43) and that it was "the most influential book" she ever read (Sandler 46). In these tales there are bloody corpses, greed, abundant immorality, and very little sugar coating. The stepsisters of Cinderella cut off pieces of their feet and have their eyes pecked out by birds. In some versions, Sleeping Beauty does not awaken until after she has had children, and, unlike the blissful ending of Disney's *The Little Mermaid*, Hans Christian Andersen's mermaid does not marry the prince. Instead, she dies a lonely, if sacrificial death. Fathers sell their daughters, mothers attempt to murder their children, and siblings often betray each other. Likewise, in myth, the age-old idea that good always triumphs over evil is also rarely in evidence. Dido's soul is only freed from agony when the goddess Iris allows her to die. Penelope, the faithful wife, is tortured by gossip of her husband's infidelities. Nymphs are raped, mortals are abused by gods and goddesses at their unfathomable whim, and earthly freedoms are granted or denied at will.[1]

In Jungian archetypal theory, the archetype is often split into a positive type and a negative type. Children's versions of myths and tales are notorious for their rigid adherence to these binary types. Virtuous virgins, brave princes, wicked witches, and wise old men populate the pages, with an occasional amoral trickster thrown in. However, adult versions, as noted above, present much more complicated characters. For example, wise old women can perform both good and evil. The witch in "Rapunzel" can be seen as imprisoning a young woman; however, she may be attempting to shelter her adopted child from the evils of the world. The fool may be the wisest of them all; Jack, of the beanstalk, manages to enrich himself and his mother, as well as outwit and slay a supernatural being. In the "unexpurgated" versions, the characters rarely maintain static dimensions; they are often "doubled," that is, they are many-layered, multi-dimensional beings who possess both positive and negative qualities, both good and evil dimensions.

True to the theorized original purposes of the stories, Atwood's narratives often serve—at least partially—as cautionary tales; however, Atwood's tales do not succumb to the perhaps easy wisdom of one-dimensional fables. For instance, in *The Robber Bride*, Zenia is both wicked witch and fairy godmother.[2] In *The Handmaid's Tale*, Offred is both temptress and virginal, and in *Cat's Eye*, Elaine is victim and victimizer. In fact, not one of Atwood's many, many protagonists can be characterized as either wholly moral or irredeemably immoral. Likewise, in the adult fairy tales, the protagonists are free characters as well. These "sinister little stories," as Sullivan contends, contain powerful ambiguities such a magic and fear, but also princesses with "intelligence, cleverness, and perseverance" (35-36). Atwood recalls, "The women in these stories are not the passive zombies they would later become in the sanitized versions" (36). The tales are indeed laced with characters that overcome the stereotypes and generally transform into better selves. The simpleton son outwits the ogre or witch and ends up marrying the King's daughter; the clever maiden accomplishes her Herculean tasks; the child escapes unspeakable evil.

Of importance, as Wilson contends, "in fairy tales, myths, and Atwood's texts, transformation is not always positive; generally, at the end of an Atwood text, transformation has just begun" (*Fairy-Tale* 21). In essence, in many of the female centered fairy tales, the transformation is a journey to and beyond the maturation process; that is, many of the tales relate the transformations to and between maiden, mother, and crone. The maiden's stories center on her purity and worthiness, the mother's positive stories—though rare—center on the protection of her child and the fulfillment of her mate, and her jealousy and impediment to maturity if she is negative; and the crone's stories tend to focus on survival and wisdom if she is a positive type, but her depravity if she is not. Not surprisingly, the majority of the tales relate the transformation from childhood to adult. Snow White transforms from little girl to marriageable maiden, though her stepmother attempts to murder her with the very accoutrements of feminine maturation: a corset, hair combs, and finally the biblical apple—the fruit of the tree of knowledge, in this case, adult carnal knowledge.

Many of Atwood's heroines have failed to undergo necessary transformations. For example, the three middle-aged protagonists of *The Robber Bride*—Tony, Charis, and Roz—have not succeeded in maturing. Tony is a perpetual child, Charis is a dreamy teenager, and Roz—the most motherly of them—cannot move beyond the young wife/mother mode. Likewise, Atwood's first male protagonist, Jimmy, in *Oryx and Crake*, has failed to achieve maturity. In fact, Atwood's frequent choice to portray inadequately integrated adult individuals is underscored by her use of transitional narrative types such as the fairy tales, myths, and legends.

*****

The essays in this volume have been written by some of the most influential Atwood scholars internationally, each exploring Atwood's use of primal, indeed archetypal, narratives to illuminate her fiction and poetry. These essays interact with all types of such narratives, from the aforementioned fairy tales and legends, to Greek, Roman, Biblical, and pagan mythologies, to contemporary processes of myth and tale creation.

While both Sarah Appleton and Carol Osborne discuss the importance of myth in *Oryx and Crake*, Sarah's essay focuses on the incorporation of apocryphal tales of extinction in her essay, "Myths of Distinction; Myths of Extinction Margaret Atwood's *Oryx and Crake*," and Carol's essay, "Mythmaking in Margaret Atwood's *Oryx and Crake*," identifies multi-levels of mythmaking.

Sarah Appleton writes not only of the plentiful allusions in the novel to other dystopian fictions such, as George Orwell's *1984,* but she also posits that Snowman's/Jimmy's experiences in *Oryx and Crake* may possibly be explained as his own fantasy, that is, his own extinction myth, self-created by the narrator to shield himself from an inhospitable existence. Thus, in his return journey to the Paradice Dome, Jimmy may be undergoing a process of reintegrating his psyche. She writes, "Indeed, Crake and Oryx may represent portions of his own psyche: superego and id, shadow and anima, mind and soul, thanatos and eros." In the end, then, his up-in-the-air decision to contact other human survivors or destroy them might be read as a decision of whether to accept reality or not.

Carol Osborne contends that Atwood explores the role of mythmaking on many levels from the protagonist and narrator's "therapeutic piecing together of his own story" to Atwood's strategy for creating a dystopian myth and the invitation for the readers themselves to "participate in the storytelling process." In her analysis, Osborne—unlike Appleton—sees the novel as realist rather than an individual's delusions; yet, she too sees a process of psychological reintegration occurring, as well as a healthy maturation process for the narrator.

Shannon Hengen's essay on the staging of *The Penelopiad* uses reviews from the cabaret show, as well as a blog from one of the production's cast members, to indicate the viable resonance of the oral tradition and myths with contemporary audiences. She writes,

> Paradoxically, in fashioning anew tales from ancient Greece, Atwood's imagination captures contemporary Canada and to a degree the UK in a most visceral and immediate way.

By invoking and recording the means by which an ancient myth may continue to inform and even delight an audience, Hengen relates the success of the staging of Atwood's re-invigorated tale.

Working also with *The Penelopiad*, Coral Ann Howells proclaims that "a whiff of scandal surrounds Atwood's woman-centered revision of *The Odyssey,*" noting how Atwood has reworked the classic, male-centered epic into a "domesticated" tale; yet, this tale is also dominated by "ghosts," the long silenced females of myth. Howells realizes that Atwood "has invented a vividly realized female community that was barely acknowledged by Homer."

Sharon Wilson's essay, Fairy Tales, Myths, and Magic Photographs in Atwood's *The Blind Assassin*, discusses the effect of photographs in the novel, concluding that

> through her magical realism and her embedded fairy tale and mythic intertexts, Atwood's novels thus record eras in meticulous detail, ironically erasing an objective reality as it is posited, and create verbal "photographs" all the more magical for calling attention to their subjective 'tints.'

Therefore, these "magic" photographs—both visual and verbal—operate at a similar level as myth itself with the ability to question time, history, and even storytelling.

Karen Stein reviews an older novel, *Life Before Man*, and discovers

> Through their emerging links with the green world of nature and the great turning cycle of the year, the characters at least temporarily find hope, experience positive emotions, and may grow closer toward their full stature as whole, feeling persons.

Stein finds a cyclical structure that pervades the novel, one that relies on ancient and native myths to explain time, fertility in relationships, and regeneration.

Theodore Sheckels' essay, No Princes Here: Male Characters in Margaret Atwood's Fiction, examines a multitude of male characters from Atwood's novels. He posits a pattern of failed princes in the texts, finding that these characters "play the prince in counterpoint to the distressed woman. Or they try to." Unlike their fairy tale equivalents, however, Atwood's "princes" suffer from human tendencies that may dilute their potential mythical aspirations.

In a nice inversion, Shuli Barzilai's essay, instead of finding the myth within the narrative, assesses the truth within Margaret Atwood's short fable, "Thylacine Ragout." Minutely researching the fate of the thylacine, or Tasmanian tiger as well as indigenous peoples, Barzilai notes that Atwood's fable is rooted more in the actual dangers of extinction, than in a simple morality tale.

In this volume's last essay, Kathryn VanSpanckeren examines an Atwood poem, "Half-Hanged Mary," through its many drafts and revisions to uncover a poetic mythmaking process. She contends that the poem "draws together crucial recurring themes" such as "uncanny women, patriarchal violence against females, female struggles for survival and autonomous identity." The poem ultimately constructs "a mythical paradigm for women that may subtly interrogate the traditional Christian message of sacrifice and forgiveness." VanSpanckeren contends that "the poem suggests that Christ's story of faith, submission and forgiveness is a gendered account that may not work for women."

In fact, as evidenced in this collection, Atwood's use of myths and fairy tales allows for an abundance of old/fresh material for contemporary readers. By reconciling, yet by also revisioning, the archetypal motifs, characters, and narratives, Atwood presents a familiar, yet unique, reading experience.

Notes

[1] Rosemary Sullivan, Atwood's biographer, relates the importance of mythology to the fledgling writer and the questions Atwood may have had in regard to the "muse" (106-110).

[2] Likewise, Madeleine Davies states that in *The Blind Assassin*, "Iris's aging body allows her to indulge in one of her favorite identities as a sinister witch or malevolent fairy godmother" (68).

Works Cited

Atwood, Margaret. *The Blind Assassin*. 2000. New York: Nan A. Talese.

—. Grimms' Remembered" in *The Reception of Grimms' Fairy Tales: Responses, Reactions, Revisions*, 1993. Donald Haase, ed. Detroit: Wayne State UP. 290-292.

—. "Most Influential Book." 12 June 1983. *New York Times Magazine*. 43.

Bettelheim, Bruno. *The Uses of Enchantment: The Meaning and Importance of Fairy Tales*. 1975. New York: Vintage Books.

Cooke, Nathalie. *Margaret Atwood: A Critical Companion*. 2004. Westport, CT: Greenwood P.

Davies, Madeleine. "Margaret Atwood's Female Bodies" 2006. In *The Cambridge Companion to Margaret Atwood*. Coral Ann Howells, ed. Cambridge: Cambridge UP. 58-71.

Hammond, Karla. "Articulating the Mute" 1990. In *Margaret Atwood: Conversations* Earl G. Ingersoll, ed. Princeton, NJ: Ontario Review P, 109-120.

Howells, Coral Ann. *Margaret Atwood*. 2nd ed. 2005. Hampshire: Palgrave MacMillan.

Sandler, Linda. "A Question of Metamorphosis" 1990. In *Margaret Atwood: Conversations* Earl G. Ingersoll, ed. Princeton, NJ: Ontario Review P. 40-57.

Sullivan, Rosemary. *The Red Shoes: Margaret Atwood Starting Out*. 1998. Toronto: HarperCollins.

von Franz, Marie-Louise. *Shadow and Evil in Fairy Tales*. 1974. Zurich: Spring Publications.

Wilson, Sharon. "Blindness and Survival in Margaret Atwood's Major Novels" 2006. In *The Cambridge Companion to Margaret Atwood*. Coral Ann Howells, ed. Cambridge: Cambridge UP. 176-190.

—. *Margaret Atwood's Fairy-Tale Sexual Politics*. 1993. Jackson: UP of Mississippi.

Zipes, Jack. *Fairy Tale as Myth: Myth as Fairy Tale*. 1994. Lexington: The UP of Kentucky.

CHAPTER ONE

MYTHS OF DISTINCTION; MYTHS OF EXTINCTION IN MARGARET ATWOOD'S *ORYX AND CRAKE*

SARAH A. APPLETON

> Whenever contents of the collective unconscious become activated, they have a disturbing effect on the conscious mind, and confusion ensues. If the activation is due to the collapse of the individual's hopes and expectations, there is a danger that the collective unconscious may take the place of reality.
> —Carl Jung, "Psychology and Religion"

In Margaret Atwood's dystopian novel *Oryx and Crake*, the narrator Jimmy (also known as Snowman) tells us an apocalyptic tale of human extinction. An alienated and troubled boy and a disassociated man, Jimmy offers his autobiography as a testament to the catastrophic events that have occurred. In a traditional sense, Jimmy delivers up an ostensible story of survival, a Robinson Crusoe epic. However, similar to many, many of Atwood's narrators and characters,[1] Jimmy's testimony rings with peals of perjury and plagiarism, whether intentionally delivered with the purpose to deceive or not.

Jimmy's alter-ego name, "Snowman," bears analysis, as it is the name he has chosen for himself. Jimmy might be referring to his frozen situation of stasis and his self-proclaimed condition of "Abominable," or he might be alluding to his lack of possible connection now that humanity has been erased. And as such, he could be equating himself with Snow White, hidden in the forest with a contingency of not quite human beings. Another possibility of his renaming of himself considers that he takes his name from Wallace Stevens' poem "The Snow Man." Jimmy tells us he is the existential "no man" of the poem who "beholds/ Nothing that is not there and the nothing that is." Although such a pronouncement may contain connotations of the devastated life of post-Paradice, Jimmy may also be cluing us into the possibility that the world he inhabits does not, in fact, exist; this world may only dwell in his imagination: it is the nothing that is.[2] As countless references in the text to a myriad of dystopian fiction attest, this post-world may have been conjured by Jimmy and composed of fragments of films, books, and video game plots.[3] Moreover, the individuals he holds responsible—Crake and Oryx—may also be mere "shadows," figments of his tortured mind. Indeed, Crake and Oryx may represent portions of his own psyche: superego and id, shadow and anima, mind and soul, thanatos, and eros.

Thomas M. Disch explains the concept of a dystopian novel:

> Dystopias are balancing acts. The best are usually applauded for being 'savagely' satiric, after the fashion of Swift, a novel in which the author continues to pile horror on horror to preposterous and appalling heights. Yet they should never be so preposterous and merely phantasmagoric as to escape the quotidian, accepted awfulness of the here and now. For their sting is in just how snugly the shoe fits. Huxley's beehive of hedonists in *Brave New World* is simply Jazz Age America unmasked, while 1984 is famously 1948 in disguise. (BW03)

Atwood writes that the events of the novel are indeed spawned by ideas that are already in progress in our contemporary world. She contends that *Oryx and Crake* is not science fiction ("It contains no intergalactic space travel, no teleportation, no Martians"); the novel is a work of "speculative fiction"—"it invents nothing we haven't already invented or started to invent" ("Writing").

To offer but a small sampling of the dystopian allusions replete within the narrative, Jimmy's sense of being watched by the corporation/government summons up George Orwell's *1984*, and Atwood's "pigoons" are infused with Orwellian imagery from *Animal Farm*. The sexual complacency of women in *Oryx and Crake* harkens to Huxley's *Brave New World*, as do certain Freudian references, particularly about motherhood. The scientific fabrication of a sentient being has its roots in Mary Shelley's *Frankenstein*, Marge Piercy's *He, She, and It*, and Phillip Dick's "Do Androids Dream of Electric Sheep?" Ideas about the destruction of humanity can be found in *On the Beach* as well as Stephen King's *The Stand*, and it is the motif of dozens of popular films and video games. Jimmy's portrayal of two different versions of dystopia can be seen in Marge Piercy's *Woman at the Edge of Time*, contrasting the edenic and hellish possibilities of different planes of existence, as well as Ursula Le Guin's *The Left Hand of Darkness*.

The dystopian references in the novel also point to another kind of dystopia: the self-created dystopia of a damaged psyche. A novel such as Ken Kesey's *One Flew Over the Cuckoo's Nest* articulates the self-construction of a personal hell. The Chief, the narrator of Cuckoo's Nest, has imagined the ward of the hospital as a mechanized "Combine," complete with systematic disemboweling of patients who are then "rewired" to become socially acceptable. Another famous novel that can be read through a dystopian lens is Lewis Carroll's *Alice in Wonderland* in which it is implied that Alice has escaped in dreaming to, then from, a world of chaos devoid of adult reason. Likewise, in Chuck Palahniuk's *Fight Club*, a young man, disenchanted with the sops and impotency of corporate consumer life, psychologically creates a violent and powerful alter ego who commands the position of anarchist. In other words, Palahniuk's unnamed narrator sublimates his ineffective ego, allowing his id and superego to enact its violent and pleasurable fantasies of power.

The inclusion of distinct points of comparison with Jimmy's narrative and these classic and well-known texts proposes the conclusion that Jimmy's tale is a fabrication. Yet, the questions remain: why would Jimmy contrive such an elaborate but clearly recognizable fiction? How much of Jimmy's tale is real and how much is imagined? And where is the point of departure into the realm of the fantastic?[4] Simply put, Jimmy is not trying to convince anyone as to the veracity of the story, except himself. Jimmy's narrative hyper-realizes that which has already occurred, thus the point of departure into an alternative constructed reality is impossible to pinpoint, yet readers may sense that Jimmy's already tenuous world is shattered with the departure of his mother. When Jimmy's mother deserts her family, Jimmy is unable to achieve compromise between his wants and needs, his conscience and his desire. Even before her departure, however, Jimmy has already sensed that she is lost to him; in remarking about the few times she appeared happy, Jimmy notices, "She was like a real mother and he was like a real child" (30). Just before she leaves, he overhears his mother saying: "Jimmy depresses me, he's turning into a …" (57), but the sentence is never finished. Thus Jimmy never discovers what his mother thinks of him; he agonizes, "he failed her in some crucial way. He'd never understood what was required of him. If only he could have one more chance to make her happy" (68).

Jimmy's mother is symbolized several times in the novel by references to doors, especially doors closing. She describes her previous profession of microbiologist as: "The bad microbes and viruses want to get in through the cell doors and eat up the pigoons from the inside. Mummy's job was to make locks for the doors" (29). Every time in the novel Jimmy shuts a door on a part of himself, the moment is signified by the sound "whuff" that he associates with his mother and her slammed doors. As a critical figure who has "shut the door" on him, Jimmy's mother cannot function properly as his anima; thus, without compensation, Jimmy's psyche may become damaged as he is unable to access, in effect, his soul.

According to Jungian archetypal theory, the mother represents the anima—the female counterpart to his psyche—in a male, which functions as his soul; the anima is at once both an archetype and a complex. The anima is also responsible for projections and is associated with eros. Jung discerned that the anima is an archetype that articulates the soul and it "mythologizes all emotional relations with [man's] work and with people of both sexes." In addition, Jung claimed that an overly "constellated" anima makes man "unadjusted" ("Concerning" 144). The character of the individual's anima can be ascertained as the opposition of the persona; in other words, the anima contains all the qualities that are missing from the man's exterior attitudes. Jung explains: "If the persona is intellectual, the anima will certainly be sentimental" ("Definitions" 804). Jung warns, however, if a man ignores his anima, "the anima is inevitably projected on a real object, with which he gets into a relation of almost total dependence" ("Definitions" 807). If the individual fails to integrate his anima into his consciousness, Jung predicts he may develop "resignation, weariness, sloppiness, irresponsibility, and finally a childish [petulance] with a tendency to alcohol" ("Syzygy" 40), conditions that apply to Jimmy. Successful integration allows the anima to "forfeit the daemonic power of an autonomous complex; she can no longer exercise the power of possession, since she is depotentiated. She is no longer the guardian of treasures unknown…" ("Mana-Personality" 374). Yet Jimmy is unable to integrate his anima as his mother has, he feels, rejected him.

Jimmy's distant father is symbolized by the knife with tools and scissors he had given Jimmy as a birthday present when Jimmy was nine, a potent Freudian symbol. Jimmy is confused about what his father expects of him, how he is to "measure up." He worries in regard to his father, "There was never any standard [to measure up to]; or there was one, but it was so cloudy and immense that nobody could see it, especially not Jimmy. Nothing he could achieve would ever be the right idea, or enough." He suspects that whatever praise his father extends is "secretly disappointed praise" (50). He fears never being able to live up to his father's indiscernible expectations.[5]

In the psyche the father plays a paradoxical role. On the one hand he is the superego: a regulatory instructor representing rationality, such as the male voices Jimmy hears in his head, urging forbearance and achievement. On the other, he is the critic, judging inadequacies and disallowing sentiment. The father figure is also represented in the image of the mind, the intellect. In Jimmy's case, his father is a brilliant genographer; his father's strength is his rational intelligence, while Jimmy's intelligence is manifested in his language. The father also can represent thanatos—the specter of death—as he is not only responsible for triggering the Oedipal complex, but also he serves as a symbol of mortality as in myths of regeneration and rebirth. Jimmy dismisses his father, unable to identify with him or enact rebellion; he forfeits his archetypal role as prince who must succeed the dying king in order to regenerate the land.

Damaged by his inability to control or remedy the tragedies in his life, such as his mother's abandonment and his father's aloofness, Jimmy concocts an elaborate fantasy means of avoiding his existential dilemma. At first he deflects his rage at abandonment into sorrow over the loss of his pet rakunk, Killer, the only creature he claims to love other than his mother. And while this deflection may assuage his childhood rage, his adult self need stronger stuff. Therefore, like Palahniuk's protagonist, Jimmy utilizes his subconscious, separating himself into three divisions of his self: Crake, Oryx, and ultimately, Snowman.[6]

Jimmy projects the father image onto Crake; likewise he projects his mother image onto Oryx. Both creations are materialized from the "shadow": the "hidden or unconscious aspects of oneself, both good and bad, which the ego has either repressed or never recognized" ("Excerpts"). Jung explains:

> It is a frightening thought that man also has a shadow side to him, consisting not just of little weaknesses and foibles, but of a positively demonic dynamism. The individual seldom knows anything of this; to him, as an individual, it is incredible that he should ever in any circumstances go beyond himself. But let these harmless creatures form a mass, and there emerges a raging monster; and each individual is only one tiny cell in the monster's body, so that for better or worse he must accompany it on its bloody rampages and even assist it to the utmost. Having a dark suspicion of these grim possibilities, man turns a blind eye to the shadow-side of human nature. ("On" 35).

Dependence on the shadow signifies the individual who has not been able to integrate his unconscious and consciousness.

Crake has a habit of materializing whenever eros has failed Jimmy. He first "meets" Crake[7] when his family has been relocated to another Compound and Jimmy is isolated and lonely and aware that his mother has been retreating further and further into herself. Jimmy, as a young boy, has resorted to playing the comic to gain his mother's attention; this is the same strategy he employs with the students in his new school. Yet Jimmy feels fraudulent and guilty about his antics; he would prefer that people— including his mother—would love him for himself; he wishes that she would "try her best with him, to hammer away at the wall he's put up against her" (21). He displaces his anger at his mother's inability to nurture her son because he fears he will be proven right; he cannot risk angering her. In addition, Jimmy's hand puppet games representing his parent's failings add to his anxiety and guilt. Enter Crake.

Jimmy's mother, by his account, admired Crake because he was "intellectually honourable" (69).[8] Jimmy cannot see himself as "intellectual" or "honourable," only hopelessly unworthy. The oppositions do not end there: Crake has "potential," Jimmy does not; Crake is never "affected" by drugs, violence, or sex; Jimmy is affected; Crake's father is gone; Jimmy's mother is gone; Crake is a "numbers" person, while Jimmy is a "words" person (75, 86). In addition, Crake introduces Jimmy to the violent video games, broadcast executions, and pornographic websites, both contrasting Crake's image as "honourable" and allowing Jimmy a vent for his own angry and violent urges.

Michiko Kakutani complains that Crake is a "cardboardy creation," a valid observation if Crake is an actual being.[9] Crake, while a genius and overtly logical, is devoid of emotional response and his obsession with death and destruction reveals his connection to thanatos. Crake represents Jimmy's superego; Jimmy complains, "Crake could be a little too instructive sometimes, and a little too free with the shoulds" (70). Jimmy also notes, "He could feel it within himself to hate Crake, as well as liking him" (75), acknowledging his ambivalence. Taken to the extreme, Crake enacts Jimmy's God Complex and also represents Jimmy's "shadow"; it is Crake who has a murdered father, Crake who directs Jimmy to the ideas that will culminate in the means to destruction, and it is Crake who ultimately annihilates civilization. Crake, therefore, contains the oedipal instinct that Jimmy desires to repress, and that the final destruction of humanity is brought about by a sexually enhancing drug is fitting in its Freudian undertones. Jimmy relegates the portion of his psyche—the shadow that represents his dark urges—to Crake.

Oryx, in contrast, is eros personified. Oryx herself is a compilation of every illicit male sexualized fantasy as she is a survivor of child pornography, a sex slave, and a prostitute. Natasha Walter contends: "Oryx is Jimmy's wet dream." She also recognizes that Oryx is "an ambiguous figure who hovers between reality and fantasy" ("Pigoons"). In fact, the name oryx spelled backwards is xyro, or zero, an indicator of her emptiness. Even Oryx, laughing, asks Jimmy, "What is my will?" implying that as a construction, or projection, she is incapable of having a will (141). Disch observes, "Oryx sometimes seems to have superhuman powers, especially in the way her italicized advisories[10] pop up with no explanation all along the way. But in fact these fleeting visions of a seemingly immaterial, possibly cybernetic Oryx are only a novelistic artifice" (BW3). However, if Oryx represents Jimmy's id and his connection to *eros*, the "advisories" are a part of Jimmy's psyche. Moreover, Oryx's "advisories" sound suspiciously like maternal advisories. The implications of this are two-fold: first, Jimmy has confused the image of his mother with Oryx, revealing that Oryx is functioning as his anima,[11] as indeed do all of the women in Jimmy's life in one sense or another. Second, the Freudian implications are obvious: as Crake, Jimmy has killed his father and he is having sex with Oryx, fulfilling the oedipal destiny.[12]

Yet, Oryx as Jimmy's id and *eros* is surprisingly devoid of emotion, and she dismisses the horrors of her past. Thus, it would seem that even though Jimmy has compartmentalized his selves, he still doesn't have the capacity to find an outlet for his emotions. However, Oryx as id is incapable of having any emotions of her own; she can only act as conduit for Jimmy's repressed emotions—if he allows it.[13] Thus, he may lavish his supposed love and real pain upon her, and she, in return, provides hedonistic and platitudinous soothings. Oryx as *eros* chides Jimmy: "Why do you want to talk about ugly things? … We should think only beautiful things, as much as we can" (144). Jimmy thinks Oryx "was not unfeeling: on the contrary. But she refused to feel what he wanted her to feel," revealing that she has an uncanny similarity to his mother (190).

However, Oryx, like Crake, represents danger to him. He suspects that "there was something—some harmful snake or homemade bomb or lethal powder—concealed within" (312). At the same time, he is obsessed with her, possibly because she is a projection of his mother:

> He could never get used to her, she was fresh every time, she was a casketful[14] of secrets. Any moment now she would open herself up, reveal to him the essential thing, the hidden thing at the core of her life, or of his life—the thing he was longing to know. The thing he'd always wanted. What would it be? (315).

That "thing" is love, of course. But Oryx isn't real, as he subconsciously acknowledges when he admits: "sometimes he felt that her entire past—everything she'd told him—was his own invention" (316). Jimmy reveals that he "preferred sad women, delicate and breakable, women who had been messed up and needed him" (100). As a young man, he attempts to be what he couldn't be as a child: his mother's healer. Again and again he reenacts this fantasy with a parade of women; however, Jimmy has trouble relating to the women who share his mother's passions for global preservation and women's causes, such as his college roommate and his final college girlfriend. It seems he only cares for damaged women, not women who maintain his mother's strengths.

It is only when Jimmy is forced to concede his mother's death that he unleashes Crake and Oryx onto the world. In the time following his graduation from college, Jimmy's life has become stale. He works in advertising, which spurs his cynicism; he suspects that all life experiences are nothing more than marketing hype. He regresses into his comedy routine cynically satirizing his own advertising campaigns. He has also found sexual connections to be little more than pointless manipulations; his social life is a "zero" (249). Finally, Jimmy must confront the specter of his mother's possible death, supposedly witnessing her execution during an interrogation by the CorpSeCorps.[15] He, unlike Crake, is able to hear her last words: "Goodbye. Remember Killer. I love you. Don't let me down" (258).[16] Rather than engendering a sense of closure within him, Jimmy is traumatized, sad, angry, depressed: "he had to dull the pain…. The pain of raw, torn places, the damaged membranes where he'd whanged up against the Great Indifference of the Universe" (260). Luckily, and in the nick of time, Crake reappears—"Let me in," he says, "And Jimmy did"—suppressing, as he always does, the effects of eros and emotion within Jimmy (286).

In aligning himself with the logos of Crake, Jimmy may subdue the pain and grief he harbors. In becoming, in a way, Crake, he accesses a coolly rational means of venting his rage: he will destroy humanity and its flaws, supplanting it with a new race of beings—beings that come fully equipped to evade the follies of the human race. In essence, Jimmy creates the Crakers—placid demeanors, gentle natures, and uncomplicated sexuality—in his own image. That is, even with all of their souped-up features, the Crakers are devoid of all of the attributes Jimmy has foisted off on Crake and Oryx: his emotions and intellect, his passion and desire, his rage and his love. In his universe, Jimmy has reasoned that it is these qualities that need to be eradicated from humanity, i.e., himself. During the outbreak, Jimmy reveals: "Nobody in the inner bubble now but himself and the Crakers" (327); he has locked everything else out. When Jimmy confronts the Crakers he has decided to change his name because, he concludes in acknowledging his purpose for all of the preceding events: "He needed to forget the past—the distant past, the immediate past, the past in any form. He needed to exist only in the present, without guilt, without expectations. As the Crakers did" (348-49). He is hoping to discard the guilt represented by Oryx/mother and the expectations represented by Crake/father.

Shortly after Jimmy has been hired by Crake to write the hype for the BlyssPluss pill, Jimmy discovers the presence of Oryx, an extraordinary coincidence. Crake reveals that he had devised a vision of his perfect woman, and Oryx was delivered by the obliging Student Services of his university. The incongruence of Crake having a lover—especially this lover—seems to appall Jimmy, as he has fantasized about Oryx for years and feels she belongs to him. Thus, a battle ensues: which one will triumph and win Jimmy's allegiance? When Jimmy asks Oryx, "You always do what he tells you to do?" Oryx responds, "He is my boss" (313), an answer that is disturbing to Jimmy. Oryx is accommodating, dividing her attentions between the two;[17] yet Jimmy demands all of her, cajoling her to leave Crake. The crisis occurs when Jimmy forces the issue and Oryx attests, "But I would never leave Crake" (321-22). Because Crake and Oryx exist in opposition to each other—that is they harbor the opposing characteristics of Jimmy's psyche, they cannot exist as powerful entities independent of each other. If Jimmy abandons Crake for Oryx, Crake will be destroyed, and the superego cannot allow its destruction, nor will thanatos lessen its grip. Likewise, while Jimmy is in thrall of Crake, he submerges his need for eros and Oryx fades into oblivion, although Oryx is weaker than Crake and does not fight as stringently for her existence. Thus, in the end, Jimmy must destroy both. He abandons their bodies in the airlock and ventures out of Paradice with the Crakers.

Jimmy becomes a prophet to the Crakers; he is Moses leading his people out of slavery. While he claims to dislike his role; the Crakers provide him with what he believes he needs. Yet, perhaps Jimmy's subconscious is foiling his project as the Crakers act as Jimmy's therapists, constantly asking him for his stories and bringing artifacts to him to identify. The stories and objects are the means to reconnection. And although Jimmy tells lies to the Craker children, he is nevertheless drawn into recognitions he had hoped to once and finally avoid. In particular, the Crakers want to know about Crake, who they consider—because of Jimmy's lie—to be a God. Therefore, Jimmy finds himself in an ambiguous position. He has killed Crake; he has attempted to permanently eradicate that which he no longer wishes to acknowledge. Yet, as the prophet of Crake, he cannot escape him. It is as if it is not only Oryx who speaks to his mind, but it is also Crake who continues make his presence known. Thus, Jimmy must admit that his new "paradise" has failed, and that he can not hold off his psyche indefinitely. As Crake and Oryx are the repositories for his memories, desires, intellect, and emotions they demand to be recognized; they will be validated. The dross of the lost civilization, then, serves as symbolic messages from the "gods": it is the trash that cannot be discarded.

Jimmy's psyche needs the oppositions that Crake and Oryx represent. There is no reality without opposition. For example, when Jimmy as Snowman attempts to explain the concept of pictures as not real to the Crakers, they ask: "What is this not real? Not real can tell us about real" (102). Jimmy, in his misery, calls out to Oryx, begging her to return if only in ethereal spirit form. However, because he has negated Crake, he has also lost Oryx: one cannot exist without the other. Jimmy has created an absence, a blankness to erase his pain, yet without pain, there is no pleasure. In essence, Jimmy yearns for his soul; however, without a mind to access the soul, appreciate the soul, and have a point of reference for the soul, he must remain soulless. He know he is able to exist by blocking the anima, living with and through his mind as evidenced by the long stretches he relied on Crake, yet he finds that he requires his wits to survive. He discovers that, just as he is unable to erase the maternal advisories from his conscious, it is also impossible to arrest the practical phrases that intermittently invade his conscious.

Jimmy is literally and figuratively starving; the resources of his world are nearing depletion: a signal that the world he has envisioned cannot sustain him. His inertia and catatonic existence are indicators that his refuge into this world is detrimental; the "snow man" must ultimately thaw. After a night of drunken self-indulgent anguish, Jimmy makes the decision: "Time to face reality" (149), and thus he ventures forth, paradoxically, into regression. The only way he can face this journey is to delude himself; he tells himself: "A quick in and out [of the Paradice dome where the bodies of Crake and Oryx lay in the air lock], a snatch and grab. Then he'll be equipped for anything," a revealing conclusion (151). He muffles his true need—to face and reclaim the separated portions of his psyche—because he fears his own extinction into the stronger aspects of his psyche, as well as the pain that this reconciliation will engender. Yet if he waits any longer, he will be extinguished anyway.

What Jimmy must face are the circumstances of his exodus into and out of Paradice. When Jimmy (ego) threatened to leave Crake (superego) to join with Oryx (id), Crake responded by killing Oryx and manipulating Jimmy to kill him, yet both have forewarned Jimmy that they might not be around to take care of the Crakers, a sign that Jimmy has already decided to banish them. Tellingly, both Crake and Oryx were then entombed in the glass air lock, capable of being seen but not touched, conjuring associations to Snow White's glass coffin. And as readers know, Snow White is not really dead, just incapacitated. Snow White needs to "move" forward in order to breathe again. And, Jimmy cannot survive missing large portions of his psyche; he must return and reconnect his selves.

Jimmy's return to Paradice reads like the plot of a video quest game of his childhood, as well as a journey into his own mind: Jimmy must traverse the "No Man's Land"—a place where there is nowhere to hide, and travel through the blasted wall, a reference to the walls that Jimmy has erected around himself. He "rejuvenates" himself at a house that is certainly symbolic of his childhood homes, and the psychological connotations of this action are intensified as Jimmy feels as if "someone— someone like him—is lying in wait, around some corner, behind some half-opened door" (229). One of the vistas that awaits him is the remains of the dead parents; another is a view of himself in a mirror where he sees a "stranger." He asks, finally, "Why does he have the feeling that it's his own house he has broken into? His own house from twenty-five years ago, himself the missing child?" (233). Thus he indicates that he is in the initial stages of reintegrating his psyche.

Threatened by the ferocious pigoons that, tellingly, contain human DNA, Jimmy takes shelter from a tornado in the checkpoint gatehouse. A psychological analysis of these circumstances might suggest that Jimmy, on his was to recovering, finds several obstacles in his way, obstacles that he most certainly has created. It is a test of Jimmy's will, then, by the strength of the obstacles and his own tenacity in overcoming them. In fact, after Jimmy leaves the checkpoint onto the ramparts, the reader is suddenly confronted with an inexplicable wound on Jimmy's foot. Remarkably, this cut has materialized just after Jimmy has heard voices on a CB radio; a radio that Jimmy conveniently (to his state of reality) forgets to bring along with him. The text implies that Jimmy has stepped on the broken glass of a Bourbon bottle, but the incident itself is suspiciously absent from the narrative. It may be that Jimmy, having overcome one seemingly impossible hurdle by escaping the pigoons has found himself dangerously close to success, as evidenced by his possibility of contact with humans; thus, he needs a possible "out" in case he changes his mind—say, a wounded foot.

Finally, at the heart of his quest lies the treasure he has been seeking, the "vulturized" corpses of his psyche, entombed within the Paradice dome. The dome itself resembles an egg that filters and breathes, a potent Atwood symbol. Moreover, Jimmy has already offered a subliminal image of the dome: "for every pair of lovers there was a dejected onlooker, the one excluded. Love was its own transparent bubble-dome: you could see the two inside it, but you couldn't get in there yourself" (165). From the aspects of psychoanalysis, Jimmy's return is the inverse of his escape from Paradice and he, in fact, is able to "get in there."

His return to the Crakers elicits revelations. The community, while it still cares for him, no longer needs him; an effigy suffices in his absence. The people have grown beyond their naiveté and are manifesting signs that are distinctly human; for example, Abraham has assumed leadership capabilities. Jimmy seems to have come to some conclusion as he recognizes, when the Crakers dismantle the "idol" and return the pieces of its construction to where they found them, "after a thing has been used, it must be given back to its place of origin" (363). In conjunction, after Jimmy has used these images and fantasies to sustain himself, he must return them to their rightful place: his subconscious. Watching them return the pieces, he feels "It's as if he himself has been torn apart and scattered" (363). The reader may surmise that the false Jimmy is being dismantled, leaving the "real" man behind. It is possible that this action symbolizes the death of "Snowman."

That Jimmy also no longer needs the Crakers is evident in the "timely" disclosure that other "humans" have been seen by the Crakers. Jimmy is compelled to find these others, although he does not acknowledge—even to himself—what he plans to do at this confrontation. Before he leaves the Crakers, he tries to come up with "a few words to remember," but nothing practical will work, especially if he is planning on facing reality, which entails consigning the race back to his psyche where it belongs. Jimmy settles on "Crake is watching you" and "Oryx loves you," a mantra to his newly restored sensibility. This mantra serves to remind Jimmy of his need to accept all that Crake and Oryx symbolize, as well as his acceptance of himself, in the form of the Crakers. That he has resolved to become whole again is evident after he plans what he will say to the Crakers: "Then his eyes close and he feels himself being lifted gently, carried, lifted again, carried again, held" (367).

The novel ends as he prepares his approach. The day of his new journey begins with almost the same words of the novel's opening chapter, but the tone is changed. "He pees on the grasshoppers, watching with nostalgia as they whirr away. Already this routine of his is entering the past, like a lover seen from a train window, waving goodbye, pulled inexorably back, in space, in time, so quickly" (372). Yet he is also anxious: "He is not ready for this. He's not well. He's frightened" (372).

The novel ends with Jimmy poised on the brink of his decision: will he or won't he rejoin humanity? This conundrum of the open ending of the novel, however, is less of the "lady or the tiger?" dilemma than an acknowledgment that Jimmy has reached crisis in his integration: Is Jimmy ready for the real world? The answer appears to be "Yes," in spite of his worries; he has already placed his feet in the footprints of his own kind.

Jimmy as Snowman asks himself,

> When did the body first set out on its own adventures? Snowman thinks; after having ditched its old traveling companions, the mind and the soul, for whom it had once been considered a mere corrupt vessel or else a puppet acting out their dramas for them, or else bad company, leading the other two astray. It must have gotten tired of the soul's constant nagging and whining, and the anxiety-driven intellectual web-spinning of the mind, distracting it whenever it was getting its teeth into something juicy or its fingers into something good. It had dumped the other two back there somewhere, leaving them stranded in some damp sanctuary or stuffy lecture hall while it made a beeline for the topless bars, and it had dumped culture along with them: music and painting and poetry and plays. Sublimation, all of it: nothing but sublimation, according to the body. Why not cut to the chase? (85)

Yet the chase has to end somewhere.

Notes

1 Grace Marks from *Alias Grace* and Iris from *The Blind Assassin* are just two of these narrators.

2 Yet Jimmy admits his ambivalence when, justifying his creation of a new "orthodoxy" for the Crakers; he allows: "he couldn't stand to be nothing, to know himself to be nothing" (104).

3 Several times during his narration, Jimmy consciously revises his text. For example, when attempting to identify one of the voices in his head, he concludes, "Some tart he once bought. Revision, professional sex-skills expert" (11).

4 Jimmy is not completely blind to his damaged sense of reality. When contemplating the voices in his head, he says, "He hates these echoes. Saints used to hear them, crazed lice-infested hermits in their caves and deserts," an apt description of himself (11).

5 However, one of the objects Jimmy ultimately retrieves from the Paradice dome is "one of those knives with the scissors," a "lost" object (357).

[6] In *The Robber Bride*, Zenia is also an entity that is conjured up out of the psyches of the protagonist.

[7] Crake has chosen his own name an extinct bird; Jimmy's codename, also chosen by Crake, is "Thickney," another extinct bird that "used to hang around cemeteries," a reference to *thanatos* (81).

[8] Yet Jimmy wonders when these "logical, adult conversations" could have taken place as he never "witnessed the two of them having such a conversation" (69).

[9] Jimmy, when asked by the Craker children to tell them about when Crake was born, tellingly responds, "Crake was never born." He adds, "He came down out of the sky, like thunder" (104).

[10] In fact, it is difficult to ascertain exactly whose voice is represented in the italicized female voices. While some of it "sounds" like Oryx, some also sounds like Ramona and Jimmy's girlfriends and female teachers—or even Jimmy's mother. As the anima represents all females, however, the inability to authenticate the voices as only the voice of Oryx makes sense.

[11] Oryx echoes Jimmy's mother in numerous places in the text. For example, when she tells Jimmy that he doesn't have "an elegant mind," the reader is reminded of Jimmy's mother's relaying that she believes that Crake is "intellectually honourable," and implication that Jimmy is not (142).

[12] The words that Jimmy hears in his head from his father are always: "Joke! Joke! Don't kill me!" words that can be construed as Oedipal in nature (247).

[13] Jimmy constantly probes Oryx's past, attempting to dredge up her pain. He asks himself, "Where was her rage, how far down was it buried, what did he have to do to dig it up?" (142).

[14] "Casketful" is an interesting choice of words if Jimmy's mother is, in fact, dead and in a casket.

[15] It could be possible that Jimmy is actually in therapy and in an extreme state of denial.

[16] It is entirely possible that these are the words she had written to him when she left home, words that Jimmy blocked out in his anger until later in his life.

[17] She explains: "Crake lives in a higher world....He lives in a world of ideas. He is doing important things. He has no time for play. Anyway, Crake is my boss. You are for fun" (313).

Works Cited

Atwood, Margaret. *Oryx and Crake*. 2003. New York: Doubleday.

Disch, Thomas M. "The Hot Zone." 27 April 2003 *Washington Post* 27, BW3.

Jung, Carl Gustav. *Collected Works*. 1968. Trans. R.F.C. Hull. 20 vols. Princeton: Princeton UP.

—. "Concerning the Archetypes and the Anima Concept," *Collected Works* 9i.

—. "Definitions," *Collected Works* 6.

—. "The Mana-Personality," *Collected Works* 7.

—. "On the Psychology of the Unconscious." *Collected Works* 7.

—. "The Syzygy: Anima and Animus," *Collected Works* 9ii.

Kakutani, Michiko. "Books of the Times, Lone Human in a Land Filled with Humanoids." 2 May 2003. *The New York Times* 3, E39.

Walter, Natasha. "Pigoons Might Fly."10 May 2003. *The Guardian* <http://books.guardian.co.uk/review/story/0%2C12084%2C951544 %2C00.html>.

CHAPTER TWO

MYTHMAKING[1] IN MARGARET ATWOOD'S
ORYX AND CRAKE

CAROL OSBORNE

The physical landscape of Margaret Atwood's *Oryx and Crake* is harsh; predatory animals, poisoned waters, and the unrelenting UV rays of the sun make survival in the rubble that remains of the old world difficult. This environment is inhabited by Snowman, presumably the only human survivor of a virus that has wiped out the rest of the population, and the Crakers, a collection of genetically-engineered beings for whom he has been asked to serve as guardian. Snowman has been given this role by his childhood friend, Crake, who masterminded the construction of the new species and the subsequent eradication of the human population. In creating his progeny, Crake attempted to eliminate key human traits, traits which had already led to an overpopulated, polluted, and polarized planet, and which he believed inevitably spelled doom for his own species, even without his release of the virus. In addition to modifying the Crakers' physical natures so that they are able to survive in an inhospitable environment, Crake also programmed them to be docile, free from racism and hierarchy, and so "perfectly adjusted to their habitat" that they "would have no need to invent any harmful symbolisms, such as kingdoms, icons, gods, or money" (305). In Atwood's depiction of the dystopian society before the apocalypse, she creates a symbolic, cautionary tale that mirrors current cultural conditions in portraying the competing perspectives of science and humanities, represented by Crake and Snowman, respectively. In her mythic portrayal of the post-Apocalyptic world, with the lone human survivor writing upon the blank slates of the Crakers, who have retained more capacity for belief than Crake intended, she provides a glimmer of hope for the future within the fictional world, and more importantly, support for the behaviors and perspectives that she sees as contemporary society's "saving graces" (Atwood "Perfect" par. 7).

At the opening of the novel, Snowman has reluctantly assumed his caretaking role by escorting the Crakers from the place of their "birth," the Paradice dome, to a more hospitable "home" (354), a location by the sea, and he is planning a return trip to Crake's compound to secure supplies. As in earlier novels, in particular *Cat's Eye*, Margaret Atwood structures *Oryx and Crake* to accentuate the fluidity of time, the continual convergence of the past and the present, and the influence of these moments in shaping perspectives of the future. The chapters alternate between the physical journey that Snowman takes to the Paradice dome and his concurrent psychological journey as he pieces together fragments of memory to form a chronological narrative of his life up to that point, with the two time settings converging in the last few chapters. Through these interlocking tales, Atwood explores the role of mythmaking on three levels. First is Snowman's therapeutic piecing together of his own story, the classic imaginative return to the traumatic past in order to merge conflicting parts of his psyche and move forward. On the second level, Atwood is creating her own dystopian myth, containing both a warning about current social trends in environmental policy, genetics, and social programming and, through a blend of the fabulous and the realistic, a validation of the values and customs that may be cause for optimism about humanity's future, even in the shadow of these threatening developments. On the third level, as Atwood invites the reader to participate in the storytelling process, *Oryx and Crake* offers an additional commentary on the power of words, on the omnipresence of myths in our cultural mindset, and on the inevitable pull of narrative in our desire to understand ourselves and our world.

In the first chapter of the novel, Snowman, formerly known as Jimmy, is depicted as living among the ruins, picking through not only the physical fragments of an earlier time, but also recalling random quotations from documents of the "old" world that has recently been destroyed. As a writer, Jimmy is a lover of words, a natural storyteller, but he is also a product of a society that has devalued the humanities and elevated the sciences, a society in which words have lost their meaning, so he vacillates throughout the narrative, as his impulse to relish the power of language vies with his profound disillusionment and cynicism. In his foray to Paradice, Crake's compound, Snowman is intent on gathering physical objects, the ruins of the old civilization, for his own survival, as he has before, but more importantly, Atwood depicts this as Snowman's psychological journey in which he sorts through the fragments of recollected lore, written materials, and past conversations; retells his own story to himself, and consequently to the reader; and struggles to define himself as storyteller, differentiating his role as mythmaker for the Crakers from the role he performed as the BlyssPluss advertiser.

After the destruction of the world as he knew it, newly aware of his own culpability in Crake's scheme to eradicate humanity and replace Homo sapiens with the carefully crafted Crakers, Snowman has sought to numb himself through alcohol. He has superficially lived up to his promise, made to both Oryx and Crake, to care for the Crakers (32-322), but he is incapable, at the point when the narrative opens, of escaping the prison of his own mind to interact with them significantly. The disjointed voices from the past are distracting enough, but even more debilitating is the perspective of the society that Snowman has internalized, the one that cynically dismisses humanistic values. Snowman, caught between two opposing myths, has submerged much of his own empathetic world view and assumed society's distrust of compassion and doubt about the benefit or even the possibility of meaningful communion with another. Working from this perspective, Snowman sees interactions with the Crakers, who lack his linguistic sophistication and a common cultural frame of reference, as more of a burden than a comfort. Snowman spends most of his time avoiding contact, drinking to prevent himself from thinking about the past and making decisions about the future. He finds, however, that he cannot put a stop to the memories, nor can he release himself from the guilt he feels for his own blind participation in Crake's plan and the despair he experiences in confronting his current situation. The trip to the compound is designed, in part, to allow Snowman to continue the self-medication, as he intends to restore his liquor supply, but it also represents a more promising development. His desire to find a weapon to keep the wolvogs and pigoons at bay shows that he has not succumbed totally to despair, but is planning ahead for the protection of himself and his wards. More importantly, the trip indicates Snowman's willingness to confront the past, a subconscious realization that he cannot move forward without first dealing with the memories that plague him.

Atwood stresses Snowman's psychological need for a narrative in which to ground his new identity by ending the first section of the novel, occurring in present time, with Snowman's admonition to himself to "'Get a life'" (12) and beginning Chapter Two with the formula of the fairy tale: "Once upon a time, Snowman wasn't Snowman. Instead he was Jimmy. He'd been a good boy then" (15). The encapsulation of Snowman's life story into this familiar format will allow him to establish his own personal and cultural mythology, just as he is constructing a mythology for the

Crakers. The end result of this constructed life story, for both the reader and Snowman, is an increased understanding of the social forces that have shaped him and evidence that he is beginning to emerge from his current disillusionment, self-doubt, and resignation. Snowman's return to the traumatic scene in which he loses Oryx and Crake, a return that is both physical and psychological, is the first step to his reconciling the discordant elements that have vied within him from a young age.

In adopting the frame structure of the fairy tale, Snowman accentuates the moral dichotomy he sees within himself. The opening statement "He was a good boy then," contrasts with his current perception of himself as "abominable" (7-8), setting up what Sherrill Grace has identified as a characteristic component of Atwood's fiction: the protagonists' "dynamic process" of breaking down established polarities within society and the self (Grace 7). It is useful to view Snowman's tale in light of Grace's assertion, based on her reading of earlier texts, that

> Atwood identifies human failure as acquiescence in those Western dichotomies which postulate the inescapable, static division of the world into hostile opposites. (5)

When we first view Snowman in *Oryx and Crake*, he is guilty of this kind of polarized thinking, symbolized through the sunglasses he wears, in which one lens is missing. Not only does he dwell on his own internal division and the old society's binary systems (science/humanities; Compounds/pleeblands, etc.), but he also accentuates the divide between himself and the Crakers, and suffers from the feelings of isolation and despair that result.

The first scene of Snowman's therapeutic narrative illustrates one aspect of his internal divide and hints at its origin. Snowman recalls a time, when he was five or six, that he accompanied his father to the bonfire of diseased animals. The young Jimmy was "anxious about the animals," worried that their suffering was "his fault, because he'd done nothing to rescue them" (18). Mixed with this empathetic concern for and connection to other living creatures, though, is Jimmy's fascination with the spectacle, a distancing mechanism that allowed him to view the fire as a "beautiful sight" and to wish for an explosion (18). The recollection of the odor of burning fur causes a switch in the narrative focus, midway through this scene, to a memory of Jimmy's parents arguing over his burning and cutting his own hair. Snowman notes the contrast in his parents' reactions, witnessing his father's cool, rational response as he explains to his son that the emotional vicissitudes of his mother are characteristic of all women, who "'always get hot under the collar'" (16).

Jimmy is encouraged to adopt the "tough guy" shell of his gender, but, aware of his own internal emotions, he is left to wonder what happens under the collars of men. This is the first of many recollected scenes from his life in which Jimmy learns to hide his emotional sensitivity and empathetic nature beneath a façade of cynical detachment.

Putting up walls as an emotional defense, Atwood suggests, is a learned behavior, shaped by society and those who are given the responsibility of communicating social expectations to children: their parents. In the middle of his psychological journey through the past, Snowman recognizes this defense mechanism in himself as he laments his blindness to Crake's plan:

> There had been something willed about it though, his ignorance. Or not willed, exactly: structured. He'd grown up in walled spaces, and then he had become one. He had shut things out. (184)

While Snowman recognizes, in general terms, the way his psychological make-up mirrors the larger society's systems of defense, Atwood points, earlier in the novel, to more specific influences at work on Jimmy in the form of children's stories. Atwood presents two examples of story-telling within the nuclear family: the fairy tale Jimmy's father uses to justify the separation of Compounds and pleeblands, and the tale his mother uses to explain her work at OrganInc Farms, both narratives clearly presenting the model Jimmy internalizes for his own survival. Jimmy's father emphasizes the historical tradition of erecting barriers for protection:

> Long ago, in the days of knights and dragons, the kings and dukes had lived in castles, with high walls and drawbridges and slots on the ramparts so you could pour hot pitch on your enemies…and the Compounds were the same idea. (28)

His mother brings the same metaphor to bear when explaining her research, casting herself as the one who "'makes locks for the doors,'" so that the "'bad microbes and viruses'" are not able to "'eat up the pigoons from the inside'" (29). The physical barriers represented by the walls of the compound and the walls of the pigoons' cells are echoed in the psychological barriers Jimmy erects to deal with the pain of his mother's distance and his father's neglect. Underneath, he is hurt by their inattention, longing for the closeness that has been denied, but on the surface, he uses humor and an ironic distancing to protect himself.

The patterns of behavior established in Jimmy's interactions with his parents are repeated in the subsequent relationships he forms during adolescence and adulthood. As Jimmy hides his emotions in order to be accepted by his father—for example, he names his pet rakunk "Killer" to cover his attachment to the animal—he adopts the same semblance of detachment in order to avoid ridicule from the seemingly emotionless Crake. Jimmy's struggle to keep his sensitive, empathetic nature in check is particularly noticeable when Crake shares the story of his father's death. Jimmy resorts to humor to cover his emotions because "he was feeling sorry for Crake, and he didn't like that at all" (183). Conversations between the two friends take the form of analytical discourse, the arena more comfortable to Crake. When Jimmy does attempt to argue his point of view, his protests fall flat against the rational arguments proffered by the "numbers man," whose perspective reflects the predominant view of the society. Often, Jimmy retreats into one word utterances or silence, concentrating on keeping his emotions under control, for "if he lost his temper, Crake won" (168).

While Jimmy conforms to the social expectations for his gender in submerging his emotions when he is around his father and Crake, in his relationships with women, he exhibits the same conflicted response first established in the nuclear family. Longing for a close connection with his mother, Jimmy tells stories to make her laugh, but her depression makes a sustained attachment impossible, so he covers his pain with his sharp wit and his facility with words, finding the negative response he provokes preferable to none at all (31-33). After his mother's abandonment, Jimmy's longing for communion with another is even greater, revealed in his obsession with the image of Oryx, based on his assumption that her penetrating look into the camera shows that she understands him completely. Oryx, at this point in his life, however, is only an image, so Jimmy pursues other women, using the same linguistic tactics employed on his mother, attracting and then repulsing each one with his empty rhetoric. He uses the story of his childhood, elevating his mother to the "status of a mythical being" (191), to enlist the sympathy of each girlfriend, but then, to defend himself from being vulnerable to their leaving him as his mother had, he pushes them away with the same rhetorical powers.

In his relationship with Oryx, however, Jimmy breaks the pattern of erecting emotional barriers to protect himself. Perhaps because he recognizes the impossibility of ever knowing Oryx or ever enjoying a relationship with her separate from her relationship with Crake, he continues to work toward the ultimate communion rather than giving up on this ideal, as he has with other women. Through a repeated image, Atwood links the three points in Jimmy's life when he allows himself to be this vulnerable: first, with his actual pet rakunk; second, with his mother, whose last words, to "remember Killer" link her to this animal, and finally with Oryx, who is holding a rakunk when Jimmy first sees her in the flesh. Critic Stephen Dunning also notes the connection among these relationships, arguing that the strength of Jimmy's desire for Oryx derives from the previous losses of his pet and his mother (97). Allowing himself to become vulnerable by letting down his defenses with Oryx, Jimmy is once again devastated when her death at the hands of Crake puts an end to their intimate connection. As a result of this loss, Snowman has erected the psychological barriers yet again, so that between the opening of the novel and the time he begins his journey, he appears in full protective mode, using cynical humor and word-play to distance himself emotionally from the only beings he knows to be alive, the Crakers. He expresses the same desire and fear he has shown previously in his relationships with women, noting how he would like to be adored by these people, as Crake is, and how touched he is by their generosity, but quickly covering this sensitivity by cursing the absent Crake, containing his own emotional reaction in a comic strip image, and admonishing himself with the internalized voice of his father, who urges him to "stop sniveling" and be a man (161-2).

Snowman's heightened defenses, in particular the self-deprecating cynicism that erupts at times in response to the self-help platitudes that play in his head, make his psychological growth during his journey to the compound difficult to observe. For instance, his insistence that he has not "grown as a person" from the challenging crisis he has faced, but instead has "'shrunk'" until his "'brain is the size of a grape'" (237) seems to belie the therapeutic value of his survey of the past. However, Atwood establishes enough markers for a reader to see beyond these surface comments and defensive gestures to witness slight, yet telling shifts in Snowman's thinking about himself and his role in relation to others.

A large part of Snowman's "therapy" centers on his confronting and coming to terms with key losses in his past. First comes the memory of losing Killer, triggered by the "pointless repinings" (45) and inchoate emotions he is feeling in the present. In his psychological condition at this point, Snowman is not consciously aware of his defenses, not understanding why he has the feeling of wanting to be let out, why he reverts to a "sniveling child's voice" (45) in begging for someone, anyone to listen to him. Atwood uses the structure of her narrative, though, to point to the connection between Snowman's current emotions, presented in "Downpour," the last section of Chapter 3, and the first time he experienced pain as a result of allowing himself to form attachments with something outside himself, narrated in the story of Killer in Chapter 4. The link between chapters and between the time periods is established by Snowman's spotting of a young rakunk as he mutters and fills his beer bottles with the runoff from the thunderstorm, which then triggers his memory of being given his pet rakunk by his father (49).

The next memory of loss comes when Snowman reaches the RejoovenEsence Compound. As in Chapter 3, when Snowman has the impression that someone is watching and listening to him before he retreats into the memory of Killer (46), Chapter 9 presents him as entering a house in the Compound, feeling "that someone—someone like him—is lying in wait" (229). He notes that he has entered the home of a "word person," like himself, and then he experiences "the feeling that it's his own house he's broken into…himself the missing child" (233). A "woman's voice" tells him he is doing well, thus supporting his therapeutic examination of his past selves, but he refutes this assessment, seeking escape in bourbon and sleep. The next segment of his reconstructed life story that this scene initiates makes him confront the pain he felt when witnessing his mother's execution through the CorpSeCorps' video. The parallels between the reaction Jimmy has upon viewing this video and the current reaction Snowman is experiencing after the death of Oryx are clear. In both instances, he has the sense of language losing its meaning, of experiencing "the smallest setbacks" as major catastrophes, and of desiring to be known and accepted by another, but fearing the danger such openness would bring (260-1). In the present time of Atwood's narrative, Snowman's dreams accentuate the lasting effect of the loss of his mother, not only through her actual death, but also through her absence as a nurturing influence during his childhood. The empty chair (265) and the closing door (277) within these two dreams remind him of the suffering occasioned by his mother's disappearance and his attempt to find comfort by dressing in her clothes and hugging himself.

Bracketing the section of the novel in which Snowman confronts the memory of his mother's death are two key moments when Snowman's thoughts turn to the Crakers, suggesting a link between his coming to terms with his childhood pain and his ability to assume fully his role as guardian. When he first explores the house in the RejoovenEsence Compound and exchanges his dirty sheet for fresh linen, he thinks of the impression the floral pattern will make on the Craker kids. Once he has resurrected the memory of his childhood image, so needy that he "hugged his arms around himself" (277) to give the semblance of his mother showing him affection, his thoughts of the Crakers change from his desire to make an impression on them to his expression of concern about how long he has been away.

Snowman has not taken this journey as an abandonment of the Crakers, but as a means for him to assume better care of them, both physically, through attaining a weapon, and psychologically, through gaining a better perspective of himself. After first witnessing the video of his mother's death, he had dismissed the internal voice that urged him to "[g]et a grip" and "[m]ake a new you" as "bland inspirational promotions vomit" (260), but Atwood gives the therapeutic project more validation through her symbolic portrayal of Snowman's growth in the present time. At this moment in the narrative, Snowman discards his single-eyed sunglasses and dons a new pair (278). Immediately afterward, armed with what promises to be a new perspective, Snowman catches his first glimpse of smoke, evidence, it turns out, of the presence of other human survivors (280). Atwood subtly suggests that the growth Snowman is experiencing in his journey will not only enable him to be more responsive to the Crakers, but will equip him to deal more effectively with other members of his own species.

The final and most difficult visit Snowman must make to the past, of course, takes place when he enters the Paradice Compound later that day and confronts the bodies of Oryx and Crake. This leg of his physical journey spurs the memories that have most crippled him, so it is not surprising that he begins this section by berating himself as a "goon, buffoon, poltroon" referring again to his self-proclaimed status as "abominable" (307). This part of his assumed identity, as he has already shared earlier in the narrative, refers specifically to the guilt he carries over his complicity in Crake's plan (8). The other adjectives Snowman uses to describe himself suggest the second issue embedded in this memory. Snowman feels foolish for having dropped his guard so much with Oryx that he became open to Crake's manipulations of him through her, but also to experiencing once again the pain that comes from the loss of a loved one. Critic Coral Howells has noted the connection between Snowman's therapeutic journey, his return to the bodies of Oryx and Crake, "scattered like pieces of a giant jigsaw puzzle left for [him] to fit together into a narrative," and "his crisis of moral realization" as he confronts "his own complicity in Crake's genocidal project" (172). The quotation Howells cites to support this change in the protagonist's perception of himself, "some of the darkness is Snowman's. He helped with it" (333), illustrates a significant departure from the child's voice that issued from Snowman at the onset of his retrospective journey, proclaiming "'Things happened, I had no idea, it was out of my control'" (45). Beyond his acceptance of responsibility within Crake's scheme, Atwood presents even more evidence of change on the part of her protagonist as a result of his return to the scene he has fought the hardest to repress. As the times of the concurrent narratives merge, we see the stark contrast between the present-time Snowman who is willing to face these memories and the Snowman who had introduced himself to the Crakers following the apocalypse with a new name in an effort to "forget the past—the distant past, the immediate past, the past in any form. . . to exist only in the present, without guilt, without expectation" (348-9).

More significantly, Snowman's acceptance of the past enables him to become more confident in his own strength, particularly as the caretaker of the Crakers. He had already demonstrated notable growth between the apocalypse and the beginning of his retrospective journey, as is clear from the contrast between Snowman's description of himself as the "improbable shepherd," leading the Crakers from the compound to the shore (353), making up explanations along the way, and the Snowman of the present, portrayed in the first seven chapters. In the first half of the novel, as Snowman prepares the Crakers for his upcoming return to the Paradice Compound, he demonstrates more foresight than he had in preparing for their initial journey to the sea. Yet, even though he acknowledges the protective impulses he feels toward the Crakers, worries about their welfare while he is gone, and rehearses the story he will use to explain his departure (153), he employs his well-honed ironic mode to keep himself at a safe distance from the Crakers emotionally. He claims that "a day in their company [were they to accompany him on the trip] would bore the pants off him" and he reads their concern about his vulnerability, since he lacks their capacity to produce urine that keeps wild animals at bay, as "offensively smug" (160-1). His communication with the Crakers is frequently interrupted by the internal voices that distract him, particularly that of the small child who plays with language by deconstructing idiomatic expressions and making puns.

When Snowman returns from the trip to the Compound, however, after completing the mythic narrative of his life, we see him putting the needs of the Crakers above his own, choosing to reassure them first before seeking sleep. The undercurrent of sarcasm has diminished considerably, and when those internal voices threaten his newly developed sense of identity and purpose, he rejects their cynicism, proclaiming aloud, "'I'm not just any dead man'" (359). Snowman's communication with the Crakers requires the same intellectual effort as before, for he must use language and cultural references that they will understand and he must remain somewhat consistent in his construction of their myths, but notably absent are the joking asides and the sarcastic quips. While distracted by the pain of his injury and speculation about the future encounter he must make with the other human survivors, Snowman's attitude toward the Crakers seems much more patient and respectful, particularly in response to their concern and care for him. He realizes the only "sermon" he needs to give them before he sets out on this mission has already been embedded in the mythology he has created for them; he has given them the assurance that he lacked: their parents and their creators, Oryx and Crake, love and watch over them. Snowman's self-confidence has been bolstered significantly by the genuine concern the Crakers have shown for him, both in developing the ritual to summon him and in caring for him once he returns. In turn, he relaxes into the comfort of being held by them, a sensation notably absent from his childhood memories. Atwood emphasizes the positive growth in the relationship between the Crakers and Snowman by repeating the same words to describe his waking the next day as she used in the first chapter of the novel, with the notable deletion of the reference to "various barricades" (3, 371).[2] The barriers Snowman had established between the Crakers and himself seem to be breaking down.

Rather than continuing to be defined by Crake, stuck in his dream (218) and serving the "evolutionary purpose" that he decreed for Jimmy of simply saving "the children" (107), Snowman prepares, in the final chapter of the novel, to create his own script as he goes to meet the other human survivors camped nearby. He has relinquished the old routines, in which he had become mired, observing them "entering the past" (372). Symbolically represented by the dismantling of his effigy, Snowman has been transformed through his therapeutic journey, and when he ventures into new territory not anticipated by Crake, he removes his sunglasses altogether (372), signifying a new perspective on the future, one of his own making. Of course, in fashioning this future, he will draw on what he knows, so the various encounters he imagines have their origin in the narratives of the old world, both the Blood and Roses catalogue of events in human history (366) and the plots of popular fiction (373-4). Although aware of the worst scenarios that could result from his attempt to meet the humans, Snowman does not dwell on these, but places them on the same level as the positive outcomes that may also develop. Snowman has progressed beyond the binary way of thinking characteristic of his former society, now merging opposites, as can be seen by his commentary on the rapture he feels when viewing the "deadly" but beautiful glow of the sunrise. That his heart is "seized, carried away" (371) by this vision points to Snowman's having regained the capacity and the desire to feel the emotions he had shut down with the death of Oryx.

Snowman's viewpoint as the novel ends lacks the innocent naiveté of the young Jimmy, who played the dupe to Crake's manipulations, but also notably absent are the emotional outbursts, the cynical dismissals, the clever word play that marked his earlier internal dialogue. During Snowman's journey, the voices of Oryx and his mother, the voices that have urged him throughout the narrative not to let them down, grow more dominant as the voices of Crake and his father, which urge him to squelch his sensitive nature, fade away. No longer is Snowman governed by a culture that privileges analytical discourse over the humanistic arts; he has the power to bring together his knowledge of the past, his empathetic understanding, and his facility with words, to shape a new world.

The re-emergence of Snowman's empathetic impulse, the one that triggered his concern for the animals at the bonfire, that enabled his attachment to Killer, and that finally led him to open up to Oryx, should not be ignored. Critics have understandably focused on Atwood's dystopian myth as a critique of contemporary cultural trends: genetic experimentation, the depletion of natural resources, overpopulation, and the debasement of the arts.[3] "What if we continue down the road we're already on?" is, after all, according to Atwood, one of the guiding questions of the narrative. Yet another line of inquiry spurred by the novel, Atwood points out, is "What are our saving graces?" ("Perfect Storms," par. 7). To identify these saving graces and thus recognize the full impact of Atwood's myth, we need to examine Snowman's transformation, his evolving relationship with the Crakers, and the mythology he creates for them.

As has often been the case in Atwood's fiction, the protagonist of *Oryx and Crake* is a gifted storyteller, one who is not only able to recall a wide range of cultural lore, but who is also creative, capable of inventing new tales that prove both entertaining and instructive for the Crakers.[4] Although discredited by Crake and the rest of society, Snowman's natural inclinations and his training at Martha Graham Academy have insured that he is well-read and sensitive to the nuances of language. He is not able to convince Crake of the necessity of the arts, but he does serve as Atwood's spokesperson in arguing for their importance within a civilization. Compare Jimmy's words, "'When any civilization is dust and ashes, . . . art is all that's left over. Images, words, music. Imaginative structures. Meaning—human meaning, that is—is defined by them" (167) and Atwood's:

> As William Blake noted long ago, the human imagination drives the world. At first it drove only the human world, which was once very small in comparison with the huge and powerful natural world around it. Now we have our hand upon the throttle and our eye upon the rail, and we think we're in control of everything; but it's still the human imagination, in all

its diversity, that propels the train. Literature is an uttering, or outering, of the human imagination. It puts the shadowy forms of thought and feeling— heaven, hell, monsters, angels, and all—out into the light, where we can take a good look at them and perhaps come to a better understanding of who we are and what we want, and what our limits may be. Understanding the imagination is no longer a pastime or even a duty but a necessity, because increasingly, if we can imagine something, we'll be able to do it. ("The Handmaid's Tale" 517)

In *Oryx and Crake*, two characters, Crake and Jimmy, possess powerful imaginations. Tellingly, Snowman is the one Atwood portrays as the steward of the future. He can create heaven and hell, a whole mythology, for the Crakers, and he can take what he has learned from the old world and use it to mold "shadowy forms of thought and feeling" that will guide the Crakers, and the other human survivors, in building the future.

Before he is capable of assuming such a role, though, Snowman must shake off the influence of a society that saw little value in his talents. In Jimmy's world, the imaginative arts have suffered from neglect and abuse. The manner in which the culture perverts art and preys on language is symbolized by the Vulture Sculptures created by Amanda, Jimmy's girlfriend at Martha Graham: she creates the shapes of words out of dead animal parts and then photographs the scene as vultures attack. As Amanda's art brings words to life and then kills them (245), the advertising industry in which Jimmy finds employment transforms language from a rich embodiment of human imagination to a tool of manipulation, so that the meaning of words is secondary to the effect they produce on the consumer. Jimmy even takes delight in the "fatuous neologism" (250), and in the act of using made-up words, sacrifices meaning altogether.

Atwood is certainly critiquing contemporary culture in her depiction of the disconnect that exists between the signifier and the signified in Jimmy's world.[5] Once the old world has been destroyed, however, the rules of communication change drastically for Snowman. In interacting with the Crakers, he must completely rethink his use of language, making certain that for each word he utters, there is a referent in their experience. For someone who delights in word-play, this restriction seems confining at first, a reminder of Crake's rule "that no name could be chosen for which a physical equivalent . . . could not be demonstrated" (7), a provision Snowman delighted in breaking when he chose his new moniker. Yet, as a corrective for his past abuse of language, the thought process Snowman must undergo in speaking with the Crakers provides a valuable retraining system. At the same time that Snowman's empathetic nature is emerging as a result of his therapeutic journey, he is also, in effect, beginning a period of linguistic deprogramming. He must separate himself from the previous roles he has played, womanizer and advertiser, in which he manipulated language to exploit others to grow into the role of storyteller and guide, whose desire is to enrich the understanding and experience of his audience. In this process, the Crakers function first as models in their straight-forward use of language and lack of guile, and second, as a powerful audience, affecting Snowman's performance through their simple trust of him. Faced with "blank slates" for whom he is responsible, Snowman can no longer afford to waste his words. He must call upon his ingenuity, as in his demonstration of the concept of chaos, to communicate with the childlike Crakers.

Atwood marks Snowman's evolution in his relationship with language through the repeated image of Alex the Parrot. Alex is the star of one of the instructional CD-ROMs Jimmy watches as a child. Jimmy delights not only in Alex's invention of new words, but also his refusal to follow the commands of his trainer (54). As a student writing term papers (195) and as an advertiser (250), Jimmy retains some of the rebelliousness and inventiveness he relished in this character, but on a deeper level, he is bothered by the media's manipulation of images and words to the point where it is impossible to ascertain what is real (82-3, 254). Alex appears again in the narrative after Jimmy learns of his mother's execution, when

> Language itself had lost its solidity; it had become thin, contingent, slippery, a viscid film on which he was sliding around like an eyeball on a plate. An eyeball that could still see, however. That was the trouble. (260)

Watching old videos of Alex on the Net on the worst nights of that period, Jimmy is saddened by the fact that Alex asks for an almond, but is given corn. Witnessing this breakdown of communication between parrot and handler, noting the misinterpretation of expressed desire, reminds Jimmy of his own relationships with women, and he longs for the kind of communion he has imagined he can have with Oryx, where the medium of language does not interfere with another person knowing him and ascertaining what he wants (261).

When Jimmy meets Oryx, he learns that his imagined relationship with her is an idealized one. Unlike the other women in his life, Oryx cannot be manipulated through his stories; she "refused to feel what he wanted her to feel" (191). She is an elusive presence, in Stephen Dunning's words "a site of perpetual mystery, a space within which the narrator (and likely Crake himself) 'writes' his own sense of the Other" (96). Oryx, in her refusal to be captured by words, to reveal the "true" story of her past, is instrumental in bringing Jimmy's frustration about the indeterminacy of meaning to the forefront. In one of the stories Oryx tells of her past, she mentions a truck with a picture of a red parrot painted on its side, and Jimmy, in his obsessive need to find factual confirmation of what has happened to her, stumbles upon Alex as he combs the Internet looking for parrot logos. He wants to find "a link between the story Oryx had told him and the so-called real world" (138), a "password" that will illuminate Oryx for him. Jimmy's desire for a real-world referent for the memories Oryx recounts is analogous to his evolving desire for language that gets to the point rather than obfuscating meaning. Jimmy's response when Crake describes the effect of the BlyssPluss Pill, for example, is a profound departure from his usual word-play. Jimmy's comment, "'basically you're going to sterilize people without them knowing it under the guise of giving them the ultra in orgies,'" (294) is dismissed as a "'crude way of putting it'" by Crake, but Jimmy shows in this interchange his evolving desire for a more transparent, honest form of communication.

After Snowman encounters the bodies of Oryx and Crake on his retrospective journey, Alex appears to him once again in a dream:

> It flies in through the window, lands close to him on the pillow, bright green this time with purple wings and a yellow beak, glowing like a beacon, and Snowman is suffused with happiness and love. It cocks its head, looks at him first with one eye, then the other. "The blue triangle," it says. Then it begins to flush, to turn red, beginning with the eye. This change is frightening, as if it's a parrot-shaped light bulb filling up with blood. "I'm going away now," it says.
>   "No, wait," Snowman calls, or wants to call. His mouth won't move. "Don't go yet! Tell me . . ." (336)

This final vision of Alex, coming where it does in the novel, seems an important signpost. The image of Alex's disintegration could be tied to the memories Snowman has of the virus's effects on the humans, and thus be a symbol for the release of his entire past, childhood through the apocalypse. What seems more important, however, is Snowman's desire for Alex to stay, to tell him something. He still longs for meaning to come from outside himself; he desires the comfort of familiar stories and routines. What he is coming to realize, however, is that he is the one who must supply meaning. He cannot depend on the old narratives; it is not enough to parrot what has come before. Instead, he must create the future through telling his own stories, fashioning new myths to guide the Crakers. Because they lack the cultural context of the old world, he must invent anew, gleaning from, but not repeating, the past. His audience is "plain and blunt" and has not "been taught evasion, euphemism, lily-gilding" (348) and other aspects of duplicitous language, so he must measure his words carefully, gradually increasing their vocabulary as he had at one timed desired to do for Alex (261).

The myths that Snowman constructs are, of course, complete fabrications. Aside from the fact that Crake was their Creator, the rest is embellishment, inspired by the "God of Bullshit" (102) and pieced together from Snowman's repertoire of lore. The key to understanding these stories, though, is not in looking at their relation to fact; they function as a mythology, not a history. Just as Snowman has had to rethink the way he uses language in communicating with the Crakers, he is also making a departure from the way he has used stories in the past. He is not trying to exploit the Crakers, to use words for his own profit. Yes, he tells stories in exchange for fish, but he has shown considerable restraint in his demands on the Crakers, and his chief concern has been the impact the stories will have on his wards. Already, the myths have established a communal code that is radically different from the ideology governing interactions in the old world. The Crakers recognize that the "bad things" (103) that occurred in chaos, murder and the unnecessary taking of animal life, are to be avoided. Through his presentation of Oryx and Crake as deities, Snowman has established the primacy of love; building on the qualities programmed into these beings and the lessons already given by Oryx, Snowman's stories reinforce the Crakers' respect for all life and for the natural environment.[6] When they do kill a fish for Snowman to eat, they act together so that no one person assumes all the guilt, thus reinforcing their communal spirit. They have even been trained to recycle the leftovers from Snowman's meals. The myths of origin have set the stage for the Crakers to reverence language, since words were created by Oryx, and their curiosity, love of repetition, and eagerness for stories suggest that they have the ability, with time, to expand their vocabularies and become more proficient communicators. What seems the most important aspect of the mythology Snowman has invented, however, is the sense of community that results from the ritual telling of the stories, for it sets a precedent for how stories may function when Snowman goes to meet the humans. One of Snowman's imagined scenarios, after all, the one he does not dismiss, involves the trading of tales, and the mutual understanding that may result from the survivors' having shared the horror of the apocalypse (374).[7]

The interactions Snowman has with the Crakers provide a barometer that predicts how he will approach "his own kind" (372) in another important way. In Snowman's empathetic treatment of his wards—his concern in anticipating their worries and needs and in communicating so they will understand, given their limited vocabulary and lack of historical reference points—Atwood shows his growing ability to work across cultural borders, a skill that will certainly bode well for future dealings with members of his own species. Snowman and the Crakers are beginning to find a middle ground. As the Crakers, in their desire for stories and their emerging use of symbolic systems, seem to be moving more toward human characteristics, Snowman is beginning to adopt some of their customs. He has already considered the use of their urine as a means of protecting himself from the wild animals, but even more significant is his apology to the slug on his way back from the Paradice Compound (334). Atwood's protagonist recognizes the constructed quality of the myth, but he is also capable of seeing at its core a principle of respecting life that he can follow by modifying his own behavior.

While Snowman's development puts him in a better position to deal with other beings in the future, his situation at the close of the novel is dire. He is fighting to survive in an inhospitable environment without the genetically engineered advantages that the Crakers have. He is injured, and he has no way of determining how the other survivors will respond to him and to the beings that Crake has left for him to protect. If the Crakers continue developing as they have, creating hierarchies and sign systems contrary to Crake's design, or if the humans are able to reproduce, then there is also a chance that the whole cycle of a civilization destroying itself could be repeated. These plot points and others have led many critics to comment on the bleak prospects for the future suggested in Atwood's ending. Although an optimistic reading of the end of the novel is not popular, Atwood does provide evidence for an alternative reading.[8] As a species, Homo sapiens have shown they have the capacity to adapt to their environment, to evolve physically over generations in response to changing circumstances. Crake's prediction that it would only take a break of one generation to insure the annihilation of a species has not come to pass; at least one woman and three men have survived, and thus reproduction is possible, even if Snowman succumbs to his infection. Atwood even dangles the possibility of the female survivor being a nurse, and medical supplies, as Snowman has shown, can be found in the compounds. The Crakers are developing the capacity to learn, and they have a teacher who knows most intimately what went wrong in the old world to guide their education. Some critics question the inconsistency of Crake's leaving Jimmy as the sole guardian of his progeny, given Crake's desire to eliminate the very features of humanity that Jimmy represents

(Dunning 96). However, this act can be explained through Crake's repeated underestimation of Jimmy's ability and his over-estimation of science's power to squelch the humanistic impulses in a newly created species. Despite Crake's efforts, his progeny retain the capacity to dream, to sing, to enjoy stories, and to develop religious rituals.

Speculation about what will happen to Snowman and the Crakers is a natural by-product of Atwood's open ending to the novel, but this is a work of fiction, so the future within that fictional world is not nearly as important as the instruction this imaginative work of art provides for the reader. The full impact of Atwood's dystopian myth, then, comes not in the potential clues she leaves for the next episode in the story, but in the way she reinforces in the reader the skills she extols in her protagonist. By focusing on Snowman's emotional growth and giving her reader access to his inner psychological struggles, she fosters the same kind of empathetic impulse in the reader that she depicts developing in the protagonist. In requiring the reader to supply the ending of the narrative, she forces participation in the same imaginative process that the gifted Snowman engages in, a process that Atwood sees as "no longer a pastime or even a duty but a necessity" ("The Handmaid's Tale" 517). In perhaps the most interesting authorial manipulation, though, Atwood trains her reader in the same linguistic and literary skills that make her protagonist outstanding. In despair that his memory is failing, Snowman makes lists of words and quotes passages from a wide range of texts. In this act of reciting his accumulated store of knowledge, Snowman provides vocabulary instruction for the curious reader and a review of cultural artifacts that have shaped our collective identity. The fact that Snowman draws from all kinds of writing, not just canonical literature, actually privileges a reader who is well-versed in a variety of disciplines and suggests that the core values that can guide us may be embedded in a range of cultural texts. As Snowman sifts through the fragments of text he remembers, searching for ideas that may help him make sense of his situation, so must the reader of Atwood's text sift through images, symbols, and mythic allusions to make sense of the narrative. In leading her readers through this process, Atwood enables them to practice the kind of thinking that will counter the current nihilistic despair, that will help them fill in the gaps created when the old master narratives failed by pulling from their experience and dreaming new mythostories that can sustain them.

In Atwood's explanation of her novel's origin, she speaks of this kind of dream vision and locates precedents for it in literature and myth:

Mary Shelley started to write *Frankenstein* because of a dream she had, and so it was with Robert Louis Stevenson and Dr. *Jekyll and Mr. Hyde*;

and most works of fiction begin this way, whether the writer is asleep or awake. There's a Middle English convention called the dream vision, and I'd say most fiction writing has to have an element of dream vision twisted into its roots. I began *Oryx and Crake* when I was in Australia, land of the dreamtime; I "saw" the book as I was looking over a balcony at a rare red-headed crake, during a birding expedition—and birding is a trance-inducing activity if there ever was one. The details of the story got worked out later, but without the vision there would have been no book. ("The Handmaid's Tale" 517)

Atwood's reference to the Aboriginal concept of the Dream Time reveals the deep roots of the "saving graces" she emphasizes in her novel. The indigenous people of Australia see all life and all phenomena as part of a vast system of relationships, all connected. Their system of belief stresses the importance of environmental stewardship, the people's responsibility for protecting all life and keeping the land fertile and alive. It also posits the confluence of all times, past, present, and future, and thus acknowledges the continued impact of the past on the present and future ("Dreaming" 479-81). Eliade writes of the medicine man's role in the Aboriginal culture, "More and better than other members of his tribe, he can reactivate the contact with the Dream Time and thus renew his world. And because he can reintegrate at will the fabulous epoch of the beginning, he can 'dream' new myths and rituals" (157). As a fictional character, Snowman functions as a medicine man for the Crakers, devising new myths and rituals for them. As his creator, and as someone who pulls from existing cultural lore to create her own vision, Atwood serves as ours. Both Snowman and Atwood, by sharing their love of words, kernels of wisdom from their vast knowledge of cultural texts, and their visions, have the capacity to help their audiences "come to a better understanding of who we are and what we want, and what our limits may be" ("The Handmaid's Tale" 517).

Notes

[1] I am admittedly using the term "myth" loosely, not wishing to enter the ongoing definitional debates that span many disciplinary boundaries. In discussing the cosmogony that Snowman invents for the Crakers, and which they, collectively, believe, I am employing the most traditional sense of myth. However, I also read Atwood's novel as a prophetic myth for our time, an attempt on her part to make our collective experience intelligible through a narrative that is a representation "of truths or values that are sanctioned by general belief" (Douglas 121). Atwood's report that her novel began with a vision while she was in Australia (517) and the connections she establishes with the Aboriginal concept of Dream Time add to the

mythic quality of her text. While I recognize the basic distinctions that separate a contemporary work of literature from a culture's mythology, I also believe that works of speculative fiction, such as Atwood's, can function as a corollary to myth, perhaps as a call for collective awareness and renewal of belief (in certain values rather than in specific religious dogma) in an age where all established master-narratives are suspect. In *The Many Meanings of Myth*, Martin S. Day writes,

> In secular guise, however, prophetic myth is rampant today as science fiction, perhaps the strongest claimant to 'myth of the 20th century.' Traditionally the 'dreamtime' of myth has been the remote past; hosts of modern myth-makers from Jules Verne to Ray Bradbury are projecting our 'dreamtime' of myth to the future. (25)

William G. Doty also suggests that there may be a "mythic dimension to such speculative fictions" (19) and that the move away from mimetic realism in contemporary literature may be "an attempt to point more vitally toward some *projected* meanings of the world" (241). In explaining the value of mythography, Doty provides an interesting parallel to what I feel Atwood is depicting in her novel:

> Mythography, critically pursued, may function as a curettage device, scalpeling away debris (from our present perspective) that should have been removed long ago. But it also may provide us with some of the tools for making moral choices among the vast range of myths that are available to us; it should provide us with a heightened dedication to forge the best possible personal and cultural mythostories, the stories that can serve as symbolic constructions of reality leading to individual freedom and social growth rather than a retreat into an automatically repeated and uncritical view of historical events that now may need to be drastically reshaped. (19)

In her depiction of Snowman creating his life narrative, and in the writing of the novel, Atwood represents this process, pulling together a wide array of "symbolic constructions" from all different kinds of texts in an effort to promote "individual freedom and social growth."

[2] Danette DiMarco notes this change, but her interpretation differs slightly from the one offered here (192-3).

[3] See Ingersoll, DiMarco, and Bouson for more in-depth discussion of these topics.

[4] See Karen Stein for a full discussion of Atwood's storytellers in *The Blind Assassin* and earlier works.

[5] Helen Mundler discusses Atwood's treatment of language at length in "Heritage, Pseudo-Heritage and Survival in a Spurious Wor(l)d," offering a more pessimistic interpretation of Snowman's discourse after the apocalypse. She sees Snowman's listing of words as "free-floating signifiers without signifieds, referentless language" (96), the history he tells as spurious, and his character as "a textual construct held together only through a web of connection to other texts" (94). Eleonora Rao writes of the relief that words and the act of storytelling afford Snowman, but like Mundler, she focuses on the loss of his skills and the gaps in his story (111).

[6] DiMarco writes that by raising
Oryx to mythological status," Snowman "constructs a vision of her that sees her as an instrument to be used to sustain community and love. She is reinvented as a goddess whose genuine concern for nature requires that its people give attention to regenerative possibilities, like returning the bones of the fish to the waters that have provided the food. (186)

[7] Both Stephen Dunning and Dunja Mohr read Snowman's capacity as a storyteller as an optimistic sign for the future. Mohr writes, "narration, story-telling, and a valorization of the multiplicity of language and words not only constitute forms of survivalist defiance, but also hope for the persistence of creativity" (18), and Dunning admits that "Although the novel is understandably coy about the status of Snowman's sacred stories, it clearly suggests that we cannot do without such tales" (98).

[8] Earl Ingersoll does not see the textual support for a hopeful outlook on Snowman's future. He writes, "it is troubling that the ending of *Oryx and Crake* may be contaminated with a similar 'optimism' for which readers may have difficulty finding any firm basis" (par. 28).

Works Cited

Atwood, Margaret. *"The Handmaid's Tale* and *Oryx and Crake* in Context." *PMLA Publications of the Modern Language Association of America* 119.3 (May 2004): 513-517.

—. *Oryx and Crake: A Novel.* 2003. New York, Anchor Books.

—. "Perfect Storms: Writing *Oryx and Crake.*" Book-Of-The-Month Club/Bookspan. London: O.W. Toad Ltd, 2003. Margaret Atwood: Oryx and Crake. 18 June 2008
<http://www.oryxandcrake.co.uk/perfectstorm.asp>

Bouson, J. Brooks. "'It's Game Over Forever': Atwood's Satiric Vision of a Bioengineered Posthuman Future in *Oryx and Crake.*" *Journal of Commonwealth Literature* 39.3 (Sept. 2004): 139-156.

Day, Martin S. *The Many Meanings of Myth.* 1984. Lanham: University Press of America.

DiMarco, Danette. "Paradice Lost, Paradise Regained: homo faber and the Makings of a New Beginning in *Oryx and Crake.*" *Papers on Language and Literature: A Journal for Scholars and Critics of Language and Literature* 41.2 (Spring 2005): 170-95.

Doty, William G. Mythography: *The Study of Myths and Rituals.* 1986. University: The University of Alabama Press.

"Dreaming, The." *The Encyclopedia of Religion.* 1987. Ed. Mircea Eliade. Vol. 4. New York: MacMillan Publishing Company. 479-481.

Dunning, Stephen. "Margaret Atwood's *Oryx and Crake*: The Terror of the Therapeutic." *Canadian Literature* 186 (Autumn 2005): 86-101.

Eliade, Mircea. *Australian Religions: An Introduction.* Ithaca: Cornell University Press, 1973.

Grace, Sherrill E. "Articulating the 'Space Between': Atwood's Untold Stories and Fresh Beginnings." 1983. *Margaret Atwood: Language, Text, and System.* Ed. Sherrill E. Grace and Lorraine Weir. Vancouver: University of British Columbia Press. 1-16.

Howells, Coral Ann. "Margaret Atwood's dystopian visions: *The Handmaid's Tale* and *Oryx and Crake.*" 2006. *The Cambridge Companion to Margaret Atwood.* Ed. Coral Ann Howells. Cambridge: Cambridge University Press. 161-175.

Ingersoll, Earl G. "Survival in Margaret Atwood's Novel *Oryx and Crake.*" *Extrapolation: A Journal of Science Fiction and Fantasy* 45.2 (Summer 2004): 162-175.

Mohr, Dunja M. "Transgressive Utopian Dystopias: The Postmodern Reappearance of Utopia in the Disguise of Dystopia." *Zeitschrift für Anglistik und Amerikanistik: A Quarterly of Language, Literature and Culture* 55.1 (2007): 5-24.

Mundler, Helen E. "Heritage, Pseudo-Heritage and Survival in a Spurious Wor(l)d: *Oryx and Crake* by Margaret Atwood." *Commonwealth Essays and Studies* 27.1 (Autumn 2004): 89-98.

Rao, Eleonora. "Home and Nation in Margaret Atwood's Later Fiction." 2006. *The Cambridge Companion to Margaret Atwood.* Ed. Coral Ann Howells. Cambridge: Cambridge University Press. 100-113.

Stein, Karen F. "Talking Back to Bluebeard: Atwood's Fictional Storytellers." 2003. *Margaret Atwood's Textual Assassinations: Recent Poetry and Fiction.* Ed. Sharon Rose Wilson. Columbus: Ohio State University Press. 154-71.

CHAPTER THREE

STAGING PENELOPE: MARGARET ATWOOD'S CHANGING AUDIENCE

SHANNON HENGEN

Canadian artists and cultural practitioners have attempted from the early years of Margaret Atwood's career to bring her works to an audience wider than the solo reader alone in his/her study, or indeed the live audience—however large—for Atwood herself reading from her work. For example, in 1981, several Canadian film producers brought an adaptation of the novel *Surfacing* to the large screen. In 1990, a US/Germany collaboration adapted her most popular novel, *The Handmaid's Tale*, into a film with somewhat greater success and wider distribution. The Women's Network (Canada) commissioned a series of six of Atwood's short stories for television in 2003, and in 2007, CBC TV in Canada aired a version of the novel *The Robber Bride*. These four ventures translated her fiction to the screen.

Canadian theatre artists have also attempted translations for the stage. David Carley's script, *The Edible Woman*, was performed in 2002 at the Canadian Stage Company, Toronto. In 1999, Clare Coulter dramatized selections from *Good Bones* in a one-woman show at the Tarragon Theatre's Extra Space in Toronto. A group of female theatre practitioners in Toronto, Company of Sirens, created and performed in several small spaces between 1985 and 1993 a piece called Penelope, the piece drawing heavily on Atwood's "Circe/Mud Poems" from the book *You Are Happy*. And in the United States, musicians at Syracuse University in New York have very recently performed and recorded some of Atwood's poetry in songs commissioned by young female US composers. Writes soprano Eileen Strempel of these musical settings: "live Atwood's texts are so dramatic (operatic even)." Audiences for these live performances have been small but receptive.

What has occurred with great success in more recent years has been the adaptation of her fiction to the large stage. In 2004 the Canadian Opera Company mounted the opera version of *The Handmaid's Tale* to appreciative audiences at Toronto's Hummingbird Centre with a seating capacity of 3,200. And in 2007, in an unprecedented collaboration with the UK's Royal Shakespeare Company, the National Arts Centre based in Ottawa, Canada, produced the well received cabaret rendering of Atwood's 2005 novella, *The Penelopiad.*

My paper will address the possibility that this movement of Margaret Atwood's work from page to stage—that is, the large stage of the Hummingbird Centre for the Performing Arts and, especially, the National Arts Centre in the Canadian national capital —deepens the place of her work in the national cultural imagination. How it does so can be described at least in part by reference to the art of oral story telling.

Atwood explained to radio journalist Carol Off in a CBC interview about the staged rendering of *The Penelopiad* that the origins of myth are always both oral and local, that myth is shaped from the beginning by its method of delivery *and* by the time and place in which it is told. Oral delivery in preliterate cultures implied a somatic or physical connection with words that we in literate cultures can only sense, according to Walter Ong in his influential study, *Orality and Literacy.* In preliterate cultures where words travel exclusively via the speech of human beings, "Words acquire their meanings only from their always insistent actual habitat" (47); furthermore, "Spoken words are always modifications of a total, existential situation, which always engages the body" (67). In the oral-formulaic tradition that Ong studies over time, tellers of tales and their listeners feel viscerally the values implied in the tales. Exchanging experiences to arrive at communal identification with local knowledge describes the ancient art of oral storytelling. Ong concludes that "For an oral culture learning or knowing means achieving close, empathetic, communal identification with the known" (45).

While we do not, naturally, enter a preliterate state when we view Classical myth in a theatre, we may reconstruct to a degree the experience of its original audience, an experience of unmediated identification that is unique to the stage. After a recent production of selections from Ovid's *Metamorphoses* at a theatre in Cambridge, Massachusetts, I was able to correspond with the play's director, Carmel O'Reilly, who is also artistic director of Súgán Theatre in Boston and Visiting Director at Harvard University. When asked to comment on the return of Classical tales to their original oral format through live theatre, O'Reilly wrote:

Distilling them [the tales] into drama allows us to access and acknowledge our own feelings to life around us. They are not about rational notions but reflect some deep part of our emotional being. . . . As creatures with imagination we may need this moment of escape not just into a kind of dreamworld but into our own often ignored feelings. It fulfills our need for union in some holy way.

When asked to comment on whether or not audience members might be more likely to sense the importance of the stories to their lives by watching the stories performed than by reading or seeing them on a screen, she responded:

In the case of Mary Zimmerman's play [Metamorphoses] the approach has been to create a rich theatrical event embracing drama, dance, poetry with water as a metaphorical agent for the play. Such an approach makes the magic possible as all our senses respond through that combination of those performance styles. When the narrator asks "Do you remember the smell of apples?" there is a collective response from the cast and then the audience. This has been noted by audience and reviewers alike. And it may have nothing to do with apples. It touches some chord of memory and personal association. . . . A single personal moment translated into a collective event. . . . What more could we ask of theatre?

My claim is that when Atwood's Penelope opens the play with the words "Don't follow my example," a warning that she would scream at us if she could scream, she is beckoning us to relive experientially and individually Penelope's neglect of her disadvantaged maids and then as an audience to discern the instances and effects of similar neglect in our time. Considering the networks of powerful and talented women who collaborated to make this co-production possible, we might conclude that the myth of Penelope holds unique appeal, and that appeal may lie in the myth's exposing the effects of the failures of our collaboration in support of vulnerable women.

About the opera version of *The Handmaid's Tale*, reviewer Tamara Bernstein of Canada's *The National Post* newspaper wrote:

The opera gives us something no novel can: the force of communal experience. It's one thing to read a novel, quite another to experience Atwood's vision with thousands of others. You could feel the cathartic power in the opening-night ovations for all . ... But when Atwood herself came onstage, the audience released the greatest roar I've ever heard from a Toronto audience. Don't miss this show. ("The Handmaid's Tale")

Bernstein attributes the opera's success in part to the timeliness of the issues raised in *The Handmaid's Tale*: the defiance and reluctant heroism of the female lead, the haunting by its Puritan theocratic origins of a nation—the US—attempting "to reinvent itself." Important current themes along with elaborate public presentation of them seem to give Atwood's work a new immediacy, indeed a new public.

Consider, then, the impact of her more recent work being produced in what has been described as a cabaret style, a mix of choral song, monologue, dialogue, and dance, a style more accessible than opera. When the content of the script becomes the tale of Odysseus's wife, Penelope, from Homer's epic, and equally the never-told tale of the twelve maids who accompany her during her twenty-year wait for her husband's return, further connections arise between audience and performers, among performers, between two national companies in two countries, and between Canada's national theatre and a group of wealthy female Canadian benefactors. I propose that the various fruitful linkings that we will now consider develop at least somewhat from the nature of the medium of oral storytelling itself, particularly its origins in the preliterate Classical world out of which the figures of Penelope and her maids come to us. Paradoxically, in fashioning anew tales from ancient Greece, Atwood's imagination captures contemporary Canada and to a degree the UK in a most visceral and immediate way.

Marcel Jousse's study, *The Oral Style*, published originally in 1924 and influential in the later oral-formulaic theory, claims that as gestural creatures we must acknowledge the beginnings of speech in the body, especially the human body's need for balance:

> A man carries the most conviction when he is able to seize his audience, rock them, as a mother rocks her child. We are essentially balancing, undulating beings. (xx)

We learn language as a visceral experience, social clichés becoming, according to Jousse, integral to our growth as organisms. Words imitate actions. In Atwood's maids' choreographed repetition of the lines "we are the maids / the ones you killed / the ones you failed . . . // it was not fair" in the second scene of the play and then again in the final scene touches the audience deeply: we recall at both conscious and unconscious levels how we first learned the concept of injustice, Jousse would argue.

Atwood adapted the script of *The Penelopiad* from her own novella of the same name, the novella having been commissioned and published by Canongate in 2005 as part of its series on myth in the contemporary world. Of the title character, Atwood writes in her Author's Introduction to the play, "Penelope . . . although somewhat weepy—is resourceful and brave, and (as befits the wife of Odysseus, master trickster) a good liar" (vii). Of her maids whom Odysseus kills abruptly upon his return home she writes:

> The hanging of these maids bothered me when I first read The Odyssey as a teenager, and it bothers me still, as it is so excessive in relation to anything they actually did. (vi)

Her chosen topic, although originating in the ancient world, might remind us of similar contemporary Atwoodian topoi: dangerous, unpredictable men; powerful, vulnerable, flawed women; power*less*, vulnerable, flawed women; troubled liaisons between them; disastrous political situations in which all are implicated. In two obvious examples, the handmaids of that tale and their male and female owners come to mind, as do Grace Marks and her companion domestics in their subservient roles in the novel *Alias Grace*.

We learn through recent media accounts of the collaboration between two powerful women that initiated *The Penelopiad* as opera and as co-production: the meeting between Phyllida Lloyd, British director of the opera version of *The Handmaid's Tale*, and Margaret Atwood, during Lloyd's stay in Toronto for the opera. Richard Ouzounian writing for the *Toronto Star* newspaper states that "Atwood let Lloyd read the still-unpublished novel. The director shared her sense of the work's dramatic possibilities, and they began working on it together" ("The Penelopiad"). We are sent both in the Ouzounian piece and in the playbill for the Canadian premiere to a blog by one of the actors, Canadian Kate Hennig (Eurycleia), where we learn of the routine standing ovations that the work received in Ottawa. For example, see this entry posted on 22 September 2007, the day after opening:

> The response of the audiences here in Ottawa is considerably different to the reaction in England. The English, and Irish women in our cast have remarked on it, too. I'm not sure what to chalk it up to, but we have had standing ovations for every show here. It's such a pleasure. Maybe it's a Canadian story? Or maybe it's told in a way that we are somehow akin to? Maybe we're really hitting our stride now? Or maybe we're just proud that this is a Canadian play, a Canadian production, a Canadian success story? Whatever it is, it feels so great to have such an amazing response from our home crowd! Yee haw. THANK YOU OTTAWA!
> (thepenelopiad.wordpress.com)

Throughout Hennig's blog we hear of close friendships developing among the international cast. Unprecedented working relationships between the creative teams of the Royal Shakespeare Company and the National Arts Centre resulted in successful runs at both the Swan Theatre in Stratford-upon-Avon, UK, in the summer of 2007 and in Ottawa, Canada that fall.

Furthermore, an unusual connection developed between nine wealthy and influential Canadian women and the play's creative team, we learn from the Canadian playbill and from Hennig's blog. The playbill reads as follows:

> In recognition of the many Canadian artists involved in *The Penelopiad*, nine remarkable Canadian women from across our country have given leadership gifts to champion The Penelopiad project and ensure that the National Arts Centre could create this valuable opportunity . . .. These donors have come to be known as the Penelope Circle. Their shared vision and belief in the power of women's leadership to effect positive social change have been an inspiration to us all. Each member of the Penelope Circle has been encouraged to engage a young woman who she believes will have profound impact on our society, as a protégé. (n.p.)

In her blog of 30 September 2007, Hennig writes that she's off to the Governor General's place to participate in a panel discussion entitled:

> Leading by Example: Empowering the Next Generation of Canadian Women. The women of the Penelope Circle were there, along with about half our cast, and Rae McKen and Veronica Tennant. There were about 120 women altogether, including many recipients of the Order of Canada, and many high power executives from business, law, politics, and the Arts. The main speakers were Zita Cobb (an amazing chick from the Rock!), Gail Asper (a family success story from Winnipeg), and Marie Chouinard (a woman whose heart speaks through her body), along with her Excellency, Michaëlle Jean [Canada's Governor-General].

Somehow the telling of a Classical tale seems to have drawn artists, benefactors, and audience together uniquely. And, all of the actors, the writer, and the director are women, as are all of the benefactors.

The play opens in the underworld with one of Penelope's several monologues. Here she intones to the audience that historically she has been "A stick used to beat other women with" when held up as inhumanly patient, faithful, and long suffering (4). Then come the concluding lines of this first speech: "Don't follow my example, I want to scream in your ears—yes, yours! But when I try to scream, I sound like an owl" (4).

Audiences must discern throughout the rest of the work which aspects of Penelope's example we are not to follow. Given the focus on the heretofore voiceless maids, especially their conspiracy with the queen to save her life, ending not in a reward but rather in their senseless slaughter, we might think that Penelope is cautioning us, as women, not to allow mutual betrayal. Indeed her suffering in Hades seems to arise specifically from regrets over her neglect of her maids' safety. About their nightly unweaving of her father-in-law's death shroud with her, we hear her say of them: "we shared riddles; we made jokes. We became like sisters" (54). Then immediately after she comments that "In retrospect, I can see that my actions were ill-considered, and caused harm."(54). Her failure to protect her maids results not just in their deaths but also in her unrelieved torment. Director Josette Bushell-Mingo explains starkly that

> Odysseus was knackered and said to his son, take them [the maids] out and murder them. They were getting hoisted up—can you see it?—and slowly dying. Penelope could have said something. She didn't. We need to capture that" (qtd. in Taylor 92).

Penelope's suffering in Atwood's version seems then to lie as much in her betrayal of her maids as in the many absences and infidelities of her husband. Odysseus in fact disappears in the play's final scene, leaving the queen and the twelve approaching her with "ropes around their necks" (81). She queries: "What do you want from me? Just tell me! The Maids titter eerily, bat-like" and respond:

> we had no voice
> we had no name
> we had no choice
> we had one face
> one face the same
>
> we took the blame
> it was not fair
> but now we're here
> we're all here too
> the same as you
>
> and now we follow
> you, we find you
> now, we call
> to you to you

Penelope responds: "They never talk to me, down here. They never stay. I hold out my arms to them, my doves, my loveliest ones. But they only run away" (82).

That the play's reception varied from the UK to Canada, as noted in Kate Hennig's blog and corroborated in a comparison of newspaper reviews, only confirms Atwood's statement that myths are both oral and local. Canadian theatre-goers frequently awarded the show with standing ovations as if, in part, to show solidarity with its author, described in a recent *Chatelaine* interview as having the power to dispense special wisdom to Canadians (Mallick). With the move to large, prestigious national stages of Atwood's fiction, in particular her rendering of Classical myth, Atwood's work simultaneously moves closer to the centre of her country's and perhaps the anglophone world's cultural imagination both because of the nature of the cautionary tale she tells and its method of delivery with roots in an ancient oral art.

Works Cited

Al-Solaylee, Kamal. 24 Sept. 2007. "A hit, but not a home run." Rev. of *The Penelopiad*, by Margaret Atwood. National Arts Centre English Theatre Company in Association with the Royal Shakespeare Company. The National Arts Centre, Ottawa, Canada. *The Globe and Mail* (Toronto) R1.

Atwood, Margaret. *The Penelopiad: The Play*. 2007. London, UK: Faber and Faber.

—. *You Are Happy*. 1974. Toronto: Oxford UP.

Bernstein, Tamara. "Handmaid opera perfectly tailored." Rev. of *The Handmaid's Tale*. Canadian Opera Company. Hummingbird Centre for the Performing Arts. *The National Post* 27 Sept. 2004. Accessed through National Post librarian, Scott Maniquet (smaniquet@nationalpost.com). 26 Oct. 2007.

Carley, David. *The Edible Woman*. 2002. Scirocco Drama/J. Gordon Shillingford: Winnipeg, MB.

Hennig, Kate. thepenelopiad.wordpress.com. 27 Oct. 2007.

Howells, Coral Ann. "Five Ways of Looking at *The Penelopiad*." *Sydney Studies in English* 32 (2006): 1-18.

Jousse, Marcel. *The Oral Style* [1924]. Trans. Edgard Sienaert and Richard Whitaker. New York: Garland, 1990.

Mallick, Heather. "Margaret Atwood." *Chatelaine* October 2007: 37-38.

Marmion, Patrick. "Don't swap this wife." Rev. of *The Penelopiad*, by Margaret Atwood. Royal Shakespeare Company. Swan Theatre, Stratford-Upon-Avon, UK. Mail on Sunday (London) 5 Aug. 2007: FB64.

Off, Carol. Interview with Margaret Atwood. *As It Happens*. CBC Radio
    1. 18 Dec. 2006.
Ong, Walter J. *Orality and Literacy: The Technologizing of the Word*.
    1982. London: Routledge.
O'Reilly, Carmel. E-mail to the author. 25 Oct. 2007.
Penelope. Adapted from Margaret Atwood's "Circe / Mud Poems" by
    Cynthia Grant, Susan Seagrove, and Peggy Semple. *Canadian Theatre
    Review* 78 (Spring 1994): 4258.
The Penelopiad. By Margaret Atwood. Playbill. Dir. Josette Bushell-
    Mingo. Perf. Mojisola Adebayo, Jade Anouka, Lisa Karen Cox,
    Derbhle Crotty, Philippa Domville, Penny Downie, Kate Hennig,
    Pauline Hutton, Corrine Koslo, Sarah Malin, Pamela Matthews, Kelly
    McIntosh, Jenny Young. The National Arts Centre English Theatre
    Company in Association with The Royal Shakespeare Company (UK),
    Ottawa, Ontario, Canada. 19 Sept.-6 Oct. 2007.
Ouzounian, Richard. "*The Penelopiad*: Margaret Atwood's novel arrives
    on British stage with help from some Canadian friends." *The Toronto
    Star* 28 July 2007: E01.
Strempel, Eileen. E-Mail to the author. 29 Oct. 2007.
Taylor, Craig. "Twelve Angry Maids: Margaret Atwood's *The
    Penelopiad* brings forgotten corners of myth to light on stage." *The
    Walrus*. October 2007: 91-93.

CHAPTER FOUR

"WE CAN'T HELP BUT BE MODERN": *THE PENELOPIAD*

CORAL ANN HOWELLS

There is darkness all around and the sound of a howling wind. Where are we? We are not in Margaret Atwood's graphomanic tent (*The Tent*, 2006) this time, but in Hades. Or rather, we are in two places at once, for we are sitting in the Swan Theatre at Stratford- on-Avon watching a performance of *The Penelopiad*, where the theatrical space represents the Underworld, the place of forbidden knowledge: "There is something down there, and you want it told" (*Negotiating with the Dead*, 177). Under a single spotlight a heavily veiled figure appears on stage, then throwing off the veil, she begins to speak: "Now that I'm dead I know everything" (*The Penelopiad: The Play*, 3). Here is Penelope the icon of wifely fidelity celebrated in Homer's *Odyssey*, but should this "edifying legend" now unveiled be wearing a clinging ruby red dress and complaining about her mythic status, "Don't follow my example" ? (*The Penelopiad: The Play*, 4) Our unease increases when her twelve maids appear, accusing Penelope as they sing their edgy little lyric:

we are the maids
the ones you killed
the ones you failed
we danced in air (*The Penelopiad: The Play*, 4).

A whiff of scandal surrounds Atwood's woman-centered revision of *The Odyssey*, and it is this rather disreputable dimension that I shall be exploring in my discussion of Atwood's dialogue with Homer through her resurrection of the faithful Penelope, the *femme fatale* Helen of Troy, and Penelope's hanged maids. This essay will develop Atwood's arguments about legendary women and myths of femininity, primarily in relation to *The Penelopiad* but also with reference to her earlier representations of Penelope, Helen, and other goddess figures in her poetry, dating back to her first privately printed volume *Double Persephone* (1961). My object is to show how Atwood's use of mythological materials refocuses the grand narratives of classical myth through women's True Confessions in ways that are both parodic of and complicitous with the old patriarchal texts. Indeed, we might see such revisioning as another of Atwood's negotiations with the dead:

> As long as you continue to write, you continue to explore the work of writers who have preceded you … So, if you are going to indulge in narration, you'll have to deal, sooner or later, with those from previous layers of time. (*Negotiating*, 178)

Not only does Atwood locate her writing within a long literary tradition, but she also engages with the resurrection of some of the female ghosts out of that tradition, giving them a voice to speak directly to us in the present time.

Her legendary women lead duplicitous lives, always shadowed by their mythic identities but vigorously resisting their entrapment as they reinvent themselves in a contemporary idiom, giving very different emphases to the classical tales. Indeed, such transformations characterize Atwood's postmodern approach to mythography in general:

> Strong myths never die. Sometimes they die down, but they don't die out. They double back in the dark, they re-embody themselves, they change costumes, they change key. They speak in new languages, they take on other meanings. ("The Myths," 35)

Those images of shape-changing and surreptitious returns form the dead also remind us of Atwood's fascination with the Gothic, where "life of a sort can be bestowed by writing" (*Negotiating*, 172). From that perspective, *The Penelopiad* might be seen as Atwood's Gothic version of *The Odyssey*, while her description of the play script version as "an echo of an echo of an echo of an echo of an echo" (*The Penelopiad: The Play*, v) could be read as either very Gothic with its whispered continuities or as very postmodern with its deferrals and indeterminacies. *The Penelopiad* is itself a shape-changing text, first appearing in what Atwood calls "the book version" in 2005, then metamorphosing through a staged reading in a London church (where the author herself played the part of Penelope) into a play script adapted by her which had its first dramatic performance at the

Swan Theatre in 2007, a spectacular production where further changes were made after negotiations between the author and the director, Josette Bushell-Mingo. Like the ancient myths or Atwood's legendary women, *The Penelopiad* refuses to be confined within a single definitive form.

Atwood's project is to retell *The Odyssey* as "herstory" for modern readers, as she engages in the kind of feminist revisionary mythmaking at which, in common with Hélène Cixous, Adrienne Rich, and other contemporary Canadian writers like Alice Munro, Carol Shields and Aritha van Herk, she is so adept (*Open Letter*, 7-8).[1] As critic Sharon Wilson has remarked in her study of Atwood's myth revisions,

> Atwood has used mythology in much the same way she has used other intertexts …Whether explicitly named or simply implied, Atwood's varied mythological intertexts are central to her images, characterization, and themes. (Wilson, 215)[2]

This is not surprising when we remember that Atwood's literary imagination was nurtured in the mythic fifties at the University of Toronto by her professors Northrop Frye and Jay Macpherson. Frye regarded myth as the key to "the integral meaning [of a poem] presented by its metaphors, images, and symbols" {Bush Garden, ix) and Macpherson's poems of the mid 1950s like "Sibylla," "Sheba," and "Isis" prefigure Atwood's where women speak out of ancient myths and legends.

Interestingly, in *Double Persephone* Atwood had not yet found a voice for her heroine; in the title poem Persephone is wordless and dying, yet by the 1970s the ghostly voice of Canada's most famous nineteenth-century woman pioneer has taken over the national historical narrative and turned it into poetic autobiography in *The Journals of Susanna Moodie*: "I have my ways of getting through" (Moodie, 60). Similarly in *You Are Happy* (1974) Circe and the Sirens tell their own version of episodes in *The Odyssey* in voices that are irreverent and skeptical as they mock the posturing of male heroes. Circe is unimpressed by Odysseus' epic wanderings after the Trojan War: "Don't you ever get tired of saying Onward?" ("Eating Fire," 161), though she also recognizes that they are both prisoners in an earlier narrative: "Don't evade, don't pretend you won't leave after all; you leave in the story and the story is ruthless" ("Eating Fire," 176). Though not in control of the stories, Atwood's women insist on challenging the authority of classical myth by voicing their points of view, like Eurydice, who would rather have gone on "feeling nothing" than be called back from the dead by Orpheus ("Interlunar," 78), and most remarkably the immortal Helen of Troy, whom we find in the 1990s doing a striptease dance in a sleazy nightclub somewhere in Europe. Forced to earn her own living in the contemporary world, Helen is still up to her old tricks, seducing male patrons with her glamorous image of desirable femininity, though she views the sexual game with unsentimental clarity. Staring back at those who are staring at her, she perceives the animosity behind the avid male gaze:

> They gaze at me and see
> a chain-saw murder just before it happens (*Morning*, 312)

Helen sells herself a male fantasy, knowing that the power of a sex goddess resides in her unattainability and the threat of female sexuality, a piquant combination which she laconically exploits in her final challenge to her audience:

> You think I'm a goddess?
> Try me.
> This is a torch song.
> Touch me and you'll burn. (*Morning*, 313)

Atwood has become increasingly interested in the techniques and consequences of modernizing/postmodernizing myth, for as she says, "Who's doing the telling and who's doing the listening have a lot to do with the slant the story's given" ("Myths and Me," 36). In the contemporary Western world where ideas of the sacred and the supernatural are viewed with skepticism, neither Helen's semi-divine status nor the Sybil's role as prophetess is likely to be taken seriously. Helen's story is reduced to parody in the prose poem, "It's Not Easy Being Half-Divine." In this version Helen and Paris's elopement, that notorious cause of the Trojan War, is translated into gossip about a small-town scandal where the beautiful young wife of the local police chief runs off with a man from the city who is passing through. Told in colloquial language by an eye witness who "lived down the street," the legend does not die but merely becomes contaminated by the popular culture of celebrity:

> Says it wasn't easy when she was growing up, being half-divine and all,
> but now she's come to terms with it and she's looking at a career in the
> movies. (*The Tent*, 49)

Rather more mythically, Helen chooses to make excursions between the Underworld of *The Penelopiad* and Las Vegas, where she seems to have lost none of her traditional powers but is still causing uproar and ruining men, though Penelope is inclined to remind her that she is really only just a myth - to which Atwood might reply, "Every myth is a version of the truth" (*Lady Oracle*, 92). The Sybil, another of Atwood's favourite mythic women from Lady Oracle onwards, has become a fortuneteller, sounding grumpy and out of sorts in "Another Visit to the Oracle":

> Why should I tell you anything true?
> Why should I tell you anything?
> You're not paying me. (*The Door*, 2007)

However, the Sybil still retains her gift for prophecy, though in a characteristic Atwoodian twist she no longer looks to the gods for revelation but at human beings and the world around her, warning against disaster to the planet:

> I tell dark stories
> before and after they come true. (*The Door*, 106).

This is the same crone voice that has always been associated with the Oracle, and it sounds remarkably like the voice of old Iris Chase Griffen in *The Blind Assassin*, reminding us again of the pervasiveness of mythic subtexts in all of Atwood's writing.

In *The Penelopiad* Atwood returns to the classical Greek Underworld where her playful reinvention of women's voices and feminine cultural history works to counterbalance Homeric narratives of male heroism and adventure. Like Virginia Woolf eighty years before, Atwood is irked by

> the masculine values that prevail … This is an important book, the critic assumes, because it deals with war. This is an insignificant book because it deals with the feelings of women in a drawing-room" (Woolf, 96).

So Atwood challenges *The Odyssey* by deliberately flouting epic conventions: instead of war she deals with domestic relations, shifting the action indoors, and dismantling the epic model by transforming it into a double-voiced female confessional narrative, interspersed with song-and-dance routines, a burlesque drama, an anthropology lecture, and a trial scene, videotaped by the maids. These shifting forms draw attention to the different generic conventions through which stories may be told, so casting doubt on the authority of any single account. Atwood is highlighting the malleability of myths and their openness to revision as she offers her gendered reading designed to focus on some of the gaps and silences relating to woman's lives in *The Odyssey*.

Atwood asks two main questions: "what led to the hanging of the maids, and what was Penelope really up to?"(*The Penelopiad* xv). Homer does not tell us, but Robert Graves does—or at least he gives some partial answers in *The Greek Myths* as he repeats ancient slanderous tales about Penelope, suggesting that she slept with her suitors—perhaps with all of them—and that she gave birth to the Great God Pan during Odysseus's twenty-year long absence at the Trojan War followed by his long journey home to Ithaca. However, like any good gossip Graves cannot vouch for the truth of these rumors, but merely circulates them: "Some say … others say …But, according to a third" (Graves, 646). Atwood appropriates these non-Homeric materials and changes a few episodes in *The Odyssey*, but her crucial addition is one which is not mentioned in the Notes (though references to it are embedded in the text), and that is Aeschylus's *The Oresteia*. The burlesque scene of Odysseus's trial and his subsequent persecution by the twelve hanged maids blurs the borders between him and Orestes, who was tried for the murder of his mother, and then like Odysseus was acquitted, only to be pursued by the Erinyes (who also appear briefly at Odysseus's trial in Atwood's version though not in Homer's). By conflating these figures Atwood not only constructs a parallel between two instances of male violence against women but she also writes beyond the ending of *The Odyssey*, deftly switching the plot by reversing traditional sexual power relations as Odysseus is stalked for all eternity by the vengeful hanged maids: "We'll never leave you, we'll stick to you like your shadow, soft and relentless as glue. Pretty maids, all in a row" (*The Penelopiad*, 193).

Both Penelope and her maids offer their own versions of events, for though Penelope's monologue is the dominant narrative, her tale is frequently interrupted and challenged by the stories of her maids, those nameless slave girls who have practically nothing to say in *The Odyssey* and whose hanging is a minor element in the story of Odysseus's homecoming. Yet, as Atwood remarks, "I've always been haunted by the hanged maids, and in *The Penelopiad*, so is Penelope herself" (*The Penelopiad* xv). While Homer does not even bother to comment on the relation between Penelope and her maids, leaving their fates to Eurycleia and Telemachus who hangs them, Atwood's feminist critique of Homer makes the relationship between these women the centre of *The Penelopiad*, and Penelope's implication in their deaths is the unsolved mystery at the heart of the narrative. Her story is paralleled and shadowed by the maids' stories, who like the Handmaids of Gilead, have been relegated to the margins of epic narrative: "From the point of view of future history …we'll be invisible" (*The Handmaid's Tale*, 240). Writing against such erasure, Atwood uses her novelistic imagination to expand Homer's text, gesturing, as in so many of her novels, towards Old Testament handmaids, nineteenth century servant girls, and contemporary Third World sex slaves. Not surprisingly, the maids' stories are very subversive, not only of the masculine values that prevailed in ancient Greece but also of Penelope's version of events. Were they hanged because they knew too much? The question hovers, for Atwood is aware of the power of a good riddle or an unsolved crime to generate suspense, while she describes her writing of *The Penelopiad* as her opportunity "not only to revisit an ancient and powerful tale but also to explore a few dark alleyways in the story that have always intrigued me" ("The Myths," 38). In the process, Atwood shifts the focus of *The Odyssey* away from grand narratives of war, relocating it in the micronarratives of women at home.

Our attention is riveted by Penelope's first words, whether spoken onstage or on the page, for this is an oral narrative: "What is written down is a score for voice, and what the voice most often does … is tell … story" (*Negotiating*,142). There is something almost sinister about this resurrection of a character from ancient myth who declares that she is a ghost speaking to us from the world of the dead, trapped in a "state of bonelessness, lipless, breastlessness," and trying to make herself heard as she puts her own spin on an old tale, "But when I try to scream, I sound like an owl" (*The Penelopiad*, 2). Where does Penelope exist? She is outside the human world of bodies and time and possibly inaudible, so how does she contrive to defy those limits, just as she resists her entrapment in patriarchal myths? The answer to this paradoxical condition of being lies in a "trick of ventriloquism" performed by the artist's creative imagination, as Atwood spelled it out in a poem over thirty years ago aptly entitled "Corpse Song": "I exist in two places,/ here and where you are"(*Eating Fire*, 155). Penelope may be robed in funereal black as Atwood was in her title role, or she may be dressed in vibrant red like Penney Downie at Stratford, but like all Atwood's vanished storytellers - and there is a long line of them from Offred to Zenia to Grace Marks to Iris and Oryx-what survives is the power of voice: "By my voice I shall be known" - an echo of an echo once again, this time Atwood echoing Ovid (*Negotiating*, 180).

The transgression of boundaries, which is one of the marks of both the Gothic and the postmodern sensibility, has characterized Atwood's poetry and fiction from its beginnings, and for her the creative writing process is always haunted by intimations of mortality:

> All writing of the narrative kind, and perhaps all writing, is motivated, deep down, by a fear and fascination with mortality – by a desire to make

the risky trip to the Underworld and to bring something or someone back from the dead" (Negotiating, 140).

In *The Penelopiad* traffic goes both ways, shifting from high seriousness to comedy as Atwood's ghosts find way of crossing the threshold, blurring the mythic and the contemporary by mixing ancient rituals, spiritualism and high tech. Penelope herself manages to escape the claustrophobic Underworld which is so like her domestic spaces in Ithaca by travelling about to look in on the world of the living via the internet, so becoming in her afterlife a fabulous voyager like her husband and more like the gods themselves who "must have had something like that at their disposal" (*The Penelopiad*, 19).

Her confession has the parodic quality of Atwood's earlier short dramatic monologues in *Murder in the Dark* (1983) or *Good Bones* (1992). In fact, Penelope sounds a lot like that other queen in "Gertrude Talks Back," where Atwood irreverently applies what Reingard Nischik calls "her technique of gender-oriented revisioning … to one of the greatest works of world literature, Shakespeare's *Hamlet*" (Nischik, 156). Homer's Penelope was praised as the model of wifely loyalty and virtue, as being skilled in handicraft (and incidentally as having "an excellent brain"); it is only the jealous suitor Antinous who dares to criticize her in her lifetime as "that incomparable schemer" (*Odyssey*, Book 1, 39), but Atwood's Penelope knows that she has been the butt of dirty jokes and scandalous tales. So, three thousand years after *The Odyssey*, she asserts her right to tell a different story, being of a "determined nature" but refusing to have her identity determined for her by others. She says she is offering us "the plain truth," but how true is it? Atwood is playing with two different levels of myth here, on the one hand is the Homeric myth of feminine virtue and on the other are popular myths about the female sex as either submissive and silent or as duplicitous schemers–and which is Penelope? Atwood highlights the contradictions posed by these gender stereotypes as she peers into some of the dark alleyways in Homer's narrative, using similar techniques as a mythographer to the ones she used as a historical novelist in *Alias Grace*, digging below official versions of history to unearth "the mysterious, the buried, the forgotten, the discarded, the taboo" ("In Search," 218). However, buried under centuries of accumulated gossip and speculation, Penelope like Grace remains an enigma, so that Atwood is free to reinvent her in a modern idiom. As she commented when writing *Alias Grace*, "Whatever we write will be contemporary, even if we attempt a novel set in a past age"("In Search," 210).

Refusing to consider the subject matter of epic except as it affects her personally (Penelope's chapter on the Trojan War is called "Helen Ruins My Life"), Penelope is concerned with the practicalities of domestic life, first as a neglected and abused royal daughter, and then with her duties as wife, mother and mistress of Odysseus's household and large estates during his long absence. This postmodern domestification of myth differs from its modernist use in a novel like Joyce's *Ulysses*, which Meletinsky describes as "the removal of the masks that cover some eternal and immutable principles...manifested in the triviality of everyday life" (Meletinsky, 275); Atwood does quite the opposite, removing the masks from the banality of life in classical Greece, thereby revealing principles which are eternal and immutable from the feminine point of view. Penelope comments on her problems with her in-laws and with Odysseus's nurse Eurycleia, on her rivalry with her cousin Helen , on her husband's long absence, and on her difficulties as a single mother with a teenaged son: "Whether ancient Greece or the contemporary world, it's all just the usual family dynamics. Remove the fancy language, and that's what it is" (Dixon, R 12).

Penelope is expert at removing the fancy language of Homeric epic, manifesting a very postmodern skepticism towards tales of heroism and the sacred. Not only does she undercut Odysseus's physical and moral stature by repeatedly commenting on his "short legs" and "how can I put this?—his unscrupulousness" (*The Penelopiad*, 3), but through her ironic mode of storytelling mythic incidents are drained of the supernatural. Odysseus's adventures with monsters and goddesses are reduced to the level of gossip and tall tales by a technique which has been described as "the collision of myth with a mimetic restitution or reality" (Dvorak, 117). His encounters with the Cyclops and the Lestrygonians are little better that drunken brawls, while the Circe legend becomes the subject of sly sexual innuendo:

> Odysseus was the guest of a goddess on an enchanted isle, said some; she'd turned his men into pigs–not a hard job in my opinion – but had turned them back into men because she'd fallen in love with him and was feeding him unheard-of delicacies every night; no, said others, it was just an expensive whorehouse and he was sponging off the Madam. (*The Penelopiad*, 83-4)

As Penelope admits, tale-telling is a "low art" practiced by old women, beggars and children—but also by Odysseus and herself. After all, it was Odysseus, the "arch deceiver" as Homer calls him (or "that crafty old codger" to use the maids' demotic phrase) who first encouraged his shy young bride to find her voice on their wedding night in order to get rid of the listeners outside the bedroom door: "Do you think you could manage a few screams?" (*The Penelopiad*, 44) And of course Penelope obliges. From the beginning they are fellow conspirators and tricksters, and if Penelope is charmed by Odysseus's storytelling it is because she can spin a good yarn herself as she weaves her web of words as deftly as she wove her father-in-law's shroud. But Penelope is also adept at unpicking, and unlike her husband she uses very feminine rhetorical strategy which Nathalie Cooke has described as "The Powerful Voice That Asserts Its Own Powerlessness" (Cook, 212).[3] She even confesses her own unreliability as a narrator ("Perhaps I have only invented it in order to make myself feel better," *The Penelopiad*, 8), or else she draws attention to her own innocent duplicities when she has to appear to be surprised by her son or her husband, notably on Odysseus' return disguised as a beggar. Here Penelope contradicts *The Odyssey*, for Homer gives the recognition scene to Eurycleia, asserting that Penelope did not recognize her husband a she was distracted at the critical moment by the goddess Athena—to which Atwood's Penelope make the tart comment: "If you believe that, you'll believe all sorts of nonsense" (P, 140). However it is in the climax of their blissful reunion that Atwood's version differs most substantially from Homer's in Book 23. In *The Odyssey* husband and wife lie in bed talking till dawn, though there is no suggestion that Penelope is anything other than loyal and true as she listens "spellbound" to Odysseus' tales, whereas in *The Penelopiad* Penelope herself tells it differently:

> The two of us – by our own admission – proficient and shameless liars of long standing. It's a wonder either of believed a word the other said.
> But we did.
> Or so we told each other. (*The Penelopiad*, 173)

Here Atwood the trickster novelist has slyly transposed Athena's words praising Odysseus, "we are both adepts in chicane" (*Odyssey*, Book 12, 210), making Odysseus and Penelope the perfect match for each other. It would appear that Penelope is the latest in Atwood's long line of duplicitous female storytellers–beginning with Joan Foster in *Lady Oracle*, continuing through *The Robber Bride*, *Alias Grace*, *The Blind Assassin* and *Oryx and Crake*—who seduce and delight their audience with their riddling tales. Perhaps we should heed Atwood's warning in her poem about "True Stories" that they are always

> vicious
> and multiple and untrue

after all" ("True Stories," 11).

A different version of the True Story is told by Penelope's maids, "those naughty little jades" whose voices run in counterpoint to her throughout, reflecting on what is the most intimate relationship in *The Penelopiad*. As slave girls they represent a different area of female experience in ancient Greece, one which lies outside all the myths of femininity, for these are the women with "no name," "no voice," "no choice," as faceless during their lives as Penelope claims to be in death. By restoring to them a collective voice (they are usually referred to as "The Chorus") Atwood transforms *The Penelopiad* into a polyphonic narrative where the maids' tale-telling casts doubt on the authenticity of Penelope's confession, extending the issue of power politics beyond the traditional male/female binary to include women's relations with one another. Hovering over the narrative and refusing to be silenced or to go away, they insist on talking about unmentionable topics, blaming Penelope for betraying them and accusing her of repeated infidelities with her suitors. Of course she asserts that she was blameless, taking refuge behind Homer's account of her ignorance of the maids' fates when like all the other women in the palace she was locked out from the slaughter of the suitors in the hall and then slept through the hangings. However, the fact remains that the maids' deaths are at the centre of her anguish. Though she admits that she was wrong to keep her plotting with them a secret, she advances so many excuses for her behavior towards her favorites and suggests so many alternative explanations for why they were hanged that we begin to suspect that she protests too much. Remembering Atwood's preference for Gothic constructions of female subjectivity where the conscious self is shadowed by its dark double, we might be inclined to see the maids in a similar role: are they the unconscious which haunts Penelope's rhetoric of truthtelling? That dimension of psychodrama is made explicit at the beginning of the play version where Penelope stands backstage wringing her hands as the maids sing their first song, and again at the end as Penelope's thoughts circle back to the image of the hanged maids who forever run away from her, though "Run isn't quite accurate… Their still-twitching feet don't touch the ground" (*The Penelopiad: The Play*, 82). In the book version the emphasis is slightly different as the weight of blame is shifted to Odysseus who is hooted at by the maids, now surrealistically metamorphosed into owls.

The maids' stories draw attention to gender and class issues which go unchallenged in *The Odyssey*, focusing on the physical and sexual exploitation of a female underclass who have no rights over their own bodies and who are the victims of casual male violence. Atwood has always been intensely aware of the cultural meanings of the female body as a concept as well as of "the sexual politics which are played out on female bodies" (Davies), explored here in the contrasting experiences of Penelope or Helen and the maids. Penelope knows that she herself is an object of male desire for the acquisition of her body in marriage represents the acquisition of wealth, and that when she marries Odysseus she is the object of male exchange, likening herself to a "package of meat" handed over by her father to her husband, but "a package of meat in a wrapping of gold, mind you" (*The Penelopiad*, 39). Helen's aura of glamour evidently survives even death, demonstrating once again the power of fantasies of femininity. She is still being pursued, much to Penelope's disapproval and chagrin, by hordes of eager male spirits: "Desire does not die with the body,' said Helen, 'only the ability to satisfy it' "(*The Penelopiad*, 155). By contrast with these royal ladies, the female slaves' bodies have no value; they are there to work or as objects to be played with or raped and abused by any male guest who chooses. In *The Odyssey* they have almost nothing to say, though Odysseus does overhear them slandering himself on his return home as they go out to meet their lovers among the suitors, at which Homer tells us, "Odysseus' gorge rose within him" (*Odyssey*, Book 20, 304)). The next day by his orders Telemachus hangs twelve of those maids for dishonoring his household, and apparently they maids go to their deaths in silence, as meekly as thrushes or doves caught in a snare. In the prose translation of *The Odyssey* this event merits only a single paragraph, though Atwood lifts that paragraph out of context, using it as the second epigraph to her book in order to highlight its significance to her argument. Here it functions as emblem of male violence and when juxtaposed against the first epigraph (Agamemnon's eulogy to "the constant Penelope") the two together signal Atwood's double focus on the condition of queens and slave girls in her revisionary reading of Homeric myth.

Unlike Penelope's carefully crafted monologue, the maids' stories are multivoiced and fragmentary as Atwood reimagines their lives through a dazzling variety of narrative forms., alternating between poetry and song, prose, and burlesque drama. There are sinister little lyrics like the opening "Rope-Jumping Rhyme," and the insinuations in these songs become increasingly threatening as the story progresses. The prose poem at the end, "We're Walking Behind You, A Love Song" may be read (as it is here) as a stalker's song addressed to Odysseus, with its distorted echoes of phrases from the 1950s popular song of the same name: "Look over your shoulder! Here we are, walking behind you, close, close by; close as a kiss, close as your own skin"(*The Penelopiad*, 192). Odysseus is their main target but Penelope does not escape; after death they are free to defy her as they never could in life. Immediately following her vigorous denial of slanderous gossip about her, the maids stage their comic verse drama, "The Perils of Penelope" accusing her of multiple infidelities and of being an accessory to their deaths, where their rhyming couplets offer an ironic counterpoint to high seriousness:

> As we approach the climax, grim and gory,
> Let us just say, There is another story." (*The Penelopiad*, 147)

They also stage an anthropology lecture which parodies both the cult of the Great Mother Goddess and the mythologizing process itself: "You don't have to think of us as real girls, real flesh and blood, real pain, real injustice. That might be too upsetting. .. Consider us as pure symbol" (*The Penelopiad*, 168). It establishes an interesting parallel with the male historian's lecture at the end of *The Handmaid's Tale*, for in both instances the particularity of women's oppression is hidden beneath the generalizations of academic discourse. However, Atwood's most ferocious satirical thrust against patriarchal values occurs in the replay of Odysseus's trial (videotaped by the maids), where myth and modernity overlap in a twenty-first century criminal court. Faithful to Homer's account, Odysseus is on trial for the slaughter of the suitors, but the script changes when the murdered maids cry out for justice. The presiding judge even consults *The Odyssey*, but finding no evidence there against Odysseus (though there is evidence of the suitors' rape of the slave girls) he throws out their case as belonging to a long vanished past where social values were different. But how different are they really? Once again the maids' deaths are marginalized, and even when they transgress *The Odyssey* by invoking the Furies, "the serpent-haired, dog-headed, bat-winged Erinyes" (Graves, 426), the judge reprimands these terrible female figures of vengeance with the curt words: "You there, get down from the ceiling! Stop that barking and hissing!" (*The Penelopiad*, 184). He even dismisses the powerful goddess Athena into the bargain, for feminine principles evidently have no place whatsoever in his court. The riddle of the maids' hanging is never solved and their stories persist, for their fates represents the dark underside of heroic epic and their voices celebrate the return of the repressed.

Unlike *The Odyssey*, or even *The Oresteia*, where a point of reconciliation is achieved by the gods' intervention, there is no sense of an ending in *The Penelopiad*. Atwood's Underworld despite its classical trappings is the Gothic territory of the Uncanny, filled with echoes and repetitions as the maids continue to pursue Odysseus and he leaves Penelope again and again to escape them. (There is however an ironic dimension to this, as Odysseus continues his fabulous voyages right into the contemporary world, sometimes disguised as a French general, and at others as a film star, an inventor, and an advertising man. And of course Penelope blames that on the maids too.) Whether we listen to Atwood's legendary women as isolated voices in the poems or in *The Penelopiad*, they all refuse to be silenced or to be constrained by their mythic identities. I have concentrated on Atwood's revisionary strategies in *The Penelopiad* as her only full-length mythographic text, for it is here that by shifting the emphasis of *The Odyssey* from the masculine to the feminine that she has invented a vividly realized female community that was barely acknowledged by Homer. In her text women speak of their domestic work, their pleasures and desires, their rivalries and antagonisms, as well as of their sufferings and pain. Moreover, whether Atwood's postmodern myth revisions are set in the ancient or the contemporary world, it is the artifice of female storytelling which is emphasized as boundaries are blurred across time and genre, between true stories and lies, and between the voices of the living and the dead. The final comment on mythmaking should be Atwood's own, as she reflects—with an oblique allusion to the Great Earth Mother—on the stage adaptation of *The Penelopiad*: "The ancient myths remain fertile ground. Who knows what might sprout from them next?" (*The Penelopiad: The Play*, viii).

Notes

An abridged earlier version using some of this material appeared in "Five Ways of Looking at *The Penelopiad*," *Sydney Studies in English* 32(2006): 5-18.
[1] This edition of *Open Letter* contains 16 essays by international scholars on contemporary myth revisioning in Canadian literature, though none on Atwood. For Atwood's treatment of the Isis and Osiris myth see Heliane Ventura, "The Invention of the Self: Margaret Atwood's 'Isis in Darkness'," RANAM 30 (1997): 1-13.
[2] For analysis of the mythic subtexts in *The Blind Assassin* see also Fiona Tolan, *Margaret Atwood: Feminism and Fiction* (Amsterdam and New York: Rodopi, 2007), 261-3.
[3] Nathalie Cooke's essay usefully analyses the power dynamics of the confessional form in a wide variety of examples from Atwood's poetry and fiction. *The Penelopiad* displays many of Atwood's characteristic strategies.

Works Cited

Atwood, Margaret. *Curious Pursuits: Occasional Writing 1970-2005.* 2005. London: Virago.
—. *The Door.* London: Virago, 2007.
—. *Eating Fire: Selected Poetry 1965-1995.* 1998. London: Virago.
—. *Good Bones.* 1992. London: Bloomsbury.
—. *The Handmaid's Tale.* 1996. London: Vintage.
—. *Interlunar.* 1984. Toronto: Oxford University Press.
—. *The Journals of Susanna Moodie.* 1970. Toronto: Oxford University Press.
—. *Lady Oracle.* 1993. London: Virago.
—. "The Myths and Me," 2005. *Read: Life with Books* (Random House) 6.1. 35-38.
—. *Morning in the Burned House.* 1995. Toronto: McClelland & Stewart.
—. *Negotiating with the Dead: A Writer on Writing.* 2002. Cambridge: Cambridge University Press.
—. *The Penelopiad.* 2005. Edinburgh: Canongate.
—. *The Penelopiad: The Play.* 2007. London: Faber and Faber.
—. *The Tent.* 2006. London: Bloomsbury.
—. *True Stories.* 1982. London: Jonathan Cape.
Davies, Madeleine. "Margaret Atwood's Female Bodies." *The Cambridge Companion to Margaret Atwood.* Ed. Coral Ann Howells. Cambridge: Cambridge University Press, 2006. 58-71.
Cooke, Nathalie. "The Politics of Ventriloquism: Margaret Atwood's Fictive Confessions." *Various Atwoods: Essays on the Later Poems, Short Fiction, and Novels.* Ed.Lorraine York. Toronto: Anansi, 1995. 207-28.
Dixon, Guy. "A Desperate Housewife in Ancient Greece: Interview with Margaret Atwood," *Globe and Mail: Review,* 22 October 2005: R12.
Dvorak, Marta. "Margaret Atwood's Humor." *The Cambridge Companion to Margaret Atwood.* 114-129.
Frye, Northrop. *The Bush Garden: Essays on the Canadian Imagination.* 1971. Toronto: Anansi.
Graves, Robert. *The Greek Myths.* London: Penguin, 1992.
Homer. *The Odyssey.* 1970. Trans.E.V.Rieu. Harmondsworth, Middlesex: Penguin Classics.
Meletinsky, E.M. *The Poetics of Myth.* 1998. Trans. G. Laroue and A.Sadetsky. New York and London: Garland.
Nischik, Reingard. "Margaret Atwood's Short Stories and Shorter Fictions." *The Cambridge Companion to Margaet Atwood.* 145-160.

Tolan, Fiona. *Margaret Atwood: Feminism and Fiction*. 2007.Amsterdam
    and New York: Rodopi.
Ventura, Heliane. Editor's Introduction to *Open Letter*. 13, 2 (Spring
    2007): 7-14. Special Issue: "Into the Looking-Glass Labyrinth: Myths
    and Mystery in Canadian Literature."
Wilson, Sharon R. "Mythological Intertexts in Margaret Atwood's
    Works." *Margaret Atwood: Works and Impact*. Ed. Reingard Nishcik.
    2000. New York: Camden House. 215- 228.
Woolf, Virginia. *A Room of One's Own*. 1992. Oxford: Oxford University
    Press World's Classics.

CHAPTER FIVE

FAIRY TALES, MYTHS, AND MAGIC PHOTOGRAPHS IN ATWOOD'S *THE BLIND ASSASSIN*

SHARON WILSON

Margaret Atwood's works incisively record, investigate, satirize, and, paradoxically celebrate North American popular culture, especially its use of mythology, fairy tales, and in the case of *The Blind Assassin*, photographs.[1] In addition to household appliances and other objects we may see everyday, Atwood uses fairy tales, myth, other folklore, photography, contemporary art, film, TV, radio, opera, songs, styles of clothing and home furnishings, architecture, advertising, newspaper and society page articles, bathroom graffiti, both urban and wilderness settings, and such popular literary genres as spy thrillers, science fiction, and romance in magical realist texts also embedding the Bible and canonical literature. Magical realism, which "may constitute the single most important trend in contemporary international fiction" (Farris, 42), is the fusion of magic and realism. It "has become a common narrative mode for fictions written from the perspective of the politically and culturally disempowered," including "women writing from a feminist perspective" (Bowers, 33), and often includes works embedding fairy tales and myths. Although not always recognized, magical realists include English-speaking writers from Canada—such as Robert Kroetsch, Jack Hodgins, Michael Ondaatje, and Margaret Atwood—as well as from the US and England.

Apparently arising from what Atwood calls the same "UR-Manuscript," *The Angel of Bad Judgment* (Margaret Atwood Papers), *Alias Grace* (1996) and *The Blind Assassin* (2000) seem to indicate a paradoxical but not uncommon direction for a postmodern writer:

increasing historical documentation that compounds textual gaps and coexists with growing magical realism, in the case of the former, blood-red flowers that appear on the ground and in the cell of Grace's prison. Drawing on popular culture, *Alias Grace* features 19th-century quilt designs, clothing, furniture, and psychiatric floor shows as backdrops for a real murder. *The Blind Assassin* parodies itself and popular taste by layering science fiction, fiction about fiction, and a romance of hidden passions and perversions underneath polished surfaces of repression to depict the war-torn thirties and forties. Atwood refers to the novel as "Jane Austen in a very black mode" and describes the Iris excised from *Alias Grace*, in a desk drawer along with other discarded characters, as popping out in a "visitation," at which time she realized that this character could tell her own story (Gussow). Atwood researched pulp magazines, unions, newspaper stories, Mayfair wedding announcements, old photographs of Simpson's and the Royal York Hotel, and even menus and catalogues from Hudson's Bay Company archives for *The Blind Assassin* (Atwood Papers). To varying degrees, the manuscripts and both finished novels, Alias Grace and *The Blind Assassin*,[2] are detailed period pieces about motherless main characters, and all are about research: the attempt to construct meaning or truth about both personal and public pasts. Both novels are puzzles about the inconsistencies between appearance and reality: the appearance of piety and propriety versus hidden murder, abuse, rape, and other violence. Like a Greek tragedy, this novel develops the falls of two great houses, the old money Chase family of Port Ticonderoga and the nouveau riche Griffen family of Toronto (Stein, 136, 145). Atwood is popular as much for her ability to record manners and mores of particular eras as for her witty and incisive social comment. Further, however, it is her recording of ordinary but magical objects, in the case of *The Blind Assassin*, especially photographs of cut off hands and popular culture stories connecting to them, that gives readers a paradoxical sense of seeing, hearing, and even touching a point in time while she simultaneously deconstructs any possibility of an objective context.

Structured like nesting Russian dolls (Stein, 135), *The Blind Assassin* is a novel-within-a novel within another novel, blending three narratives interspersed with newspaper clippings, a letter, and society announcements. The first narrative is the frame one, a self-reflexive memoir of Iris Chase's life in Port Ticonderoga and Toronto, Canada, predominantly in the 1930s and 40s, including her writing of all three narratives. The second, also called "The Blind Assassin," is a novel published under Laura Chase's name. Although the protagonists are identified only as "he" and "she," readers are led to believe that it records the love affair of Alex Thomas and Laura Chase, Iris's sister. The third is an unfinished science fiction pulp" magazine" or novel, including a "Blind Assassin" story, that the "he" and "she" appear to compose together within this novel.[3] It is set on the planets Zycron, Xenor, and Aa'A with tongueless sacrificial maidens and blind assassins, lizard men wearing flammable shorts, and luscious peach women who ripen on trees. As Atwood says, the male lover uses Zycron "as many science fiction writers used the genre before him—as an oblique critique of his own society, in which there is child labour, exploitation and different classes" (Sylge).

The novel as a whole interlaces allusions to fairy tales with the Bible, *The Aeneid*, *The Metamorphoses*, *Tristan and Isolde*, stories of Persephone, Leda, Europa, Danae, Medusa,[4] Medea, Circe, Helen, Arthur, and the Queen of Sheeba and the poems of Tennyson, Keats, Coleridge, Fitzgerald, and E. Pauline Johnson, among many others, to explore the ways that we all blindly "assassinate" in personal and political wars. Alternately playing a dragon, a troll, a sibyl, Ariadne trying to solve the puzzle of the labyrinth, Rapunzel captive in a tower and brushing her hair, Scheherazade, a mouse in a castle of tigers, a Little Red Riding Hood who contains both grandma and the wolf, a Fate spinner (283), both the Grimms' Cinderella and the Girl Without Hands, both Fitcher or the Robber Bridegroom and the Robber Bride or Fitcher's Bird, Sleeping Beauty and her godmother witch, and, especially, the mythic Iris, Iris both doubles and foils Laura and the other characters. Not only Iris, but Laura, Aimee, Winifred, and Sabrina are connected to the "Sleeping Beauty" fairy tale. Early in the book, the beautiful Iris, bewitched by Winifred's pose as a parody fairy godmother (318), passively marries Richard to save the family business. Iris, later a fairy godmother, too, has a daydream about Winifred and her friends, with wreaths of money on their heads, gathered around Sabrina's bed bestowing their godmother gifts. "I appear in a flash of sulphurous light and a puff of smoke and a flapping of sooty leather wings, the uninvited black-sheep godmother." Rather than a prince, it is Laura's notebooks and finally Iris's own regained feelings that awaken Iris. Her gift is the truth (439). Laura, far more questioning than Iris, is also still blind or asleep. Angry at Laura's ability to "subtract herself," Mr. Erskine yells, "You're not the Sleeping Beauty" as he throws her against the wall. Associating the pool at Avilion with the bridge Laura drives off, Iris realizes that she should have kept her mouth shut and not interrupted "a sleepwalker" with the news that Alex was dead. She "pushed [Laura] off" (164, 488). On the other hand, Laura would also be an uninvited fairy at Aimee's christening if she said that Aimee wasn't Richard's child (432). Laura, like Iris both victim and victimizer, is captive princess, Dido, and Persephone raped and spirited to the underworld, but she is also partly responsible for Iris's captivity. Iris's, Laura's, and other characters' fairy-tale and mythic roles in what might appear a "realistic" situation create the novel's magic realism.

In addition to depicting the struggle for survival that she identifies as the major theme of Canadian literature (*Survival* 1972), Atwood's visual art, including watercolors, posters, a comic strip, and book illustrations or cover designs sometimes used in Canadian editions, also has sources in popular culture, including stories of Anne Boleyn and Amnesty International, the Frankenstein legend, Persephone and harpy myths, and the "Fitcher's Bird" or Bluebeard fairy tale. Toronto restaurants and bars often feature copies of Atwood texts that mention them, and Atwood walks are even offered for those curious to see the places she has made famous.

Atwood speaks of herself as a highly visual author (Lee video), and many readers recognize how her watercolors, collages, and book cover designs featuring goddess, fairy-tale, and other mythic intertexts illuminate her writing (Wilson, *Margaret* 35-81). I have elsewhere detailed the way she and her characters visually "photograph" scenes and people, freezing reality in order to hold onto it and sometimes to distance themselves from pain or human contact. Actual and figurative photographs have previously had four functions in Atwood's work: as neutral recorders of experience, as an apparent cause of a character's sense of fragmentation or segmentation, as narcissistic "proof" of existence, and as lenses distilling and focusing experience toward possible metamorphosis (Wilson, "Camera Images" 30-32). Atwood's photograph and closely related fairy-tale and mythic imagery in *The Blind Assassin* again record and verify the characters and their world: ironically like war memorial statues, photographs are both monuments to the past and critiques of it. Photographs illustrate not only the raging passions and sacrificial, fairy-tale amputations of both the characters and their society, but their efforts to heal. If, however, there is no objective reality, these actual and figurative photographs of amputated hands and heat may themselves deceive in this trickster text embedding an inner novel that deliberately misleads us about the frame story, which is also deceptive, may contradict itself, and may contradict the other narratives.

It is Atwood's startling imagery that sets *The Blind Assassin* apart from the popular genres and techniques she both uses and parodies. Many of these images are ordinary objects residing in a magical larger object, a usually locked honeymoon steamer trunk that contains the novel itself and its overlapping major pieces.[5] The combination of these pieces is also magical and subject to different interpretations. Iris's memoir presumably includes everything else in the trunk since all exists in the book we read. But, as in *The Handmaid's Tale*, we may imagine different possibilities, such as Myra or Sabrina's adding the novels-within-the-novel and the clippings to the memoir or even placing some chapters out of order. In addition, the trunk contains the novels-within-the-novel and materials associated with them: the manuscript and corrected proofs, letters from the publisher, hate mail about the book, and five published copies in dust jackets picturing Cleopatra. It also contains the newspaper clippings and Laura's five notebooks of knowledge—one including her print of the tinted Button Factory picnic photograph. As Iris prepares to leave Richard, she also mentions packing what she can, including her photographs and Perennials for the Rock Garden, into the steamer trunk and suitcase. In the early manuscript, "The Angel of Bad Judgment," all of the tinted photographs are in a trunk; and in another version, the novel-within-a novel and its pieces are stored in a locked, glass-topped wooden box used as a table that the "nosy parker," a visiting writer named Stuart McCrae, considers breaking into for his next book (Atwood Papers). But if the novel and its materials are all locked within the trunk, the novel itself is also, paradoxically, a magic trunk,[6] and it is often difficult to distinguish the fiction within the fiction from the frame narrative's supposed "reality." The trunk also holds the dark and empty space of a marriage in which trousseau signifies trussed. In one of the many memory fragments she reconstructs as a mosaic of the past (67), Iris uses the word trousseau as the title of the chapter describing her parents' marriage, which, like her own, involves sacrifice, including the loss of her mother's life after giving birth to a still-born child, the loss of one of her father's legs and eyes, and the death of two of his brothers in the war.

Along with time and the blind gods Eros and Justice (497, Atwood Papers), Iris is one of the novel's Blind Assassins. For her, Laura's notebooks are the doors to the forbidden knowledge of the "Fitcher's Bird" or "Bluebeard" fairy tale. These notebooks function similarly to the red plastic purse and cat's eye marble in *Cat's Eye*, again hidden in a trunk suggesting the subconscious. In the fairy tale, the Grimms' "Fitcher's Bird" or Perrault's "Bluebeard," the third sister, Fitcher's bride, discovers the dismembered pieces of her sisters, the previous brides, behind the locked door. When Elaine Risley of *Cat's Eye* opens a trunk in her mother's basement, finding the red plastic purse and the cat's eye marble within, she sees "her life entire" (Wilson, *Margaret* 311). Similarly, Laura Chase's notebooks, first used when Laura and Iris study with their tutor, Mr. Erskine, reveal to Iris her blindness and her complicity in her sister's death. Although Iris withholds knowledge about the notebooks from readers until "The Golden Lock" chapter near the end of her memoir, she says she discovers them in her stocking drawer the day Laura dies, too late to keep her from uttering the words that send Laura over the bridge.7 The Latin notebook contains a translated passage from Virgil's *Aeneid* about Dido after Aeneas has gone to war and, having stabbed herself, is lying on the burning pyre. Iris remembers the ripped out passage about the yellow-winged Iris for whom she was named: Iris releases Dido from her body by cutting off the golden lock that sends her to the Underworld, and Iris Chase had told Laura that the hair was an offering, "a thing she had to do" (499). The Geography notebook has a short description of Port Ticonderoga; and the French one, thought to be burned and now stripped of French, lists words Alex wrote while in their attic. Laura's math notebook contains the list of dates on which Richard tried to force, and eventually succeeded in having, sex with Laura. Laura's important photograph of Alex, herself, and Iris's hand is pasted into the history one.

Thus, figuratively, this trunk, which brings Iris into and out of Richard's life, ultimately "contains" the era pictured and critiqued; in other words, it contains the past, which creeps into the present in the same way that Iris's detached hand, one of the active hands that writes the book we read, subversively creeps across another magical object--the picture of Laura and Alex--and across the whole landscape of the book. Iris says she wrote down "What I remembered, and also what I imagined, which is the truth. I thought of myself as recording. A bodiless hand, scrawling across a wall." As Iris points out after teasing Laura that God's left hand might have been cut off in a war, "Laura was my left hand, and I was hers. We wrote the book together. It's a left-handed book. That's why one of us is always out of sight, whichever way you look at it" (512-13). But Iris also imagines writing with the index finger of the right hand and erasing with the left (283). The book is figuratively written with the "extra" "left" hand that each sister possesses, that of folklore (Thompson D996), of Atwood's "Third-Handed" (*Good Bones*), and, in this case, of the sister missing from each picture.[8]

The trunk is pale yellow on the outside--the color associated with Laura--but blue on the inside, the same color that Laura associates with its owner, the sleepwalker who ignores the "trail of dusty white footprints" left by her fairy-tale victim sister abandoned in the "forest" of Richard's sexual abuse. As Iris says when she sees someone placing a white flower on Laura's grave, "Laura touches people. I do not" (192). Of course, in this neo-gothic world of suppressed and hidden violence, Iris cannot touch in a double sense. Others do not find her suffering touching. Often gloved and dressed smartly in clothes picked out by this novel's wicked stepmother, Winifred Prior, whom she more closely resembles in manuscripts (Atwood Papers), she seems to have exactly what she has bargained for: wealth, status, and power. Symbolically, however, resembling Atwood characters and narrators in *You Are Happy*, *Life Before Man* and *Bodily Harm* (Wilson, *Margaret* 136-228), her "hand"--her ability to express feelings openly--is lying unmissed in Laura's photograph until she takes responsibility for her actions near the end of the novel. When Iris does so, she reveals Laura's notebooks, including Laura's copy of the main photograph, and her own willful blindness.

At least five central and many secondary photograph images structure the book: 1) the black-and-white photograph of the inner novel that appears at beginning and end, 2) the narrative photograph of the hard-boiled egg picnic in this narrative, 3) the prototypical newspaper photograph of the Button Factory picnic in the frame narrative-- self-reflexively mirrored in the other picnic, 4) Laura's tinted and cut print for Iris of the Button Factory picnic, and 5) her differently tinted and cut photo of the same picnic for herself. The alternation of narratives and time periods seems designed to blur lines between different time periods and layers of fictions and, recalling *You Are Happy*'s "Siren Song," to lure readers into reading parts of the memoir into the inner novel, and vice versa. As Atwood frequently reminds us in essays and addresses as well as her fiction and poetry, the artist always lies ("Essay"). Paradoxically, the photograph in the Prologue and Epilogue of the embedded novel, "The Blind Assassin," like the second, "narrative photo" in the inner novel's first chapter, seems to originate in a different dimension of the novel's "reality": the frame narrative's Button Factory picnic, one of the few places in this narrative that we see Alex. As the reflector narrator of the inner novel, that for convenience I will call a further fictionalized "Iris," begins her novel-within-a-novel, she puts a black and white photograph of what was once three figures on the table, feels its heat, "and stares down into it, as if she is peering into a well or pool--searching beyond her own reflection for something else, something she must have dropped or lost, out of reach but still visible, shimmering like a jewel on sand." According to Earl Ingersoll, she is looking for her paradise lost ("Waiting" 551).We read both inner and outer novels through "this square, lighted window of glazed paper," so that layers of fiction and time continuously interpenetrate one another. If we are to believe that the narrator of the inner novel has only a "single photo" in the Prologue and Epilogue, black and white rather than tinted, this photo apparently pictures "Iris," the sister who has tucked in her skirt, with "Alex"; and the hand in the left corner appears to be "Laura's," significantly "Laura's" only appearance in this inner novel, [9] ironically assumed to be written by her.

Like the toaster, red plastic purse, and cat's eye marble in *Cat's Eye*, the photographs in *The Blind Assassin*, especially the tinted ones, "possess the inexhaustible magic of magical realism, . . . a term used by Franz Roh to describe German artists of the. . .new objectivity movement [to portray] the imaginary, the improbable, or the fantastic in a realistic or rational manner," in Atwood's works often used to "combine elements of dream, fairy story, or mythology with the everyday" (Wilson, *Margaret* 296-97). All of the book's actual and narrative photographs are also associated with fairy tales, heightening the magical realism. The first photograph, "Iris"'s in the inner novel that has "picnic" written on the back, is in a brown envelope labeled "clippings"[10] and is hidden in the pages of *Perennials for the Rock Garden*, a book that deceptively appears in the frame narrative as well but does not contain a photo there. This "mutilated" photograph, easily confused with the partly tinted one Laura colors in the frame narrative, cuts off all of the other sister except for one of her hands. The second "photograph," in the first chapter of this inner novel and titled "The Hard-Boiled Egg," features one of the book's many narrative "photos," in this case of another romantic picnic, this time with hard-boiled eggs, which cannot be the picnic of the first photo since it involves just the inner novel's nameless "he" and "she": characters we presume are Alex Thomas, who is making up the first science fiction stories, and Iris Chase, who has chosen not to reveal her identity.[11] Vulnerable under a watching apple tree, "Iris" ironically imagines a protective line drawn around them with chalk, as in "The Girl Without Hands" fairy tale, a disguised incest story embedded in several Atwood texts (Wilson, *Margaret* 140). In this tale, a father accidentally sells his daughter, who is standing close to an apple tree, to the Devil. To protect her, he cuts off her hands and draws a chalk circle around her. In *The Blind Assassin*, Iris and Laura's father sells both of his daughters to devil Richard Griffen, who abuses both girls but steals the father's business anyway. In the tale, a King who falls in love with the maiden makes her silver hands and, by the end, because she is good, her hands grow back. In the novel, although Iris transforms through knowledge and suffering, Laura sacrifices her life.

In the "The Button Factory Picnic" chapter of the frame narrative, Elwood Murray takes the third, supposedly prototype flash photograph of the three main characters at that picnic. Along with ones of best dog and baby and Norval Chase at the podium, this photograph is printed in the newspaper. Although Laura takes the negative and reprints one copy for herself and one for her sister, neither print appears in the inner novel, which does not, of course, have a Button Factory picnic. On each side of Alex, "like bookends" (192), are the two sisters who grow to love him, Laura to the right and Iris to the left, what has been called the book's "spiritual" narrator and its main one, the person we eventually discover is the actual writer of the embedded novel, "The Blind Assassin." But this photograph for the Herald and Banner, significantly captioned "Miss Chase and Miss Laura Chase Entertain an Out-of-Town Visitor," depicts also Port Ticonderoga's class, gender, and political divisions, the violence submerged under the surface of both city and era. Rennie thinks that Alex, a union organizer who puts his hand partly in front of his face as gangland criminals do, looks like "an Indian--or, worse, a Jew" or even a Communist and that Laura and Iris, who shouldn't be "rolling around on the lawn in full view of everyone," look like "lovelorn geese" (192). Because Iris, who at least has her skirt tucked in, is smoking, Rennie, repository of Port Ticonderoga standards, thinks that she looks like a tramp. When the Laura of the memoir hand-tints pictures, choosing colors to match people's souls, the pictures become misty and ultrareal. When she colors this fourth photo for Iris, she cuts herself out of it except for her hand, which she colors pale yellow and which seems to creep across the grass toward Alex "like an incandescent crab" (220).

Laura has the fifth "mutilated picture" that the Iris of the memoir finds glued into the history notebook in her stocking drawer after Laura is dead. It shows what Laura wants to remember, Alex and her colored light yellow with all of Iris except for her disembodied blue hand cut out (500). Although it's hard to tell whether it is Iris's right hand in this picture and Laura's left hand in hers, or vice versa, the scissored off hand in the left corner appears to be Laura's. Since Iris was to the left of Alex in the Button Picnic photo, presumably it is her right hand in Laura's photo and Laura's left hand in hers. On the cover Atwood commissioned for *The Robber Bride*, the cut-off hand is also the left one. But is Iris to Alex's left or on the left as we look at the photo? Or are we attempting to get our bearings from within the photo? In a postmodern world, from a different point of view, what was right becomes left. Much more deceptively, however, the inner novel has only one "actual" photograph--"Iris's"--and it is black-and-white, apparently without the tinting Laura uses in the frame narrative. Thus, the photo that fascinates us from the beginning of the novel we read appears to be a print of the one at the Button Factory picnic but, although it suggests and may be based upon this photo, it is not one of the two tinted prints; and the picnic in the inner novel's "The Hard-boiled Egg" chapter is not actually photographed. If this is so, then "Iris," and "Alex" are possibly not the same characters as in the memoir either.

   Atwood deliberately uses different time sequences for the frame and
"Blind Assassin" narratives and alternates inner and outer narratives so
that readers, still expecting realism and wanting to believe in the illusion
of reality tradition, have difficulty separating narratives and remembering
the sequence of events in each. Ironically, they are even encouraged to
construct their own master narratives, flawed by associating the many
mirroring but slightly differing details, including those concerning
photographs and picnics, in the different strands. Despite its "blind
assassins" and sacrificial victims that mirror those in the other two
narratives, "Alex"'s story is admittedly science fiction and is, of course,
written by Iris. Trapped in the novel's Palace of Knossos maze, readers
desire the Truth, but this desire "blinds" us, too, putting us in the path of
the Minotaur. "The Blind Assassin" inner novel does not reliably reflect
events of Iris's life, but, of course, neither does her memoir, as she admits.
We read the narratives as we read our lives. Iris is an unreliable narrator,[12]
as we all would be if contained in fiction. Like any author, she selects and
orders what she will include. Nevertheless, in the frame narrative, the
reality of the novel we read, each sister functions as the other sister's extra
"left" hand, the disobedient, unclean, morally questionable, anarchistic,
but creative hand.
   In the caption accompanying the newspaper photograph, Laura's
personal name but only Iris's family name are given, enforcing Iris's
subservient identities first as daughter and then as wife of the book's
primary "blind assassins." Both Iris and Laura suggest the dutiful daughter
of the Grimms' "The Girl Without Hands." In the novel's incest story in
which both sisters are abused, Iris, unlike Fitcher's "Bird," is unable to
revive her sister. Unlike The Girl Without Hands, since there is also no
angel to restore Iris's hands, Iris seems to count on those of her
granddaughter, Sabrina, or friend and caretaker, Myra, to open the trunk,
this book's forbidden room of secrets, to disclose the manuscript in which
she finally speaks. Alex is the unnamed stranger, an alien matching the
aliens of his science fiction stories. In the unseen background are Richard
Griffen and Norval Chase exchanging Iris and Laura for what proves to be
all of the button factory business, leading to Laura's later similar "bargain"
with God to preserve Alex's life. Richard Griffen is the "devil" of new
money, mythologically the Griffin monster with the head and wings of an
eagle, the body of a lion, and sometimes the tail of a serpent, that guards
treasure (Leach, 467). He is also a fairy-tale wolf and ogre. In *The Blind
Assassin*, after Laura and Alex have died, the three characters momentarily
live again within this Button Factory picnic photograph reproduced in
three variations, and, in a sense, the entire novel lives within it as well.

Iris likens the display of photos to other efforts to memorialize ourselves, including, by implication, printed texts, which she, like Atwood, seems to think of as "scores for the voice" (Barnes and Noble interview):

> Even while we're still alive. We wish to assert our existence, like dogs peeing on fire hydrants. We
> put on display our framed photographs, our parchment diplomas, our silver-plated cups; we monogram
> our linen, we carve our names on trees, we scrawl them on washroom walls. It's all the same impulse.
> What do we hope from it? Applause, envy, respect? Or simply attention, of any kind we can get?
>   At the very least we want a witness. We can't stand the idea of our own voices falling silent finally,
> like a radio running down (*The Blind Assassin* 95).

Thus, it is hardly surprising that Iris and her narrator in the second narrative, "Iris," both writers, analyze and create verbal photographs. The evil fairy godmother's husband, Mr. Prior, who is thought to be stuffed, exists only in photographs. Other photos in *The Blind Assassin*, including those of various ancestors, the Button Factory blow-ups from the town archives, Iris and Laura's mother, the sisters in their velvet dresses, Laura on the inside jacket flap of "The Blind Assassin" novel, Iris's wedding, and Iris's daughter Aimee, also depict the dismembering violence under the surface of life, illustrating the atmosphere of control and repression that Iris accepts as "reality." After Laura learns how to make and tint photographic prints from Elwood Murray, Iris discovers that Laura has had the nerve to tint the framed photographs of ancestors in the library, including the prime ministers with which they are sometimes posed, making their faces mauve, green, pale orange, and light crimson and giving them a misty look. She had planned to color Grandmother Adelia steel grey and the dead uncles gold for glory, in each case revealing the colors of their souls.[13] In an early Atwood manuscript, the Iris character calls these photos her household gods, and the place they are stored, her altar to household spirits (Atwood Papers). The Button Factory, on the east bank of the river Louveteau, displays archival blow-ups of grandfather Benjamin and dignitaries, father Norval in his eye patch, with a wreath in front of the War Memorial, looking "as if he's facing a firing squad" (50-51), and the briefly prosperous factory itself. In "The Trousseau" chapter, a snapshot of the self-sacrificing, short-sighted woman named "our mother" shows her as "a boyish buccaneer" in a sealskin coat, laughing with friends. Iris "picture[s]" the time of her parents' pre-WWI engagement at a skating party as "so blank, so innocent, so solid to all appearances, but thin ice all the same. Beneath the surfaces of things was the unsaid, boiling slowly" (68-69).

Both actual and narrative photographs continue to reveal such depths under surfaces. In the portrait of the two sisters in their velvet dresses, Laura tints Iris light blue, a color their mother also wears, because she is "asleep" (194-95), a Sleeping Beauty, a condition that Iris overlooks for much of her life. Laura always sees her sister as sleepwalking, but Iris is also Cinderella, Rapunzel, and Little Red Riding Hood's Granny, containing her own wolf (332, 465, 366). Ironically, Iris is wearing what is probably this same, now too small, dress when Alex has dinner with the Chase family. Above the biographical sketch of Laura on the flap of the novel she supposedly wrote, Laura appears tragic in the publicity photo, a gifted writer who died too young in an accident. At the time of the Alumni Association presentation of the Laura Chase Memorial Prize, when this photograph runs in the paper, Iris comments that Laura is beautiful, "touchingly untouched. An advertisement for soap. . . .A tabula rasa, not waiting to write, but to be written on" (46). But after we find out how negatively she has been imprinted, Iris's view seems altered: this same photograph looks "flyspecked" by the attention of moralists, pulpit-thumpers, local biddies, and other "corpse flies" caught up in the political scandal. Ironically, Iris says she studied the newspaper photos of the BellaVista Clinic where Laura and Richard's child was aborted "with interest: it . . . was said to have some rather fine stained glass windows" (509-10). Iris invests a lifetime in keeping her feelings locked up, as if, along with the notebooks and memories of the past, they are in the honeymoon trunk.

Iris's wedding photos reveal a central image of violence and the "blind assassins" who perpetuate it. The one of Iris published in the newspapers is labeled "A Beautiful Bride": "In her case beauty was mandatory, with so much money involved" in this sale to the devil. Iris speaks of herself as "her" since she doesn't remember being present, as if she is simply the other girl's "outcome." On her wedding night, she even sprays herself with a fragrance named after Liu, a slave girl in an opera. In the group portraits, "much the same for weddings as for funerals and headwaiters," Laura is scowling and has moved so that she is blurred, "like a pidgeon smashing into glass," or is standing in "dappled light." Not only is she gnawing on a finger—highlighting the book's metaphoric cannibalism; even the wedding bouquet is grabbed greedily,"as if it were food" (239-40.) Later, Laura alters two photographs in the wedding album as a clue for Iris to Richard's abuse, one Iris tragically but possibly deliberately fails to understand. After Rennie tells Iris that Laura left her a clue, one Iris again withholds from readers until shortly before she lets us know about the notebooks, Iris remembers Laura's excision of the family Bible, deleting parts she didn't like. In the group shot of the bridesmaids and groomsmen, the figures are entirely obliterated by a coat of indigo, leaving only Richard, Iris, Winifred, and Laura. Laura tints Winifred and Richard green--suggesting greed--Iris is again blue, and Laura is radiant in brilliant yellow. Significantly, in the formal shot of Richard and Iris, Iris's face is bleached out, "so that the eyes and the nose and mouth looked fogged over," signifying her erasure from their marriage (Bouson, 25) and Iris's life as an unaware Sleeping Beauty and Bluebeard's or Fitcher's victim. McCombs suggests that Iris's bleached-out face in the wedding portrait recalls the decorated skull bride in the "Fitcher's Bird" fairy tale, in Atwood's 1970 watercolor, Fitcher's Bride (Plate 3, Wilson, *Margaret Atwood's*), and in Josef Scharl's illustration for this fairy tale (219, Hunt and Stern). Richard is "on the verge of a smile, as if at some secret, dubious joke" (239). Richard's face is dark gray, with flames shooting up from inside his head, "as if the skull itself were burning." His hands are also red. He is the burning man, "a Bluebeard on fire" (McCombs; see my f. n. 13), emblem of lust, greed, and hidden violence. Because the background is blacked out, the two figures appear to be floating in a dark night (451). In "Old Notes" for the manuscript, Iris is wearing a "Brides of Dracula" veil for her wedding to Richard Waterford (Atwood Papers).

   In a narrative photo, Laura also sees her father, Norval Chase, as a burning man. As a child, when her father appeared in an improvised Santa Claus suit, with burning candles on his head, presumably in celebration of winter solstice and the return of spirits of the dead (Leach and Fried 230), his head appeared to be on fire. She had thought that "this was what he was really like. . . That underneath, he was burning up. All the time," and only pretending otherwise (Atwood, Blind 385). Since Laura always associates particular colors with people, it is possible that this very sensitive child sees auras, and red auras may resemble flames. As a child, Iris also sees her father as a man with his head on fire. She reads aloud from her alphabet book to her parents and imagines that her father, a symbolic werewolf and ogre (82,165), who was supposed to be fighting for a boring "fireside idyll," is watching houses, towns, and people go up in smoke:

> F is for Fire,
> Good servant, bad master
> When left to itself
> It burns faster and faster. (81)

The book is illustrated with a picture of another man whose head is on fire: "a leaping man covered in flames--wings of fire coming from her heels and shoulders, little fiery horns sprouting from his head." Wearing no clothes and smiling mischievously, the man seems beyond hurt, and Iris says she is in love with him for this reason. But like Alex, Iris's father does get hurt by fire. He loses one eye, limps, and can no longer "reach" his family (78, 81-82).

In myth, fire usually is a positive image, suggesting the original fire of mankind, phoenix rebirth, the sacred altar or hearth fire purification, cleansing, the continuation of civilization, or a chastity or suitor test (Leach and Fried, 389). In Hilda von Bingen's *Scivias* (1142-52 AD), the first medieval manuscript other than the *Beatus Apocalypse* to reveal images of supernatural contemplation, the flames that pierce the woman's head suggest a divine vision and may indicate a future sainthood or halo (Chadwick Plate 18, 52-53). In some of Atwood's early watercolors, including her cover design for *Power Politics* (Wilson, Margaret Atwood's Plate 8) and unpublished work, both female and male figures appear to have fiery halos. Although Iris says that she may just have needed glasses, when she sees Laura at Diana Sweets after the war has ended, Laura herself appears as a haloed, suffering Christ. Having sacrificed too much, she resembles a photograph "leached of colour": she is "translucent--as if little spikes of light were being nailed out through her skin from the inside, as if thorns of light were shooting out from her in a prickly haze, like a thistle held up to the sun" (483). In the chapter, "The Man with his Head on Fire," Iris also is associated with a head "on fire" but ironically without any enlightenment or passion when she dreams she is wearing a hat of lurid plastic flowers lit inside by tiny light bulbs. The silver fox furs on the black chiffon cape she wears to the Royal Garden Party are arranged in the form of rays (380, 456), but at this point, she is trapped in social surfaces.

Thus, the photograph of Richard and related descriptions of burning heads may have several meanings. Fire is also associated with hell and the devil or Satan (Thompson 287-89), and the height of a fire has been an index of madness or sickness (Leach and Fried 389). Richard, Iris's father, and Alex certainly contain the violent sickness of their era. The novels-within-a novel suggest that, under the polite surface of Port Ticonderoga's social life, far away from battle scenes of WWII, war rages nevertheless, not only in Sakiel-Norn but in Iris' reality, as in our own. Although for those on the sidelines the war seems to take place in black and white, like a newsreel, for those actually in it it is always "too red and orange," and "events have no mercy" (463). When we first see "Alex," "Iris" warns him that he may set fire to himself (10). Even before he dies, his fingers are smoke-stained and he is "charred" (252). When "Iris" has a vision of "Alex" after the war, after he is dead, he looks "half-toned; two-dimensional, like a photograph. . . .he wavers, like a candle flame but devoid of light." He says that they had to "fight fire with fire" but nobody won. The city is in flames and will be erased (468-69). In the frame narrative, Iris watches a young woman set fire to herself to protest an unspecified injustice, and she wonders about young girls with "a talent for self-immolation" uselessly defying blind tyrants or blind gods and sacrificing themselves upon theoretical altars (433). Laura becomes the Dido of her Latin notebook and throws herself upon a symbolic burning pyre: she drives through the danger signs to become the "burned woman." The division between assassins and sacrificial virgins, however, is not as clear in life or even in Iris's frame narrative as in her novels, including "Alex's" science fiction. Thus, it appears that Alex, Laura, and Iris's burning heads identify them as blind assassins as well as sacrificial victims. In "The Golden Lock" chapter of her memoir, apparently the present of the novel and, unlike "Threshold," in present tense, Iris symbolically releases herself as well as Laura from the tragic plot. She says she has to hurry and "can see the end, glimmering far up ahead of me." She admits that, like Hansel and Gretel and other fairy-tale characters, she is "Lost in the woods, and no white stones to mark the way, and treacherous ground to cover," but she has learned a few tricks and will set things in order (497-98). Iris finally chooses the fire of enlightenment: she puts her hands into the flames of knowledge when she opens the notebooks and leaves the trunk of words (494). Even though she expects the manuscript of the novel we read to burn as well, it conveys, if not Truth, knowledge.

The photograph of Iris's daughter Aimee helps Iris to enlightenment. She uses it as a ruse to explain her visit to Rennie, who tells her the clue Laura has left her. Earlier resembling the white foxes on her neckpiece that have glass eyes and "only bite their own tails," Iris shows Rennie Aimee's photograph in Betty's Luncheonette and realizes that she has been eyeless and heartless as well as handless (445-46). Because she learns to read the "code" of bruises with which Richard's bad touch marks Laura's body, and the code of dates in Laura's notebook with which Laura similarly records his abuse, Iris, like Laura, stops being the wife of Gilman's "The Yellow Wallpaper": Laura's abuse, like that of Iris, is no longer "papered over" (508), and Iris is not the tongueless victim of her characters's science fiction story but the bride who speaks out in "The Robber Bridegroom" fairy tale. The person who appears to be "Laura's odd, extra hand, attached to no body. . . . , [this] prim-lipped keeper of the keys, guarding the dungeon in which the starved Laura is chained to the wall" (286), leaves a steamer trunk of words. Near the end of the novel after Iris tells Laura that she and Alex were lovers and that he is dead, Iris feels "angry and thwarted and also helpless." She resembles the June bug that she sees "blundering against the window. . .like a blind thumb" (489). But she and her protagonist, "Iris," are no longer mute, sacrificial virgins or Blind Assassins of the science fiction story or handless, helpless females. As in "The Girl Without Hands" fairy tale, Iris's cut-off hand symbolically grows back; as in the "Fitcher's Bird" fairy tale, Iris is able to reassemble the dismembered pieces of herself. White-gloved Laura takes Iris's car keys to drive off the bridge only in the frame narrative, but "Iris" of the inner novel also gains vision: she recognizes that everything in the photograph with which she began her inner novel is drowned and that the

> picture is of happiness, the story not. Happiness is a garden walled with glass; there's no way in or out. In Paradise there are no stories, because there are no journeys. It's loss and regret and misery and yearning that drive the story forward, along its twisted road.

Having taken her hand out of the trunk, presumably the right one cut-off in Laura's photograph, and also using Laura's amputated left hand, this time deceptively referred to as the "hand that will set things down" (517-18), the author Iris writes the story of the story and the story within the story with both restored hands. Suitably in this postmodern trickster narrative, her death notice in the Herald and Banner is sandwiched between the conclusion of the inner novel and the ending of the frame story, which shifts into future tense. Since all of the clippings except the article about the Queen Mary are made up (Atwood Papers), this verification of Iris's death is as fictional as everything else. Seeming to depict the modernist theme of the eternity of art against time (Ingersoll, "Waiting" 551), The Blind Assassin again blurs any distinction between reality and fiction or art and renders absurd questions about who actually assembles the novel's many pieces and whether Iris dies before or after finishing her manuscript. Seeming to pinpoint time and to verify her fiction as history with newspaper clippings and references to well-known historical events, this metafiction rearranges time according to the aesthetic goals of its narrator-inside-narrator-inside frame narrator-inside-author. Despite our dated but lingering desires to make fiction autobiography and history—parodied here and elsewhere in Atwood's texts—and to create Truth out of stories, we are left, finally, only with fiction, but glorious fiction nevertheless.[14]

Although war sacrifices and "assassinations" in *The Blind Assassin* are revealed as similarly meaningless, Iris's and readers' struggles to create meaning in art and life are paradoxically meaningful. Through her magical realism and her embedded fairy tale and mythic intertexts, Atwood's novels thus record eras in meticulous detail, ironically erasing an objective reality as it is posited, and create verbal "photographs" all the more magical for calling attention to their subjective "tints."

Notes

I'd like to thank Margaret Atwood and the Thomas Fisher Rare Book Library at the University of Toronto for the use of the Margaret Atwood Papers.

[1] This article is based on a brief paper delivered at the Popular Culture Conference, Toronto, 14-16 March, 2002, and published in "Margaret Atwood and Popular Culture: *The Blind Assassin* and Other Novels." *Journal of American and Comparative Culture*. 25:3-4 (Dec. 2002): 270-75.

[2] Motifs important in both *Alias Grace* and *The Blind Assassin,* and even *The Robber Bride*, emerge from this manuscript. Frances teaches History of Textiles at Amity College (alternatively, runs Amity Museum of Daily Life), has done a book called "Buttons and Bows: Trims and Accessories in the Age of Victoria" (alternatively, "Dress Fabrics and Daily Costume in the Nineteenth Century"), and is invited to fill the Penelope Loomis Chair for Domestic History in the University of Toronto Modern History Department. In constructing Grace and the characters of her story, she begins with a "road, with a young woman walking along it" to Nancy's house. Although Frances doesn't trust newspapers, she finds herself believing when there are photographs: "The mere existence of a photograph, in a newspaper, leads credibility to everything that's printed underneath it. But for the Kinnear murder there are no photos, only two smudgy line drawings." She dreams that she is bargaining for one of her hands with a man in a homespun cloak or cowl, whose face she cannot see, and he is dangling its wrist, like a glove. When she sees that she does have two hands, she thinks "So this third hand must belong to some other woman. It must have been cut off (Atwood Papers).

[3] Although several critics still parallel the love story in "Lizard Men of Zenor" to the supposed romance of Alex and Iris in the frame story, the published magazine version mockingly removes the romance (401).

[4] Iris imagines Sabrina as a Medusa, "her long dark hair coiled like sleeping serpents." Unlike many of Avilion's residents, Sabrina is more than a marble fireplace ornament and, at least in Iris's vision, is able to meet a patriarchal gaze (288, 58).

[5] Earl Ingersoll questions whether the manuscript ever gets into the trunk since Iris dies in the garden where she has been writing, possibly with the manuscript by her (553). But the novel, deliberately confusing time sequence, is far from this simple. Ending the book in future tense, like *Bodily Harm*, the "Threshold" chapter, where Iris says she will put the manuscript in the trunk, is placed **after** Iris's obituary and

could be prior in time to the "The Golden Lock" chapter. See also n. [7].

[6] When asked how she would describe *The Blind Assassin,* Atwood says that "A novel is a very very capacious container" (Gussow).

[7] Although she says that she puts the notebooks into the drawer on the day that Laura dies, in "The Golden Lock" chapter of her memoir, Iris assures us that the notebooks are in the trunk, "along with everything else" (497-98). In the following chapter, "Victory Comes and Goes," however, she says that she has put the notebooks back into the stocking drawer. Since her memoir sometimes takes time leaps backwards and forwards, some details seem contradictory.

[8] Other magic hands in Atwood's work are those of the grandmothers in *Bodily Harm* and *The Robber Bride.*

[9] In addition to this photograph's being deceptive because it is not tinted, as we may expect, the Prologue says the cut-off hand is "[over to one side," but the Epilogue says it is to the left. Since readers have just discovered that Laura's copy of the Button Factory Picnic photo was in one of the hidden notebooks, and since the Epilogue photo is in a chapter titled "The Other Hand," they may inappropriately read the picnic photograph into the inner narrative. Iris is to the left of Alex in the Button Factory picnic photo, and the cut-off hand in Iris's copy of that photo is Laura's. If Laura's hand is the cut-off one in the Epilogue photo, "The Other Hand," "The hand that will set things down" appears to be Laura's. At the end of the preceding chapter, however, Iris admits, "As for the book, Laura didn't write a word of it." As previously mentioned, she adds, "Laura was my left hand, and I was hers. We wrote the book together"(512-13, 517). If so, that paradox is the explanation for how the book can be written metaphorically with two "left hands."

[10] A brown envelope also appears in the "Attic Windows" chapter for "Grace" from the Ur-Manuscript. Flora (earlier Frances) Mabee, is married to Richard and has an affair with Alex. She finds a photocopy of James McDermott's execution in a brown manila envelope hidden in her grandmother's hat box (Atwood Papers). Atwood says that when she was writing *Alias Grace,* Iris, under a different name, "'had something in a box. Originally it was a hatbox. It turned into a steamer trunk. Things transmute in alarming ways when you're writing a book.' Having discovered the trunk, [Atwood] 'looked' inside and found a manuscript and other material" (Gussow).

[11] It is, of course, quite possible that, like any author, Iris might make up an affair between characters who have only slight correspondence to people in her life.

[12] Although Earl Ingersoll sees an unreliable narrator as evidence of *The Blind Assassins's* and other novels' "modernist faith in a truth outside the narrator's storytelling" ("Modernism" 9), neither modernist nor especially postmodernist fiction characteristically demonstrates faith in any external truth, and, if anything, an unreliable narrator is virtually a requirement in postmodern narratives.

[13] "The Angel of Bad Judgment" manuscript for *The Blind Assassin* provides background about tinting and evidence of fairy-tale intertexts. Geraldine, who has a "bad leg" from polio, like Flora Mabee in the early "Grace" manuscript, has a mother who colors photographs. "The colouring does not make them look more real: rather, ultra-real, citizens of a lurid, shadowy half-country where realism is

beside the point" (Atwood Papers, "Grace," ch. 6, 5). Geraldine's mother hand tints photographs and keeps hers locked in a trunk. As in *The Blind Assassin*, her father, this time supposedly missing in the war, once took her to Betty's Luncheonette. In a chapter titled "The Man with a Burning Head," her Aunt Iris finds the trunk with altered photographs of the family and says that her sister created the dragon wings, tails, blue teeth, and other effects, for revenge. Father Clyde's head appears to be on fire in her parents' wedding photos, and in one, his hands are red, flames shoot up from his head, and the bride's face is bleached. Atwood has a handwritten note on the back of this sheet saying "Cinderella, fairy godmother." In "Old Notes," the dossier of tinted photos is described as "like the pictures in fairy-tale books, vivid and fantastic." The Geraldine (Jeraldini) character describes the war as "a huge fire" and feels trapped in a fairy tale, without evil sisters, a fairy godmother or handsome prince—only a mother, Sleeping Beauty, who drinks. She (later Myra, as in the published novel) runs an antique shop named The Gingerbread House (alternatively, Seraphim) and, characterizing herself as a witch and addressing a "you," says that "you would be wise to distrust the story because the old like to eat the young up and remain immortal." Her grandfather had married into a button factory and her mother, at one point named Laurel, drives off a bridge when she is 13 ("The Angel of Bad Judgment," Atwood Papers).

[14] Bouson assumes that Sabrina finds and assembles the novel we read. Myra would not necessarily, of course, set fire to it. And, since Iris's death is every bit as fictional as her life, she is very likely to have "assembled" pieces that are as "real," but no more real, than the photographs, the trunk, or the written words.

Works Cited

Atwood, Margaret. *Alias Grace*. 1996. New York: Nan A. Talese Doubleday.
—. *The Blind Assassin*. 2000. Toronto: McClelland and Stewart.
—. *Bodily Harm*. 1982. New York: Simon and Schuster.
—. *Cat's Eye*. 1988. McClelland and Stewart: Toronto.
—. *The Edible Woman*. 1976. New York: Popular Library.
—. "Essay." http:// www.randomhouse.com/features/atwood/essay.html.
—. *The Handmaid's Tale*. 1986. Boston: Houghton Mifflin.
—. *Lady Oracle*. 1976. New York: Avon.
—. *Life Before Man*. 1979. New York: Simon and Schuster.
—. *Papers*. "The Blind Assassin" Manuscripts, 2001. Gift. Thomas Fisher Rare Book Library. University of Toronto, Toronto, Canada.
—. *The Robber Bride.1993*. McClelland and Stewart: Toronto.
—. *Surfacing*. 1976. New York: Popular Library.
—. *Survival: A Thematic Guide to Canadian Literature*. 1972. Toronto: Anansi.
Barnes and Noble Chats and Events. Interview of Margaret Atwood by

Jennifer. 12 September 2000.
http://www.barnesandnoble.com/community/a...script.asp?userid=2KA
I9UKJZZ&eventId=2291.

Bouson, J. Brooks. "'A Commemoration of Wounds Endured and
Resented': Margaret Atwood's *The Blind Assassin* as Feminist
Memoir." Spring 2003. *Critique: Studies in Contemporary Fiction.*
44.3. 251-69.

Bowers, Maggie Ann. *Magical) Realism: The New Critical Idiom. 2004.*
London and NY: Routledge.

Chadwick, Whitney. *Women, Art, and Society.* 1990. World of Art.
London: Thames and Hudson.

Farris, Wendy B. *Ordinary Enchantments: Magical Realism and the
Remystification of Narrative.* 2004. Nashville: Vanderbuilt UP.

Gussow, Mel. "An Inner Eye that Shines Light on Life's Mysteries." 10
Oct. 2000. *New York Times* 10. NYTimes.com.

Hunt, Margaret and James Stern, trans and ed. *The Complete Grimm's
Fairy Tales.* 1972. Illus. Josef Scharl. NY: Pantheon.

Ingersoll, Earl. "Modernism/ Postmodernism: Subverting Binaries in
Margaret Atwood's *Alias Grace* and *The Blind Assassin.*" Sept. 2007.
Margaret Atwood Studies 1.1. 4-16.

—. "Waiting for the End: Closure in Margaret Atwood's *The Blind
Assassin.*" 2003. *Studies in the Novel* 35.4. 542-58.

Leach, Maria, ed. and Jerome Fried, assoc. ed. *Funk and Wagnall's
Standard Dictionary of Folklore, Mythology, and Legend.* 1984. San
Francisco: Harper and Row.

Lee, Hermione. "Writers in Conversation: Margaret Atwood." Interview.
VHS Video film. Roland Collection No. 43, 52 minutes, Color.
Northbrook, Illinois.

McCombs, Judith. "Of Sacrifice and Sacrificers: History, Literature, and
Myth in Margaret Atwood's *The Blind Assassin.*" December 27 2002.
Margaret Atwood Society Session. Modern Language Association
Conference.

Stein, Karen. "A Left-Handed Story: *The Blind Assassin.*" *Margaret
Atwood's Textual Assassinations: Recent Poetry and Fiction*, ed.
Sharon R. Wilson. 2003. Columbus: Ohio SUP. 135-53.

Sylge, Caroline. "An Iterview with Margaret Atwood." *Fiction and
Literature.* http://www.uk.bol.com/cec/cstage?ecaction=boldlvie.

Thompson, Stith. *Motif-Index of Folk Literature.* Revised and Enlarged
Edition. Six Volumes. 1955. Bloomington: Indiana University Press.

Wilson, Sharon R. "Camera Images in Margaret Atwood's Novels."
Margaret Atwood: Reflection and Reality, ed. Beatrice Mendez-Egle.

Living Author Series 6. 1987. Edinburg, Texas: Pan American University. 29-57.

Wilson, Sharon Rose. *Margaret Atwood's Fairy-Tale Sexual Politics.* 1993. Jackson: UP of Mississippi.

Zamora, Lois Parkinson and Wendy B. Faris, ed. *Magical Realism: Theory, History, Community. 1995.* Durham and London: Duke UP.

Zipes, Jack, trans. *The Complete Fairy Tales of the Brothers Grimm.* 1987. New York: Bantam.

CHAPTER SIX

IT'S ABOUT TIME: TEMPORAL DIMENSIONS IN MARGARET ATWOOD'S *LIFE BEFORE MAN*[1]

KAREN STEIN

Life Before Man is a complex and problematic work. Its narrative strategies—multilayered structure, dated entries, grounding in mythology, juxtaposed narratives of time—work to interrogate the conventions of realism: all deserve more attention. This essay aims to produce a richer understanding of the novel by exploring its complicated use of time and its use of a mythic subtext.

This novel is perhaps Atwood's least studied work.[2] Many readers find the book bleak. To that charge, Atwood responds that she gives her readers hope, "If you think the world is Disneyland, my book is depressing; if you think it's Buchenwald, it's *Anne of Green Gables*" (Freedman 1980, E1). Carol Beran summarizes arguments about bleakness versus affirmation in her discussion of the of the novel's critical reception (Beran 1993, 16-25). She concludes that "although not a joyous affirmation, [the book] does offer hope that life before man—that is, a life yet to come—will not be totally bleak"(Beran 1993, 25).

Scholars disagree about the novel's form. Some read the text as a realist fiction. Giving support for this view, in an interview with Elizabeth Meese Atwood states that *Life* "stays very firmly within the boundaries of realism" (Meese 1985, 89). But we need not take Atwood entirely at her word. Some critics hold different positions. Annette Kolodny reads it as "a transitional text" in Atwood's evolution from romance to realism (Kolodny 1990, 95). Kolodny argues that the book uses a background of "mythically prehistoric monsters" such as Lesje's fantasized dinosaurs and Chris the demon lover as "reminders of the romance narratives that preceded it," and as counterpoints to the realistic foreground (Kolodny, 90). Gayle Greene observes that the novel has more affinities with modernist than with realist fiction: the structure problematizes time and reality ... and Atwood's lyrically and imaginatively textured style draws attention to itself rather than offering a transparent medium on a knowable reality" (Greene 1988,66).

Sharon Wilson has done extensive research on the fairy tale intertexts that underlie Atwood's novels. According to Wilson, there is usually a mythic intertext that promises hope, rebirth, or restoration in Atwood's novels. Her analysis of *Life Before Man* finds references to many fairy-tale and mythic intertexts, and primarily to L. Frank Baum's *The Wizard of Oz* in which the main characters search for and ultimately find the qualities they were previously lacking (Wilson 1993). Following Atwood's promise of hope, and the leads of these critics, especially Greene, Beran, and Wilson, I set out to find both the sources of hope and a critique of realism in Atwood's use of mythic intertexts underlying this work.

I suggest that the novel juxtaposes two contrasting narratives, a mythic and a realist one. The surface narrative is the realist fiction in which time drags on and the characters are bored and disillusioned. The other narrative is a mythic subtext in which the characters act out a cyclic pattern of birth, death, and rebirth, following the cycle of the year. The novel sets a gray world of contemporary urban culture in contrast to a green world of nature. The gray world is the world of realism and linear time, the boring existence of the novel's characters, who experience their lives in a black, white and gray world, drained of color and vibrancy.[3] Nevertheless, the characters are linked to the green world of nature through their fantasies and through a pattern of dates that evoke mythic and naturist/neo-Pagan rituals and ceremonies. Subtle clues to the characters' possible transformations recur throughout the text in language that alludes (although sometimes parodically) to the sacral and heroic. Images of the green world achieve weight and symbolic power by their repetition, their psychological value, and their placement in the text. The urban and natural images resonate against each other, suggesting the conflict humans face in searching for the places where they are most comfortable, most at home. I would like to explore here the idea that the novel's relation to realism holds a clue to its apparent pessimism, and its mythic intertexts open the possibility of hope.

The Novel's Relation to Realist Narrative

Life Before Man makes use of realist narrative conventions both to shape the novel and to critique the assumptions that underlie those conventions. Addressing the issue of the novel's realism, Coral Ann

Howells notes that Atwood compares *Life* to George Eliot's *Middlemarch*. Howells claims that both novels argue against scientific determinism and for a variety of "individual human responses" (Howells 2005, 91). Analyzing Eliot's style in *Middlemarch*, David Lodge demonstrates that her use of free indirect discourse "obscures and complicates the distinction between the two types of discourse," mimesis and diegesis (Lodge 1990, 49). The result is that the reader is made "aware of the indeterminacy that lurks in all efforts at human communication" (Lodge 1990, 56). In *Life* Atwood follows a plan similar to Eliot's, using realist devices to reveal the shortcomings of the realist convention which pretends to objectivity and scientific validity. This critique is articulated primarily through the motifs of time and spectacle. In counterpoint to realism's deterministic and constricted perception and its linear view of time, the novel propounds a multiplicity of viewpoints and a cyclical view of time. The narrative devices of realism—attention to detail, an emphasis on time as duration and succession, and the presentation of streams of consciousness as a revelation of the experiences and feelings of individual characters—may work in *Life* to parody and to undermine the realist conventions. The novel thus calls into question the realist tradition (which is linked to pessimism and violence), and insinuates a covert subtext, a mythic story of cyclical death and rebirth that offers a more optimistic vision.

On the realist level *Life Before Man* is a minimalist novel; there are few characters, little action occurs in the narrative present, and it is set in a limited space and time. Well into the book Lesje exclaims in frustration, "nothing has happened yet." Other readers share Lesje's frustration; critics have remarked on the sameness of events, the lack of differentiation of characters. Sherrill Grace remarks on "the boring sameness of these people" (Grace, 1980b,136) who accomplish next to nothing. She comments that the book seems to argue that "history, public and private, is pointless" (Grace, 1980a,168). Davidson and Davidson argue that there would be little change if the events were placed in a different order (Davidson and Davidson 1981, 205-21). The feeling is one of boredom and disaffection. Atwood remarks that all the events occur within one "square mile in which nothing enters and only a dead body leaves" (Wilson 165). Indeed, the sites depicted in the novel are relatively small enclosed spaces: the Royal Ontario Museum (known as the ROM), small bedrooms, offices, or tacky hotel rooms. Moreover, the characters seem stagnant, locked into deadening relationships.

Carol Beran and Gayle Greene observe that the novel minimizes plot. The major actions occur in the past, or elsewhere. Beran notes that "Atwood marginalizes the rites of passage—births, deaths, marriages, sexual initiations—that often form the climactic moments of novels by having them take place off-stage" (14). Greene argues that Atwood "has actually accomplished what [Virginia] Woolf and other modernists strive for: she has freed the narrative from plot so that she can focus on the inner events that are the real adventures" (67).

The inner adventures that comprise the novel unfold in the present tense through the reported actions, dialogue, and streams of consciousness of three main characters: Elizabeth Schoenhof, an exhibit planner at the museum; her husband Nate Schoenhof, by turns a lawyer and wooden toy maker; and Lesje Green, a paleontologist at the ROM. Other characters are Chris Beecham, Elizabeth's lover who killed himself shortly before the novel's beginning; Elizabeth's Auntie Muriel; Lesje's lover William, and Nate's former lover Martha.[4]

The novel's most immediately striking narrative strategy is the use of present tense dated text blocks, each centered on one character's point of view. Sherrill Grace comments that these dated entries suggest field notes of a scientific observer whose distanced gaze "attempts to sum up the species it purports to describe" (168). This stance of objective, scientific reality is the perspective of the realist novel. As Linda Nochlin explains, realists tried to imitate scientific attitudes

> impartiality, impassivity, scrupulous objectivity, rejection of a priori metaphysical or epistemological prejudice, the confining of the artist to the accurate observation and notation of empirical phenomena and the descriptions of how, and not why, things happen" (43).

But in *Life Before Man* the use of three centers of consciousness disrupts the reader's expectations of a consistent and objective point of view. In her study of realism in the English novel Elizabeth Ermarth analyzes the implications of the lack of an objective narrator: "there is no stable narrator standing safely outside the frame and implying the possibility of connections without having to draw any in particular" (Ermarth 1983, 51). Additionally, the present tense narration

> brackets out the future and the past, in other words it brackets out the linear coordinates that make possible relative measurements in a stable world, and the continuous present thus destroys the continuity of time and democratizes all moments and all viewpoints" (Ermarth 51).

Thus Atwood's use of multiple centers of consciousness and the present tense may be disrupting realist narrative conventions.

The setting of the natural history museum, the Royal Ontario Museum, amplifies the perspective of scientific observation, and one of the central characters is a paleontologist who classifies fossils. The museum, a collection of animal and fossil remains, reminds us that humans have lost the immediacy of their relationship to the natural world, and that institutions such as museums and zoos came into being to simulate those now unattainable relationships. The collection of animals and fossils for human observation sets up a system in which human observers obtain gratification, a feeling of power gained from understanding and from sheer longevity: the dinosaurs have become extinct, but we are here now (Berger 1980). Yet, as Grace reminds us, the human characters who populate the novel are the ones being observed. To help us account for the observing eye of the viewer and reader film and narrative theory may offer useful insights.

Film theory analyzes the scopic intrusiveness of films, and critics have extended this analysis to narrative, analyzing the ways that realism represents its characters as subjects of observation. John Bender, for example, argues that Jeremy Bentham's model of a penitentiary, the Panopticon, is "the ultimate in realism—the ultimate representational system" (Bender 1987, 40). The invisible narrating observer is emphasized in *Life*, carrying the pretext of scientific observation to an extreme. Through its technique of free indirect discourse the novel reveals the characters' thoughts and emotions—not from within as in first person narration, but from the perspective of a distanced observer. In its choice of viewpoints, the novel exaggerates the intrusiveness of the observing narrator. Thus the reader also becomes a voyeur, intruding into the characters' consciousness.

The characters here are especially vulnerable to judgmental surveillance. It is instructive to note that Atwood wrote *Life* as the first of a group of three novels in all of which the observer's gaze is powerful and destructive. In the second novel of this sequence, *Bodily Harm* (Atwood 1981), violence against women escalates from the scopic violence of pornography to rape and brutal beating. The third novel, *The Handmaid's Tale* (Atwood 1985), explicitly equates surveillance with power and violence: the handmaids are warned "to be seen is to be penetrated," and the secret police force of the totalitarian state Gilead is known as Eyes. In *Life* the violence of observation is psychological rather than political. The characters are self-conscious in the face of observation, fearing that they are inadequate. Nate is uncomfortable when Elizabeth watches him in the bathtub. In public, Lesje hides her mouth with her hand, afraid that her teeth are too large. Elizabeth, on the other hand, derives her power from

careful observation; she watches her colleagues at work and learns their
jobs better than they do. She makes sure to become friends with her
husband's lovers so as to monitor the progress of the affairs. After Nate
has left her and moved in with Lesje, Elizabeth walks by their house in
order "to see it, that's all." She wants to be seen as well: "look at me, I'm
here, you can't get rid of me that easily" (291).

Time and The Mythic Intertext

We must now turn to explore the novel's use of time, for its critique of
realism centers on time. We have seen that a series of dated entries
comprises the text of the novel. Additionally, frequent mention of time
punctuates the text. Textual analysis reveals a predominance of temporal
phrases. For example, a page chosen at random (page 8) contains
seventeen adverbs or adverbial phrases relating to time, including:
Saturday, now, tonight, used to, tomorrow, the next day, when,
meanwhile, former times, olden days, bygone era, once a week, before. In
these and similar phrases throughout the novel, we can almost hear the
clock ticking, a metronome beating out the rhythm. Time seems to drag
on. In another example, the first time that Nate and Lesje arrange a rendez-
vous in a hotel, we expect some passion. We are led to believe that they
have planned to make love, but this does not happen. Indeed, little seems
to happen; however, the characters are acutely aware of time's passage.

> They've been here two hours and she still has all her clothes on. . . . He
> kisses her again, tentatively, lingering. Then he asks what time it is. He
> himself has no watch. Lesje tells him it's five-thirty. [He has to take his
> children to dinner at his mother's at six.]. . . 'There's lots of time, love,' he
> says. 'Next time will be better.' . . . She doesn't believe there is lots of
> time. There is no time. (143-44)

Their second assignation, in Elizabeth's bed, is again replete with
references to time. The novel appears to argue that time has become
commodified, and clock time has replaced seasonal time to the detriment
of the characters' wellbeing. Slaves to time, the novel's characters drag
out their days, nervously checking their watches, regretting the past,
fearing the future, and escaping into fantasies of other temporal
dimensions.

Although many critics have commented on the dated entries, no one
has asked why these dates? I shall argue here that the dates chosen develop
a cyclical pattern of annually repeated death and rebirth. The action takes
place within a two-year period, from October 29, 1976 through August 18,

1978 (with two brief flashbacks to a time several months before the action starts). Atwood has written that she wanted the book to have a tight triangular structure, three characters who each believe that their position is correct and the others are wrong. In fact, it has an almost circular temporal structure: it begins and ends at the harvest season.

****

A brief sidestep is needed here, as we contextualize the concurrent developments of the realist narrative and the modern concept of time in Western society. With the shift from rural community to urban individualism came the shift from myth to realist narrative, and from the cyclic to the linear construction of time. The eighteenth century witnessed both the rise of the novel and the scientific revolution. The paradigmatic shifts that accompanied these changes gave us new concepts of realism, of science, of religion, and of time. As the scientific method developed, mechanistic concepts of the universe and a new focus on time arose. Scientific experimentation led to a greater emphasis on precise observation and measurement of events over time. Leonie Kellahar notes:

> time and space only came to be invested with new meaning in the Newtonian age, during and after the eighteenth century. Newton, and others like him saw time and space as absolutes in themselves. . . . at this point the human lifespan came to be construed within time" (Kellahar 1994,2).

Time and narrative are inseparably linked as our temporal experience reaches consciousness in the narrative form. Realist fiction arose in this milieu.

Mikhail Bakhtin explains that the development of realist narrative is linked to our perception of linear time (Bakhtin 1981). He traces this development to the movement from an early agrarian economy and communal society to capitalist individualism. The time of the early agricultural economy is unified time, in which nature's rhythms predominate. Mircea Eliade finds a uniquely religious relationship to time in this world view:

> Sacred time appears under the paradoxical aspect of a circular time, reversible and recoverable, a sort of eternal mythical present that is periodically reintegrated by means of rites. This attitude. . . suffices to distinguish religious from nonreligious man; the former refuses to live solely in what, in modern terms, is called the historical present; he attempts

to regain a sacred time that, from one point of view, can be homologized to
eternity (Eliade 1987, 70).

On the other hand, "repetition emptied of its religious content
necessarily leads to a pessimistic vision of existence. . . . When it is
desacralized, cyclic time becomes terrifying" (Eliade 107 emphasis in
original). In "Women's Time" Julia Kristeva notes that women have often
been identified with these rhythms in "cyclical" and "monumental" time,
while men's time has been the linear time of history and politics (Kristeva
1981). As Bakhtin explicates this evolution of temporal consciousness, in
agrarian communities personal time is not yet differentiated; people
believe themselves part of the collective, the unity, a social body. Death is
part of a cycle of life, connected to regeneration and new birth. This time
is not separated from the earth or from nature.

The literature of the agrarian community is grounded in myth, in the
stories that explain the culture's origins and its relationship to the divine
beings that pervade and control nature and human life. This unified
agrarian time becomes fragmented as culture evolves from a classless
society to one based in property ownership and capitalism. Individuals
become isolated. The newly emerging middle class needs fiction that
instructs it in the proper ways to function in social life. Bakhtin tells us
that

When it was appropriated for the making of plots, [time] bifurcated.
There were not many personal plots to choose from, and these could not be
transferred into the life of the social whole (the state, the nation); the plots
of history became something specifically separate from the plots of
personal life (love, marriage) (Bakhtin 1981, 208).

Thus, the realist novel must focus on the individual, stressing the
personal history, the events of the individual, private life: birth, sexuality,
and death. These events now assume a great significance for the
individual, but the characters are also alienated, isolated both from the
larger community and from the green world, the natural rhythms of the
year. Nature itself becomes a backdrop: "it was turned into landscape, it
was fragmented into metaphors and comparisons serving to sublimate
individual and private affairs and adventures not connected in any real or
intrinsic way with nature itself" (217). According to Bakhtin, the time of
the realist novel "moves in narrow circles . . . and almost seems to stand
still. . . . It is a viscous and sticky time that drags itself slowly through
space" (248). His comment here captures the feeling of stagnant time in
Life. The characters are concerned with the passage of time, because they
see it as leading to an end, to death. Just as there was an end to dinosaur
time, there may be an end to human time: to each individual human life,

and quite likely to the species. Bakhtin conjectures that this sense of time as an absolute end derives from the separation of the individual from the community.

The new concept of time pervaded all domains of social thought, even religion. The Deistic concept of creation employed a new and rather strange, analogy: the Creator of the universe became conceptualized as a cosmic clockmaker, the first cause that set the universal clock ticking. Thus the universe was construed as a smoothly functioning machine, operating within time. Similarly, the machine analogy became a way to describe increasingly alienated human behavior. Interestingly, in an early draft of *Life*, Elizabeth Schoenhof thinks that she used to function well, like an automaton; set her in motion and she will keep going. This scientific, mechanical, time bound worldview contrasts dramatically with the naturistic concept of time as cyclical, and divinity as immanent in an organic universe created from nothing or from natural materials such as mud and water. Whereas agrarian people may have measured events according to natural cycles such as movement of the moon, the stars and the seasons, we now measure time in ever decreasing intervals: years, months, weeks, days, hours, minutes, seconds and nanoseconds. The speed-up locks us into linear rhythms and removes us from the natural world. This disjunction between a time-bound urban world and the cyclical world of natural plenitude resonates throughout Life to critique the realist narrative and to develop a mythic intertext.

*****

Each of the novel's three main characters is associated with one or more cyclical temporal cycles, and with a particular place. Lesje Green, the paleontologist, works in the enclosed room of the fossil laboratory within the museum. Her job is to classify fossils, and thus raises the suggestion that she herself is stagnant and fossilized. But her first name conjures up the heroine of *Alice in Wonderland*, a young woman associated with other dimensions of time and space, and with transformation. Her surname, and her fantasies of the world during the time of the dinosaurs, link her with geological time, a larger natural world, and with life before the evolution of humans. Elizabeth Schoenhof, the exhibit planner, is also situated in small enclosed places, such as her bedroom, where she lies inert thinking of her dead lover. But her fantasies and her visit to the planetarium connect her to astronomical time, and to the expanding universe of stars and planet. At the novel's conclusion she experiences an empathic connection to the agrarian world of Chinese peasants. Nate is interested in politics, the present of linear historic time. But his fantasies are of a tropical island where natives dive for pearls. Thus, the novel juxtaposes four cycles of time: the astronomical time of Elizabeth's star fantasies, measured in light years; the geological time of Lesje's fantasies, measured in eras; the seasons of the natural world, measured in solstices and equinoxes; and twentieth century human time, measured by clocks and calendars. In each case the character starts his or her fantasy from association with the commodified (or fossilized museum specimen) version of the natural world: Elizabeth from her visit to the planetarium, Nate from his purchase of loofah sponges, and Lesje from the museum's fossil collection. From these seemingly trivial encounters, they imagine themselves in more direct contact with the actual natural phenomena indicated by the commodified versions—the stars, the sea, a prehistoric world.

The twentieth century dates that mark the novel's sections have a two-part structure. One series of dates establishes the linear rhythms of the historical and political worlds: Remembrance Day; the election victory of Parti Québecois; Elizabeth's birthday. Another series of dates links the narrative to the cycle of the natural year and to the holidays derived from the wheel of the seasons, including the solstices and other dates that commemorate the cruxes of the annual cycle. The events that occur at these times are occasionally dark parodies of the holidays' significance: Martha pretends that she has tried to commit suicide at Christmas, the holiday that celebrates birth and renewal; two near-rapes occur near Valentine's Day, the holiday of love. And, as it moves through these dates, the novel traces a subtle and ambiguous movement from despair to hope, from death to rebirth.

The novel's structure foregrounds the seasons. Part One takes place in autumn, Parts Two and Three in winter, Part Four in spring, while Part Five takes approximately a whole year. The mood of parts one and two is elegiac; lost life, lost loves are mourned; relationships between Elizabeth and Nate, and between Lesje and William deteriorate. Parts Three and Four are times of transition; the new romance of Nate and Lesje begins. Part Five is the resolution, a time of potential reconciliation and muted hope.

Each of the characters is connected with a season. Elizabeth's lover Chris, for example, is identified with summer. His surname Beecham suggests the green world of growth, and his first name indicates a God-like quality. Indeed, Chris is a nature god. Redhaired and passionate, he appears in the novel on a burning August afternoon in 1975, to flaunt his affair with Elizabeth. But in October 1976, when the affair has ended and the year approaches its end, he kills himself, symbolically enacting the death of the fertility god who dies at harvest time so that new life may grow in the following season. His job as a taxidermist at the museum points to his connection with the world of animals, and suggests the figure that the neo-Pagan theorist Starhawk has described as "the Dying God [who] puts on horns and becomes the Hunter" (Starhawk 1989, 113). According to Starhawk, the Hunter

> embodies all quests. . . . He is both the bright sun, the light-giving, energizing force, and the darkness of night and death. The two aspects . . . are complementary, not contradictory. . . Both are part of the cycle, the necessary balance of life. (113)

Moreover, each character is associated with one of the traditional "four elements," earth, air, fire and water. Chris, with his red hair, his fiery temperament, described by Elizabeth as hot and passionate, is fire. He is associated with energy, spirit, heat, flame, explosions, sun, volcanoes. Elizabeth, whose astrological sign is Cancer, is water; her season is autumn. She wears a fish pendant. Her clothing and furniture are in shades of blue, green, gray; the light in her living room is "underwater light" (Atwood 1979,18). She is linked with emotions, feelings, sorrow, intuition, the unconscious mind. Lesje is spring and earth: as a paleontologist she is connected with caves, rocks, bones. She is the one who will become the new mother, continuing the cycle of life. Nate is associated with the north and with air, which stands for "the mind, . . . knowledge, abstract learning" (Starhawk 1989, 251). Air is also East and dawn, and, unlike Chris who dies, Nate will live and procreate.

*****

At the start of the novel, the characters are looking backward, thinking of the ends of romantic relationships: Elizabeth mourns the death of her lover Chris; Nate laments the loss of love in his marriage to Elizabeth, and pays a disappointing visit to his former lover Martha; Lesje "wanders in prehistory," since her relationship to William in current time is unrewarding and uninteresting. In her fantasies, life before man refers to the eras when dinosaurs roamed the earth. She looks mostly toward the past, yet her actions eventually propel her into the future.

Part One of the novel takes place in autumn and devotes fifty-five pages to this occasion, taking place over a three-day span October 29-October 31,1976 leading up to and including Hallowe'en. The novel draws upon the religious significance of the holiday, and utilizes themes of neo-

Pagan rituals connected with its celebration. At the time that Atwood wrote this novel, neo-Paganism, or recovery of pagan naturist religions and rituals, including wicca or witchcraft, was spreading in the US, Europe and Canada. Because of her interest in spiritual practices such as the tarot, and in myth and folklore, Atwood may well have known about this naturist revival. Interestingly, in 1979, the year that *Life* was published, two major books about neo-Paganism were also published, the first edition of Starhawk's *Spiral Dance* and Margot Adler's *Drawing Down the Moon*. Thus, these ideas were circulating in North American culture when the book was being written.

The motifs of part one, like those of All Hallows Eve, or the neo-Pagan Samhain, are death, mourning and children. There are eleven entries in Part One; three are from Lesje's point of view, four from Nate's and five from Elizabeth's. The language, as Carol Beran and others have pointed out is a mixture of realism and fantasy. But the more fanciful language often hints at the supernatural, the mythic, or at the possibility of transformation. For example, Elizabeth will later hear voices she calls "angel voices" (64). Discussing these mysterious sounds Beran explains "the world beyond physical reality is making itself felt again, and Atwood is emphasizing it by repetition" (40).

Initially, each character thinks of him or herself negatively: Elizabeth is "like a peeled snail;" Nate is a "feeble minded creep," and Lesje a lonely observer hiding in trees to watch the dinosaurs. The characters are passive and inactive. Elizabeth is depressed, and lies in bed wondering: "I don't know how I should live" (3). This backward looking and mourning is congruent with the rituals of Samhain (related to the Christian All Hallows Eve, celebrated as the secular children's holiday of Hallowe'en), the solemn Sabbat that both ends and starts the neo-Pagan calendar. On this occasion people celebrate their ties to their beloved dead who have recently died." The ceremonial rituals include the possibility of speaking with these souls, for at this time the veils separating life and death are thin. Candles, darkness, gifts of shared food, bowls, all are part of the celebration.

> At Samhain [the god] arrives at the Land of Youth, the Shining Land in which the souls of the dead grow young again, as they wait to be reborn. He opens the gates that they may return and visit their loved ones (Starhawk 1989, 193-4; 218-19).

The novel repeats these motifs in Elizabeth's monologue addressed to newly dead lover, her references to darkness, the food for the trick-or-treaters, and two sets of bowls. She thinks about her porcelain bowls "meant to hold offerings. Right now they hold their own space, their own beautifully shaped absence" (Atwood 1979, 20). Another set of bowls holds the "offerings" that will be distributed to the children who come trick-or-treating. Elizabeth makes explicit connections to the holiday's spiritual overtones: she thinks the children do not know "what night this is or what, with their small decorated bodies, they truly represent" (54). Answering the door to the trick-or-treaters, she makes the connection to the Pagan holiday:

> All Souls. Not just friendly souls but all souls. They are souls, come back, come back, crying at the door, hungry, mourning their lost lives. You give them food, money, anything to substitute for your love and blood, hoping it will be enough, waiting for them to go away. (34-35)

Elizabeth spends most of her entries in this section remembering her dead lover Chris. Distraught at his recent suicide, she laments "I don't know how I should live. I live like a peeled snail" (3). She wants to have her shell back, to feel less vulnerable. Her ties to life are her children, but they seem remote and distant from her now, just as her husband Nate seems remote.

Lesje's section starts with her fantasy of "wandering in prehistory" because she finds her present life unsatisfying (12). Her thoughts about the dinosaurs raises concerns that humans may become extinct as well. Perhaps, just as there has been life before man evolved, there may also be life after man has become extinct. Lesje realizes that in her fantasies "she's regressing. She's been doing that a lot lately" (13). As a teenager she fantasized about dinosaurs, and then about men. But thinking about men now is "unrewarding." She does not fantasize about her lover, William, although perhaps she did previously. The Samhain rituals include a turning, a time to think of new birth. Thus, while Elizabeth laments Chris's death, Lesje thinks about her own desire for children. She would like a child, but her partner William would not.

Nate also has a mourning ritual in this part of the novel. His section starts "he doesn't know what 'love' means between them any more" (7). He mourns the end of the love he and Elizabeth once shared. He previously thought of her romantically as a "Madonna in a shrine, shedding a quiet light... holding a lamp in her hand like Florence Nightingale" (50). He visits Martha, his former lover, and feels defeated in the face of her anger at him for breaking off the affair. Yet he experiences a turning and new beginning as well. There are hints that he will next begin a relationship with Lesje, whom he is now romanticizing. He places a call to her from a pay phone, and thinks of her as "his one hope of salvation . . . [her] fingers upraised in blessing" (34). He imagines himself transformed; he goes into a phone booth like a "feeble-minded creep" and comes out like Superman, as in the comics. He later thinks of himself as Spiderman, climbing Lesje's wall to meet her (77). Nate's tendency to romanticize and sacralize the women to whom he is attracted may be perceived on two levels. On the mundane, realist level, he is unrealistic, and creating overly romantic expectations. Yet on the mythic level, he is hinting at the sacral dimension that the novel repeatedly evokes, weaving a tapestry of the sacred through threads of metaphor and allusion.

Part Two takes place in winter, covering two months and two weeks, from November 12, 1976, the day after Canadian Remembrance Day, through December 28, 1976, just after Christmas. The action of this part stresses separation and connection, life and death. The narrative moves through the Christmas season, the holiday of birth and renewal, the celebration of light returning from darkness, of life emerging from death. Atwood handles some of these events parodically: there is little joy or celebration for any of the characters. This part begins with Elizabeth again remembering Chris. On December 23 she goes Christmas shopping. But the act is now an empty one for her; she thinks that the wrapping paper will be too bright and intrusive. She feels passive, apathetic. Nate's presence is like a ghost to her; "like light from a star that moved on thousands of light – years before; a phantom" (110).

In a darkly comic reversal of the birth of the Christ child, Martha lies to Nate at her Christmas party, telling him that she has attempted to commit suicide, taking all the pills in her medicine cabinet. The last entry of Part Two is Lesje's, on December 28, 1976. She buys a bottle of wine to celebrate the Christmas holiday belatedly with William, who spent Christmas with his parents, thus increasing his separation from her. Unexpectedly, she encounters Nate in the liquor store. In a symbolic gesture of healing, Lesje touches the wound on Nate's forehead where Martha hit him. Nate and Lesje embrace. Her wine bottle drops, but it does not break. In this ceremonial moment, the connection between Nate and Lesje starts (128). She thinks that "he is making a gift of himself" to her (128).

Part Three continues in winter from January 3, through February 16, 1977, that is, just after the start of the New Year through Valentine's Day. Elizabeth thinks "I live my life despite [Auntie Muriel] and I will continue to live it" (137). She later conducts a burial ritual, symbolically scattering fur scraps in a ravine (170) as a memorial for the taxidermist Chris. The estrangement of William and Lesje continues while the connection between Nate and Lesje grows stronger. Around the time of Candlemas in early February, a holiday that Starhawk calls the "feast of the waxing light," a time when seeds that will later grow first begin to sprout (186), Lesje and Nate first make love. After this Nate imagines a future with Lesje.

In a parodic inversion of the romantic myths of Valentine's Day, February 16 has two entries describing unromantic sexual intercourse. Elizabeth remembers seducing a boy she picked up when she was a teenager. She thinks of their sexual urgency as "time squeezed together" (204). In the narrative present Elizabeth has manipulated William, hoping to force a confrontation between William and Lesje that would lead to a reconciliation and end Lesje's affair with Nate. But Elizabeth's plan backfires: William attempts to rape Lesje, who escapes him by locking herself in the bathroom.

Part Four takes place in spring, over a period of four months, from Wednesday, March 9 through Saturday, July 9, 1977. This is the season of spring, the time of new growth, the season of rising desire, proceeding through the balance of the equinox, and the triumph of light at the summer solstice. In keeping with the motif of growth and fertility, this section is built around growing sexual desire, rape, and seduction, much of it darkly comic. Lesje leaves William and moves into a rented house, expecting Nate to join her. But even though he tells her he will, and says he'd like them to have a baby, he delays. Meanwhile Elizabeth seduces William. And, on May 14, Elizabeth arranges to meet a man who tried to pick her up. In a parody of her first sexual encounter in her teens, he attempts to seduce her in his car, but she fends him off.

Images of fertility and sterility characterize Lesje's thoughts on April 29, the day before May Day, the pagan holiday of Beltane, the day that celebrates the marriage of the god and maiden. Nate's children are coming to spend the weekend with Lesje and Nate. Lesje dreads their arrival, and feels barren, "in the desert without, isolated, single, childless" (259), excluded from the "verdant little oasis" of Nate, Elizabeth and the children (259).

June 22 is the summer solstice, the time when light triumphs and then immediately begins to decline; the Sun King embraces the Queen of Summer and their marriage is consummated. The entry for this day is Lesje's. Although Lesje (now the supposedly triumphant Queen of Summer) has won Nate (the new Sun King) from Elizabeth, her mood is unhappy. She thinks "Elizabeth should have felt deserted and betrayed and she herself should have felt, if not victorious, at least conventionally smug. Instead, it seems to be the other way around" (276). However, Elizabeth is not happy either. On her 39th birthday, she begins to feel old. She resents

Nate's freedom and feels herself "locked into this house while the roof leaks and the foundation crumbles and the earth revolves and leaves fall from the calendars like snow" (290).

Part Five covers almost a full year, from September 3, 1977 through August 18, 1978. Although it begins with entries in which all three protagonists are unhappy and dissatisfied, it ends with at least a temporary resolution of their concerns. In contrast to its elegiac start the novel ends in muted celebration, although characteristically for Atwood, the conclusion is somewhat ambiguous. Its concluding sections, set on August 18, 1978, are a time of fruition presented in images of harvest, fertility, pregnancy, renewed desire, and utopian yearnings. Each character experiences a connection to the green world and new hope. Notably, there are fewer references to clock time.

Part Five ends on Friday, August 18, 1978, almost 2 years from the start. Late August begins the harvest season, and each entry on this day suggests harvest, fertility. Lesje is now identified with summer. She tries to enter her familiar fantasy of the living dinosaurs, but "she can't do it," perhaps because she is too tired, or perhaps because she is more firmly attached to her own present life (361). No longer afraid of Elizabeth, she believes they ought to make peace with each other (359). At the end of May she threw away her birth control pills in a fit of anger, and, having missed two menstrual cycles, she believes she is pregnant. Thus she will take Elizabeth's place to continue the cycle of generation. She thinks getting pregnant may be a "stupid thing . . . or she may have done a wise thing for a stupid reason" (361). She is unused to thinking of herself as having power of agency, but now affirms her place in the museum as a "guardian" of the past with its "whole chunks of time, . . . golden and frozen" (357). Although she worries that her child may have horns, the impregnation with a horned baby suggests the mythic horned god, who will continue the cycle of death and rebirth (341). The horned baby also reminds us of the conclusion of Atwood's novel *Surfacing* when the unnamed narrator engages in a ritual outdoor mating and believes she may be giving birth to a horned, godlike, new kind of being.

Nate thinks of going "out into the country" with Lesje to "make love, slowly and gently, under some trees or in a field" (363). He goes to meet her at the Museum, uncertain of her response to his unexpected arrival and thinks "In any case, they will go home" (365). Thus in his section, the man who felt displaced from his wife and bed now feels he has a love and a home they share.

For her part, Elizabeth has come to revel in her strength and her survival. She is glad that "she has built a dwelling" even if it is "over the abyss" (352). At the museum, she looks at the Chinese Peasant painting exhibit she has arranged. Able now to think of others and to enjoy a more technicolor world than her previously black and white world of depression, she is unexpectedly moved by pictures of women harvesting glowing purple eggplants and ripe orange persimmons. The Chinese paintings represent a utopian state of agrarian community and connection to a fertile, blossoming nature. Elizabeth is aware of the contradictions of Communist China. The utopian China of the paintings "does not exist. Nevertheless she longs to be there" (368). Newly able to experience deep emotion, she plans a front porch picnic for her daughters, a connection to the green world she has until now rejected.

*****

The novel formulates a critique of realism by showing realist narrative strategies as invasive and open to interpretation rather than scientifically objective, and by fracturing and problematizing the point of view. It posits a mythic subtext that inserts an epic story of loss and renewal, of connection to ritual and community. Moreover, by juxtaposing the two types of time, linear / mundane time and cyclical / sacral time, the novel suggests possibilities of healing and transformation through connection to nature and to a sacral worldview. Through their emerging links with the green world of nature and the great turning cycle of the year, the characters at least temporarily find hope, experience positive emotions, and may grow closer toward their full stature as whole, feeling persons.

Notes

[1] Margaret Atwood, *Life Before Man* 1979. (New York: Ballantine,). All references to this novel are taken from this edition. This essay is a revised and expanded version of my chapter on *Life Before Man* in *Margaret Atwood Revisited*, 1999, Twayne, and appears here with permission of Gale, a part of Cengage Learning, Inc.

[2] For one recent example, *Margaret Atwood: A Critical Companion*, devotes two paragraphs to the novel in a book of 155 pages.

[3] See, for example, Elizabeth's view of food as the black and white magazine diagrams of its fat content, *Life Before Man* 6.

[4] Atwood chooses characters' names carefully, and her choices suggest mythic possibilities. Lesje is Ukranian for Alice (99) which means "truthful one" and hints at Alice in Wonderland, the girl who enters a strange universe; Elizabeth means "dedicated to God;" and Nate (Nathanael) means "a gift of God" as his mother explains to Elizabeth (51). Chris comes from Christian or Christopher which means "follower or believer in Christ." Green refers to the green world; Schoenhof

is "beautiful place," and Beecham is beech trees, woods. William, Lesje's lover's name comes from the old German meaning strong protector. Auntie Muriel's name derives from the Greek for myrrh, bitter, and Wilson postulates that she is linked with the Auntie Em from *The Wizard of Oz*. Martha comes from the Aramaic for lady, mistress, and is connected with the Biblical Martha, sister of Lazarus and Mary. The name choices here suggest alternative worlds, the inverted realities of *Alice in Wonderland* and *The Wizard of Oz*, and the spiritual possibilities conveyed by the Biblical and naturist allusions.

Works Cited

Atwood, Margaret. *Life Before Man*. 1979. New York: Ballantine.

—. *Bodily Harm*. 1981. Toronto: McClelland and Stewart.

—. *The Handmaid's Tale*. 1985.Toronto: McClelland and Stewart.

Bakhtin, Mikhail. 1981. "Forms of Time and Chronotype in the Novel," in *The Dialogic Imagination*. Ed. Michael Holquist. Trans. Caryl Emerson and Michael Holquist. Austin, Texas: University of Texas Press, 184-258.

Bender, John. 1987. *Imagining the Penitentiary*. Chicago: U Chicago P.

Beran, Carol. 1993. *Living Over the Abyss: Margaret Atwood's* LifeBefore Man. Toronto: ECW Press.

Berger, John. "Why Look at Animals,"1980. *About Looking*. NY: Pantheon, 1-26.

Cooke, Nathalie. *Margaret Atwood: A Critical Companion*. 2004. Westport, CT: Greenwood Press.

Davidson, Arnold E. and Cathy N. Davidson. "Prospects and Retrospects in *Life Before Man*."1981. *The Art of Margaret Atwood: Essays in Criticism*. Toronto: Anansi. 205-221.

Eliade, Mircea. *The Sacred and the Profane: The Nature of Religion*. 1959. Trans. Willard R. Trask. San Diego: Harcourt Brace, 1987.

Ermarth, Elizabeth Deeds. *Realism and Consensus in the English Novel*. 1983. Princeton, NJ: Princeton University Press.

Freedman, Adele. "Happy Heroine and 'Freak' of Can Lit." 1980. *Globe and Mail* (Toronto), 5 October, E1.

Grace, Sherrill. " 'Time Present and Time Past': *Life Before Man*." (Winter 1980-81). *Essays in Canadian Writing* 20 165-70.

—. *iolent Duality: A Study of Margaret Atwood*. 1980. Montreal: Vehicule Press.

Greene, Gayle. "*Life Before Man*: Can Anything Be Saved?" 1988. *Margaret Atwood: Vision and Forms*. Eds. Kathryn VanSpanckeren and Jan Garden Castro. Carbondale, Illinois: Southern Illinois University Press, 65-84.

Howells, Coral Ann. *Margaret Atwood*. 2005. NY: Palgrave Macmillan.

Kellahar, Leonie. "Aging and Time." 1994. *Encyclopedia of Time*, ed. Samuel L. Macey. New York and London: Garland.

Kolodny, Annette. "Margaret Atwood and the Politics of Narrative." 1990. *Studies on Canadian Literature: Introductory and Critical Essays*. Ed. Arnold E. Davidson.NY: Modern Language Association, 90-109.

Kristeva, Julia. "Women's Time," trans. Alice Jardine. 1981. *Signs* 7:1. 13-35.

Lodge, David. *After Bakhtin*. 1990. London: Routledge.

Meese, Elizabeth. "An Interview with Margaret Atwood," Fall 1985. *Black Warrior Review* 12. 89. Interview conducted April 1985.

Nochlin, Linda. *Realism*. 1971. Harmondsworth, Middlesex, England: Penguin.

Starhawk. *The Spiral Dance: a Rebirth of the Ancient Religion of the Great Goddess*. 1979. Reprinted. San Francisco: HarperSanFrancisco 1989.

Stein, Karen. 1999. *Margaret Atwood Revisited*. NY: Twayne..

Wilson, Sharon Rose. *Margaret Atwood's Fairy-Tale Sexual Politics*. 1993. Toronto: ECW Press.

CHAPTER SEVEN

NO PRINCES HERE: MALE CHARACTERS IN MARGARET ATWOOD'S FICTION

THEODORE F. SHECKELS

Many have noted how Margaret Atwood's fiction centers on female characters, with male characters shoved into the background. The relative few who have attended to these marginalized males have offered rather different interpretations of them: they are victimizers, whose limited space in the narrative does not necessarily reduce their patriarchal power (Rigney); they are shadowy reminders of largely missing father figures in the heroines' lives (Hudgens); they are, just like Atwood's women, surviving in a world fraught with trouble (Heinimann). And there is truth in all of these interpretations. Not surprisingly, which one seems truest depends on the Atwood male one has in mind. Peter in *The Edible Woman* is a predator; West in *The Robber Bride* does seem to echo Tony's suicidal father; and Nate in *Life Before Man* does seem as adrift as either Elizabeth or Lesje.

Perhaps there is no single thread that unites Atwood's males, but I would like to propose one, one that rests in the structures of Atwood's stories and the role that fairy tale motifs play as intertexts in these structures. Sharon Wilson has extensively studied Atwood's use of fairy tale motifs in her earlier fiction. Atwood clearly has many motifs in her mind, with a few more dominant than others. One of the dominant ones, found in tales such as those dealing with the characters Cinderella, Rapunzel, Sleeping Beauty, and Snow White, is the entrapped heroine rescued by her prince. As satirized by Stephen Sondheim's delightful musical comedy *Into the Woods*, there are princes a-plenty (all in "Agony") in the fairy tale woods intent upon rescuing their designated ladies. Atwood plays off of this motif in structuring her fiction.

Atwood's fiction has some comic princes, like the ones Sondheim has singing before us: the Polish Count and "The Royal Porcupine" in *Lady Oracle* (1976) come to mind. But, what seems to unite Atwood's would-be princes is that they are not really princes. They sometimes lack the goodness, and they sometimes lack the power. Either way, they afford Atwood's heroines with little by the way of rescue.

These would-be "princes," I would suggest, fall into four categories. There are those who pretend to offer rescue but are actually quite dangerous; there are those who pretend to offer rescue and seem genuine but, ultimately, prove less than noble. Then, there are those who are good, but comically ineffective; and there are those who are good, but sadly impotent. And there is a fifth group: the would-be princes the status of which Atwood leaves ambiguous. For no other purpose than clarity in this essay, I will call the four types "dark princes," "shadowy princes," "comic princes," and "sad princes." The fifth group, "unfinished princes."

Dark Princes

Peter in *The Edible Woman* (1969) very much reflects the traditional assumptions about male and female roles that characterized Canada during the transitional 1960s. A young lawyer aspiring to climb higher in his firm, he desires the proper wife, for whom he has certain expectations. She will dress a certain way; she will act a certain way; and she certainly will not work. Within the novel's consumer culture context, Peter seems to be engaged in wise consumer behavior as he surveys the available goods and selects Marian. It is no wonder then that she feels she is a product, a foodstuff about to be consumed. Peter, the wise consumer, is disturbing to Atwood's early 1970s readers with proto-feminist ideas. But Peter is a darker character. He has two hobbies: collecting cameras and collecting guns. Both, of course, are objects to shoot with, and they become quickly synonymous. So, when Peter wants to shoot Marian in her to-order sexy red dress, the reader quickly jumps from photography to pornography to murderous predation. The three possibilities blur.

But how is Peter a rescuer, a prince in the archetypal sense? One only has to reflect on the world of "the office virgins" in the novel. They—and women like them—are waiting to be saved from prospective spinsterhood by a marriage proposal. It is into this world that Marian has gone upon graduation from college. One does not detect in the novel a strong emotional bond between Marian and Peter. He is handsome; he has fine prospects; he is acceptable to her parents. He will do as a rescuer from the world Emmy, Lucy, and Millie are settling into. So, Peter occupies a rescuing position within the novel's structure, but he is more an entrapper than rescuer.

David in Atwood's *Surfacing* (1972) is not as obviously a rescuer. He offers no woman salvation; however, he does position himself as being able to rescue art from bourgeoisie crap and the Canadian nation from nasty American imperialism. His "enlightened" rhetoric, however, is quickly forgotten when we realize both how self-absorbed and dangerous he is. He is psychologically if not physically abusive toward his wife Anna. In a scene that feels like rape, he coerces her into stripping for his movie camera. Then, he proposes that he and his buddy (with Anna's cooperation) rape the narrator so that they can add a sex scene to the inane movie, *Random Samples*, that the two men are making. Neither his anti-establishment words nor his goofy laugh should deflect the reader from recognizing David's dangerous sexism.

The Commander in *The Handmaid's Tale* (1985) would like Atwood's heroine, the unnamed handmaid, to think of himself as a rescuer. In the "Time Before," there was rampant pornography and sexual violence directed against women. The Republic of Gilead has saved women from these threats—given them "freedom from." Now, they are treated with reverence. The cost, of course, is their "freedom to." They cannot read; they cannot write; they cannot freely speak. And their bodies are used, without their giving free consent, for the reproductive purposes of the nation's elite. Although "the ceremony" they endure may not look like rape, it is. And the handmaids are not the only women in Gilead who are sexually used. There are also the women at Jezebel's, the only somewhat underground nightclub/brothel we are introduced to late in the novel. The commander may strut about there and in other Gilead circles in a princely manner, but he is not a rescuing prince.

Richard Griffen in *The Blind Assassin* (2000) presents himself to both Iris Chase and her near-bankrupt father Norval as rescuer. Shortly after he marries Iris, both Iris and her father discover the truth. He is a physically abusive husband, and he is a businessman intent on obliterating, not saving, Norval's family company. Worse, Richard uses his role as Iris's spouse to gain control over her younger sister Laura, who he, first, rapes repeatedly and, then, commits to a mental hospital. Thought, even at his death, to be a pillar of Canadian society, Griffen is a victimizer.

Crake in Atwood's more recent futuristic novel, *Oryx and Crake* (2003), takes his name from an extinct species. We naively may think that he has sympathy for the near-extinct, just as we may naively think he has sympathy for the victims of sexual violence because he has managed to embrace the young woman now named Oryx, whom he has somehow extracted from the child pornography and prostitution she was entrapped in. In reality, Crake is amoral, intent on using science for ends that seem god-like and demon-like. He and Oryx will create a new Eden, as well as a new, better race of humanoid creatures; but they will also play a role in the pharmaceutical plot to infect the developing world before saving the developed and making a huge profit. When the latter plans runs horribly amok, Crake ends up not a rescuer of humankind but as its destroyer.

All of these dark princes, it should be noted, possess power. Atwood's males are sometimes critiqued as powerless, but that critique certainly does not apply to these five. Although the kind of power they primarily possess varies from social (Peter) to psychological (David) to political (the Commander) to economic (Richard Griffen) to scientific (Crake), it is power nonetheless that they wield. Atwood furthermore establishes that one kind of power often entails others, so Griffen, for example, uses his economic power to gain social and political. All of these men victimize the less powerful, and the less powerful are most often gendered female.

Shadowy Princes

Not all of Atwood's males are, however, so obviously powerful and so obviously evil. Like the "Dark Princes," they occupy a rescuing place within the novel's stuctures. They, thus, seem to be rescuers, but the reality is rather different.

Duncan in *The Edible Woman* is a counterpoint to Peter. Whereas Peter is the well-dressed establishment male with his very male cameras and guns, Duncan is the pathetically thin, scruffy graduate student in English with an obsession with therapeutic ironing. Marian meets him at the laundromat, and she gradually falls into a rebellious relationship with him. The reader undoubtedly finds little long-term hope in a Duncan-Marian relationship: they are, after all, so very different. Nonetheless, the reader does hope that Duncan might rescue Marian from Peter. All along, Duncan makes his selfishness clear. However, it seems benign, especially because he presents himself as somewhat sexually naïve—not necessarily virginal but, nonetheless, not predatory. The truth, we discover after he beds Marian, is that he is accustomed to sexual conquest and that his pose is a part of the disarming charm he uses to gain sexual advantage.

Billy in *The Robber Bride* (1993) is also deceptive. We, of course, see him entirely through Karen/Charis's eyes, eyes that perceive him as needy. He is the American draft dodger she adopts, like an orphaned puppy. The reader is pleased at her generous spirit, and, given how wounded Karen/Charis is because of her traumatic adolescence, the reader is probably glad that a love relationship seems to develop between the two. Billy might rescue her from the after effects of that trauma. When we discover that sex with Billy is a dreaded ordeal and, in addition, is sometimes violent, we become uncomfortable with this supposed prince. When we realize that he not only slept with Zenia but (probably) killed Karen/Charis's beloved chickens before abandoning her for Zenia, we see his potentially nefarious side. I say "potentially" because we have only Zenia's version of Billy to set against Charis's perception, and Zenia is notoriously unreliable.

Much the same analysis might be offered of Mitch in *The Robber Bride*. Roz certainly seems less in need of rescue than Charis, but , despite her strong personality, she feels weakened by her ethnicity and by the shadowy ways in which her family escaped off society's margins and insinuated itself into the economic elite. Mitch, with the "right" ethnicity and "old money," rescues Roz from her nagging sense of inferiority. Princely, he might appear, but we discover rather soon that his behavior is far from such. He proves to be quite the womanizer until he meets the woman, Zenia, who throws him for a suicidal loop. Roz tolerates his indiscretions; she even, in a perverse way, thinks she gains power in the relationship by being able, almost on cue, to rescue him from the flings by throwing a tantrum. In the end, however, Roz realizes how the social respectability Mitch had offered her just was not worth the indignities that went along with it.

Neither Duncan nor Billy nor Mitch is quite what he initially seems to be. The same is true of Jimmy (a.k.a. Snowman) in *Oryx and Crake*. He is Crake's co-conspirator as a young adolescent, but, lacking Crake's mathematical, scientific aptitude, he is relegated to a lesser educational path in the arts. He creeps back on the scene, but he is clearly kept at a distance from where the true action is. In fact, inaction becomes characteristic of him, as he shies away from any involvement with his mother's rebellion against the economic/political "system" that seems to be calling the shots in the future world Atwood has created. But what if Jimmy had had Crake's "smarts" and a bit more assertiveness? Is Jimmy nothing more the Crake's weak reflection? His willingness to have sex with Oryx allies him with those who had sexually exploited her earlier in her life. In addition, it has him perhaps betraying his friendship with Crake, since it is unclear whether Crakes has assented to their liaisons or not. Furthermore, once the novel's apocalypse has passed and he becomes the teacher of the new breed Crakers, he feeds them repeated lies about past, present, and future. He, perhaps, feels the princely need to rescue them, but his actions belie that need.

Comic Princes

There is little that is amusing about Jimmy, Mitch, or Billy, despite Atwood's tendency to inject comic notes—dark ones—even at some of her more serious moments. Duncan, on the other hand, is comic for a good bit of *The Edible Woman*. His ironing is funny, and so is his graduate student lifestyle, along with those of roommates Trevor and Fish.[1] Ultimately, however, Duncan, like the wolf in "Little Red Riding Hood," reveals his what big teeth he has. Two other Atwood males, however, remain always comic.

The Polish Count in *Lady Oracle*, although he does take sexual advantage of young Joan Foster, proves benign. She is able to leave him and, later, laugh at the situation she had naively stumbled into. The Count becomes almost a caricature of old royalty, now down on its luck. He, therefore, offered her no real rescue from the economic hardship she had fallen into after she rebelled and left home. At best, in his appreciation of her fuller figure, he may have rescued her a tad from her self-image problems but from little else.

Also comic is Joan's relationship with The Royal Porcupine, a.k.a. Chuck Brewer, in *Lady Oracle*. It also takes a sexual turn. However, older, Joan is more in command of this relationship. He was, perhaps, looking for the moment to seduce her, but it is quite likely that she was looking for a way out of the life she had thus far crafted when she had sex with him. But the sex leads to nothing, no relationship and no rescue. In fact, post-sex, he becomes much more Chuck Brewer to her than "The Royal Porcupine." The suggestion of prince-ness in his silly nom de plume vanishes once the deed is done. He offers no way out and, therefore, she concocts her plan to fake her death and flee to Italy.

Sad Princes

Lady Oracle is probably Atwood's most comic novel. Thus, it is not surprising that we find the comic princes within it. Most of her fiction is either frightening or depressing or both. And within these novels, in addition to the dark and shadowy princes, we find many sad ones.

Life Before Man (1979) is probably Atwood's saddest book insofar as there is very little that is uplifting in the lives of any of the characters, male or female. The latter, then, certainly need rescuing; the former, caught in the same ennui, are scarcely able to be rescuing princes.

There is Chris, not a major character in the novel because he's dead before it begins. He was the lover who was supposed to have rescued

Elizabeth from her emotionally dead life. But Chris had troubles of his own, troubles that led to his suicide. Elizabeth's husband, Nate, was, of course, part of her troubles, so it is ironic when he becomes the would-be rescuer of Lesje, who is in a dead-end relationship with William. Nate's sensitivity nonetheless causes us to hope that he will indeed be able to play the role of Lesje's prince. He has renounced his potentially lucrative career as a corporate lawyer and has turned craftsman, creating children's toys out of wood. Both the law and the corporate dissatisfied him, and his crafting represents his way of enacting his anti-establishment rebellion. He is not, however, much of a rebel.

Lesje waits to be rescued, as Nate wavers between her apartment and Elizabeth's house, not fully living in either. Finally, she acts to force the issue by discarding her birth control pills and, then, becoming pregnant. Maybe now, she seems to think, Nate will fully choose her and rescue her from the limbo she is living. We never know if he does, for the scene in which Lesje tells Nate she is pregnant with his child is not in the novel: it is set to occur after the novel ends. This sad prince may run away, or he may rescue her. Or, perhaps, "rescue" is the wrong term, for, given all of the novel's failed couples, why should we think Lesje and Nate will prove to be any happier (for the moment or ever after) than Elizabeth and Nate or Lesje and William or Elizabeth and Chris.[2]

After *Life Before Man*, Atwood's fiction takes a pronounced political turn. The situations that the characters, the female characters, need to be rescued from therefore shift from ennui and emptiness to third-world prisons and right-wing republics. In the first of the two overtly political novels, *Bodily Harm* (1981), "soft" Canadian journalist Rennie Wilford finds herself on a Caribbean island that is slowly dissolving into civil war. Unfortunately, Rennie has unwittingly involved herself in the conflict. As a result, although innocent of political intent, she finds herself at-risk if the chaos takes the wrong turn. And, as it turns out, she ends up in a gruesome prison.

As the novel moves toward its in-prison finale, the island nation and she are both depicted as looking for rescue from the potentially oppressive forces. The island (personified female) looks to the political figure known simply as "Prince" to save it. "Prince" fails. Rennie looks to Paul, a politicized figure whose allegiances are not entirely easy to figure out, to save her. He becomes a romantic interest, and he eventually becomes her lover. Although he may help Rennie overcome her self-consciousness over her recent partial mastectomy and resulting poor body image by making love with her, Paul cannot help her escape the political chaos. He can barely help himself. So, he proves no rescuing prince, and the novel's use of popular romance elements which position him as lover/rescuer makes his failure to be an effective prince even more striking. So, Rennie ends up in prison. There, she and her cell-mate Lora are in a situation where they are compelled to trade their bodies for "favors" from the guards. Lora offers hers, to save Rennie the indignity, and, although this act does not rescue Rennie from the prison, it is a far more princely gesture than any made by the male characters in the novel.[3]

Chris, Nate, "Prince," and Paul are sadly ineffective for somewhat different reasons: in *Life Before Man*, the emotional states they are trapped within; in *Bodily Harm*, the political states. The young psychologist, Dr. Simon Jordan, in *Alias Grace* (1996) is sadly ineffective for yet another set of reasons: first, he's weak and, second, he becomes disempoweringly enamored of the woman he might have rescued. His role in the novel, of course, is not to rescue her, only to study her. He takes on the rescuing role because of the emotional attachment he develops for her. That attachment, however, destroys his objectivity. The only route he had to rescuing her or her reputation was through his standing as a psychologist. Once his objectivity is gone, so is that standing. Ironically, the emotional attachment that made him want to rescue her made it impossible for him to do so. Sadly, the princely role cannot in the end be his

Alex Thomas in *The Blind Assassin* needs help himself. A social activist (i.e. a communist), he becomes a suspect for arson and is, in and out of shadows, fleeing authorities. The focus of the novel, however, is not on his plight but that of sisters Iris and Laura Chase. For both of them, he represents a romantic escape. For Iris, the escape is real: she and Alex become lovers, and, in his arms, she is able to escape—albeit temporarily—the horrors of marriage to Richard Griffen. For the younger Laura, the escape is something she imagines. Alex, however, cannot rescue either of these desperately needy women. He is both endangered in Canada and committed to a global sociopolitical cause, the cause that will eventually cost him his life. When news comes of his death to Iris, her hopes for rescue end. More poignantly, the battered Laura's hopes end, for she now feels not only the lost dream but the betrayal by her sister and drives herself off a bridge to her death.

Unfinished Princes

All then seems rather bleak for would-be princes in Atwood's fictive world. They are dark or shadowy and threaten rather than help. Or they are comically or sadly ineffective. However, there are a handful of male characters who come closer to playing the archetypal prince's role.

Atwood does not let them do so completely. Nonetheless, they do qualify the otherwise bleak picture her fiction presents.

The first of these more optimistic figures is the other male in *Surfacing*, Joe. Said by the novel's narrator to have potential, she chooses him to father the fetus who will replace the one she was compelled to abort by her teacher/lover. Joe joins in many of David's games, but lacks his coarseness. Joe is also quite "furry," suggesting his alliance with the natural world, and he is a fellow artist, although one who cannot quite find the beauty he is seeking in the pottery he crafts. He seems, more than either Anna or David, intent on finding her and bringing her back to the civilized world of Toronto. As the novel ends, the narrator imagines that she will indeed return with him. She offers an indifferent evaluation of that prospect, leaving the reader to wonder if the prospect is a good one or a bad one. Perhaps, Joe will be her rescuer from not only the island but the psychopathology violations of nature—and her violation of nature—have driven her to. Perhaps.

Nick in *The Handmaid's Tale* is similarly ambiguous. We know only what "Offred" knows. She has come to believe that Nick is part of the "May Day" resistance to Gilead, and we accept that as likely the case. He has become her lover—ostensibly to impregnate her, something her sterile commander cannot, but the emotional bond between them has grown. When Serena Joy discovers that "Offred" has gone to Jezebel's with the Commander and is about to use the power she has against the offending handmaid, Nick's cronies—we think—swoop her up and carry her to safety. We do know she reached a safe place because scholars have the tapes she recorded after she reached relative safety. We do not know, for certain, if she escaped from Gilead or if she ever saw Nick again. We know she was rescued long enough to record the thoughts the book is a supposed edited transcription of, but that is all we know.[4]

West in *The Robber Bride* is ambiguous in a different way. Unlike Billy and Mitch, he is still there in the end: he and Tony are married. They survived Zenia, but, until her final end, Zenia remains a threat, at least in Tony's mind. The relationship between West and Tony is fragile. Without West, Tony would have lived alone in her turreted house, a Rapunzel figure without the long hair. She would pursue her academic work, recreating famous battles and writing about the soldiers' attire. She would be in her academic tower very much alone. West rescued her from that loneliness. However, West, the musicologist, is in the tower too. Furthermore, although he dwarfs the diminutive Tony, he lacks her strength. He must, as Tony sees matters, be protected—rescued, as it were, from the forces outside the tower (including Zenia) that might threaten him. So, Tony is as much West's prince as West is hers.

Atwood offers one last unfinished prince in the title character in *The Blind Assassin*. The literal title character is curiously minor. He is buried in the interpolated tale Alex tells Iris during the course of their love affair. The tale takes us to a remote kingdom where things have gone wrong. Rugs are made by young male slaves. They are, along the way, sexually abused, and, when they have outlived their productivity, blinded so that they can practice the carpet-making art (for others) no more. Many of these blinded carpet weavers have joined a guild of for-hire assassins. At the same time, the ritual sacrifice of young virgins continues although no one believes in the theology the sacrifices were based on any longer. In addition, because the young virgins can bring a price, they are routinely raped by the highest bidder the night before their execution. Also, the girls no longer hail from the kingdom's noble families; rather, they are underclass surrogates for the once-required well-born girls. The ritual is then, in a number of ways, corrupt. The girls, through the years, realized its corruption and ceased going quietly to their rape and death. So, they are now muted by having their tongues excised. In the tale Alex tells, a blind assassin rescues a muted young virgin before her rape and murder. Bravely, using his deft sense of touch and her vision, they escape the kingdom together.

The escape leaves them in the wilderness, and we are not told, definitively, what fate befalls them there; we are, instead, given three versions: the pessimistic one offered by Alex; the optimistic one offered by Iris; and a published one that erases the blind assassin and the muted young virgin entirely from the story. Given this deliberate refusal on Atwood's part to commit to a happy ending and given all we are told about this wilderness and given the escaping couple's disabilities, we must be dubious about their fate. However, they have escaped: the blind assassin did, prince-like, rescue the sacrificial virgin. The "happily-ever-after" part is the part that is in doubt. Of course, if this story is intended to mirror that of Alex and Iris, then we know that there will be no "happily-ever-after.")

Conclusion

Wilson and others have made the argument that fairy tale motifs inform Atwood's fiction. Atwood's own comments on her novels suggest as much. So, it should not be surprising that a pattern as fundamental as that found in tales such as "Cinderella," "Rapunzel," "Sleeping Beauty," and "Snow White" informs her work. Atwood specifically draws attention to one of these when in *Survival* (1972) she describes "the Rapunzel Syndrome" that characterizes realistic novels about women—in Canada and elsewhere. In this pattern, she notes, we find "a handsome prince of little substantiality who provides momentary escape" (209). These princes are ineffective, and "Rapunzel is in fact stuck in the tower." "[T]he best thing she [the female character] can do is learn how to cope with it" (209).

The comic princes and the sad princes fit "the Rapunzel syndrome" perfectly. The dark princes and the shadowy princes offer a disturbing variation on it in which the prince is not just ineffective but, in fact, dangerous. In only a few cases does Atwood suggests that the syndrome might be over-come, and all of those are qualified. We don't know what lies ahead for Joe and unnamed narrator in *Surfacing*, Nick and the unnamed handmaid in *The Handmaid's Tale*, or the blind assassin and the muted sacrificial virgin in *The Blind Assassin*. The only story that may get us beyond the syndrome is that of West and Tony, where gender barriers dissolve and the two become victims both and rescuers both. Only in that mutuality is there a possible escape from the tower.[5] And, although West and Tony may mutually escape from tower-as-metaphor, they are still in their literal tower. So, even in this case, Atwood complicates the picture.

Men in Atwood's fiction are neither monsters nor father figures, although there may be instances of both. But neither are they just chromosomally different variations of the same pattern that defines her women. They play a different role in the motif or pattern that underlies Atwood's fiction; they play the prince in counterpoint to the distressed woman. Or they try to. Because they are bad or inept, they really cannot play the role. And, when they come close, it is still not clear that they did the job. Atwood's fiction features many the distressed female, but there are no princes to be found here.

Notes

[1] *The Edible Woman*, written when Atwood was a graduate student in English, contains much humor that an academic audience especially appreciates. Many who pursued graduate work in English can attest to the Trevors, Fishes, and Duncans they knew.

[2] There is even a moment in the novel when a relationship between Elizabeth and William, an unhappy one, seems in the offing, turning the plot into something of a relationship merry-go-round.

[3] Rennie seems, in the end, to be rescued by a male official representing the Canadian government. However, Atwood's verb tenses as well as the manner in which Atwood begins the novel have suggested to many that this rescue is but her in-prison fantasy.

[4] The motion picture version of the novel gives us a more definitive sense of rescue. We know what Nick's role is, and we see Kate (She has a name in the movie!) after she has escaped. But, even in the feature film, there is ambiguity about the lead character's ultimate fate.

[5] Many have suggested—and Atwood confirmed the idea to a point when she addressed a large group at the MLA conference in Toronto—that Tony is as close as Atwood has come to putting herself in one of her novels. That she and Graeme Gibson present a tall-and-short picture much like Tony and West gives additional credibility to this notion. The mutuality in the Tony-West relationship, then, may be Atwood's veiled way of suggesting that she and Gibson have come closer to getting "it" right than any of the couples in her novels.

Works Cited

Atwood, Margaret. 1972. *Survival: A Thematic Guide to Canadian Literature.* Toronto: Anansi.

Heinimann, David. Autumn 1997. "Ironized Man: *A Jest of God* and *Life Before Man.*" *Canadian Literature* 154. 52-67.

Hudgens, Brenda. 1997. "Faded Photographs: The Elusive Male in Margaret Atwood's Fiction." *Publications of the Missouri Philological Association* 22. 47-56.

Rigney, Barbara. 1987. *Margaret Atwood.* Totowa, NJ: Barnes and Noble.

Wilson, Sharon Rose. 1993. *Margaret Atwood's Fairy-Tale Sexual Politics.* Jackson: University of Mississippi Press.

CHAPTER EIGHT

UNFABULATING A FABLE, OR TWO READINGS OF "THYLACINE RAGOUT"

SHULI BARZILAI

...like those who dine well off the plainest dishes, [Aesop] made use of humble incidents to teach great truths, and after serving up a story he added to it the advice to do a thing or not to do it.
—Flavius Philostratus, *Life of Apollonius of Tyana*, Book 5:14

Don't worry about the world coming to an end today. It's already tomorrow in Australia.
—Charles M. Schulz

First Impressions

That myths, folktales, and fairy tales abound in Margaret Atwood's writings is, by now, a critical commonplace. From brief but pointed allusions to full-scale revisions, Atwood frequently draws on these venerable genres and recasts familiar motifs and stories into contemporary forms. On occasion, however, Atwood does something else. She tells a story that only appears to belong to one or more of these categories. Rather than a reinterpretation and rewriting of an earlier tale, it becomes clear on closer examination that the tale is her own invention. She is not pouring old wine into a new bottle. The text may look like a folktale or fable, may even have the characteristic markers of the genre but, in fact, it's all fact. The question of why Atwood uses this narrative strategy is one to which I shall return in the course of this discussion. However, as a preliminary hypothesis, I would propose that her mode of storytelling in such instances has a calculated two-pronged effect: while it initially defuses or de-intensifies (and sometimes temporarily masks) her social, political, and environmental engagement, the strategy ultimately serves to heighten an often devastating critique.

Atwood's short-short story, "Thylacine Ragout," is a case in point. It first appeared in *Bottle*, a limited edition of prose pieces, produced in support of the Hay-on-Wye Festival in 2004. It was republished two years later in *The Tent*, a collection of short fictions that the book jacket celebrates as "vintage Atwoodian tales—monologues, pretend histories and autobiographies, animal fables, and condensed science fictions." The word "pretend," as already suggested, also describes "Thylacine Ragout," a two-page text with several generic components that characterize the Aesopic tradition of the fable: "a brief, succinct story, in prose or verse, that features animals, plants, inanimate objects, or forces of nature which are anthropomorphized...and that illustrates a moral lesson (a 'moral'), which may at the end be expressed explicitly in a pithy maxim" ("Fable"). To be sure, Atwood dispenses with an explicit maxim at the end of her story. Nevertheless, "Thylacine Ragout" conforms to the category of animal fables not just in length and featured character; it also provides the audience with ample "opportunities to laugh at human folly" through its presentation of "behaviors to be avoided rather than emulated" ("Fable").

Yet another component is the surprise twist that typically occurs at the end of a fable. To extend the metaphor of Philostratus, the tables are somehow turned, as in the tale of a lion and a bear who fought to exhaustion over the carcass of a fawn: "Noting the helpless condition of the two beasts, the impudent fox stepped nimbly between them, seized the fawn...and with never a 'thank you' dragged it away to its den." Thus fools are caught off their guard, we are taught, "while a rouge runs off with the dinner" (Aesop 110). "Thylacine Ragout" gestures toward this literary model by ending with an analogous turn of events. In effect, Atwood's narrative compounds the surprise insofar as it also provides a startling instance of the discrepancy between a naïve reading and an informed reading of the same text. Rather than an autonomous, allegedly timeless and universal tale that requires no "external" socio-historical contexts for an adequate interpretation to be achieved, in the case of "Thylacine Ragout," I would argue, context is everything. Familiarity with the traditional fable is only one of several points of reference with (and against) which Atwood plays in recounting the tale of the thylacine.

The first of the story's three paragraphs begins by announcing the conclusion of a successful cloning project:

> They cloned the Thylacine. They got some DNA out of a bone and they emptied the nucleus out of the egg of a Tasmanian devil and they put the Thylacine bone DNA into the egg, and it grew, and they implanted it, and

it didn't work, and they did it again, and it didn't work, and they did it
again, again, again, and they tried it a little differently, and they tweaked it
this way and that, and finally they cloned the Thylacine. (73)

Much depends upon whether or not the reader has encountered the
word "thylacine" before reading the story. To the uninitiated, the word
may sound, as it did to me, like one of those neologisms that Atwood is so
adept at inventing. The thylacine, I thought, is probably an offshoot of her
contemporary "fabulist" imagination—except for the fact that mention is
soon made of a silent film, which could imply a preexistent referent,
something actually there in the real world:

> Out it came, the baby Thylacine, and they nurtured it tenderly and with
> great interest and there it was, running around with stripes on, frantic, as in
> the only remaining film of it, where it runs and paces and utters silent yelps
> because the film is a silent film, and it stops to gaze into the camera with
> an expression both poignant and severe. (73-74)

Nevertheless, since Atwood is a self-confessed, avid reader of pop-science
books and journals, it seemed to me no less probable that the thylacine—
not unlike the genetically-spliced "pigoons," "wolvogs," and "rakunks" in
her dystopian novel *Oryx and Crake*, published the year before *Bottle*—
was a creature similarly conceived in a satiric spirit for the allegorical
instruction of her readers.

Moreover, for the reader who has somehow managed to avoid any
exposure to Taz, the Warner Brothers' popular Looney Tunes cartoon
character based on a real-life species indigenous to Tasmania,[1] Atwood's
allusion to "the egg of a Tasmanian devil" also fits into the same fanciful
frame of reference. Accordingly, the thylacine amounts to a far-fetched
hybrid, and the text titled "Thylacine Ragout" is in itself a literary splicing
between ancient myth and fable. It seems as if the storyteller has put, say,
a unicorn instead of a stag into an animal fable. After all what is a ragout if
not a mixture of different ingredients cooked up for the appreciation of its
consumers? Thus read without the mediation (or prejudice) of prior
contexts, "Thylacine Ragout" represents another one of the varied ways in
which Margaret Atwood answers to the calling of a "con-fabulator," that
is, a consummate teller of tall tales about legendary lands and other things.

The opening sentence of the second paragraph confirms and amplifies
this interpretation by putting an additional clue into place:

> The event made the headlines...and they named the Thylacine Trugannini,
> a name you see on restaurant menus in that part of the world, as a gesture

of respect perhaps, or a way of selling something, or a commemoration, as on tombstones. (74)

Word-games, of course, are a signature or "vintage Atwoodian" ploy. If the name "Trugannini" has no referential specification for the reader—and I was still safe from, or not guilty of, knowledge—it may be reasonably construed that the first syllable "Tru-" suggests none of it was. That "Thylacine Trugannini" is far from true may also be inferred from the third and final paragraph in which the tale-teller recounts the implausible fate of the creature:

> Crowds visited. A documentary was made. Prizes were awarded. Then what happened? The Thylacine disappeared. It vanished. One day it was there, in solitude, in singleness, in its cage, or rather its large tastefully landscaped compound,...and then it was gone. It didn't die of solitude, however. It was sold. A bent scientist retired to Bermuda on the proceeds. A very rich person with refined tastes ate the Thylacine. He ate it in the form of a ragout. He had a yen for the unique, he wanted to be the only person ever to eat a Thylacine. It did not taste very good, despite the care taken in the preparation of it – well, there were no recipes – but it tasted very expensive, and the man who ate it wrote in his secret diary that it was good enough value for the money. (75)

Recall the nimble fox who dragged the fawn away to its den. Atwood gives a distinctly postmodern edge to the institutionalized literary model associated with Aesop. On the one hand, it is impossible to miss the tone of irony and critique of modern technology, of human greed and ruthless egotism, informing her text; on the other, with no supplementary information, "Thylacine Ragout" presents itself as a cautionary fable for adults, loosely based on current technological advances and premised on a future-oriented possibilities.

But the sad fact, as already indicated, is that almost nothing in this story is untrue. Everything it describes has already happened or could be happening right now. "Thylacine Ragout" is a transposition of real animals, people, and events into a form of narrative fiction. Thus the disparity between an uninformed reading of Atwood's story and an informed one corresponds to two general types of information gap. Unlike a murder mystery, for instance, in which the gap ("who did it?") lies in the text itself, "Thylacine Ragout" immediately identifies the perpetrators and their motives. Its *moralité*, although unstated, is also unambiguous. Atwood holds a mirror up to a brave new world in which laboratories and ledgers are the governing principles: the scientist who sold the thylacine and the person who ate it epitomize the cannibal commercialism of the age that bred them. Information gaps, however, are sometimes located not in the text but rather, and for a variety of reasons, in its audience. "Thylacine Ragout" makes sense, albeit incomplete sense, and its moral lesson remains the same even to an imperfect and naïve (or, perhaps, ideal) reader such as I was, still uncontaminated by facts and contexts. An informed reading not only changes the generic identification of "Thylacine Ragout" but also enables the critical perception that the "fabulous"—in the dual sense of fable-related and remarkable—aspect of this story is not the animal after which it is named.

In what follows I propose to retrace a passage or, more precisely, an expulsion from ignorance to knowledge that entails, ironically enough, a considerable reliance on twentieth- and twenty-first century information technologies whose profit motives and ambitions have also supported the actual project to recreate the vanished thylacine. First, you snuff it out and, then, you try to resurrect it. In describing how Atwood's supposed fable became unfabulated for me and how my generic "coping mechanisms" were undone, I shall also provide a more detailed account of the three histories packed into her very short text.

The Thylacine's Story

Before putting Atwood's mini-fiction aside, I decided, just to be certain, to go to Google. What I expected after typing in "Thylacine" was a polite "Did you mean: _____" query, followed by a redirection to the website for, perhaps, an antibiotic or the like. Instead, I found myself rapidly transported to *The Thylacine Museum*, an impressive online reference guide devoted to the marsupial species (*Thylacinus cynocephalus*) popularly known as the Tasmanian tiger. Fossils of the thylacinid family, I learned, have been discovered dating from the late Oligocene epoch (about twenty-eight to twenty-three million years before the present). The modern thylacine, a canine-looking animal with stripes on its back, made its appearance about four million years ago and roamed all over continental Australia, spreading north from Papua New Guinea and south to Tasmania. Yet the thylacine is currently classified as extinct by two world authorities on the preservation status of plant and animal species: the International Union for the Conservation of Nature and Natural Resources (IUCN) and the World Wildlife Fund (WWF) (Campbell). Cameron R. Campbell, author and curator of *The Thylacine Museum*, summarily explains:

> Out of misunderstanding, irrational fear and simply because it was
> perceived as a threat to economic interests, a genocidal assault was waged
> against the species. Thus, thousands of Thylacines were destroyed by man
> during the 19th and early 20th centuries. (Campbell)

Nonetheless, despite the open and unrestrained slaughter of the species, two thylacines feature prominently on the Tasmanian State Coat of Arms, granted by King George V in May 1917. "It is tragically ironic," as Campbell points out, "that the Tasmanians chose as their state symbol the very animal which they sought to exterminate." The Coat of Arms shows a shield with emblems of Tasmanian industry, supported by a pair of magnificent thylacines, with a motto beneath, *Ubertas et Fidelitas* ("Fertility and Faithfulness"). The history of the Tasmanian tiger utterly belies the official heraldic image.

After the European colonization of Tasmania in the early 1800s, not only was the thylacine's natural habitat subjected to invasion and incremental destruction; the species was poisoned, snared, shot, skinned, or captured for display in zoos for over a hundred years until it expired of unnatural causes. In the mid-nineteenth century, the British naturalist John Gould already foresaw the fate of the species:

> When the comparatively small island of Tasmania becomes more densely
> populated, and its primitive forests are intersected with roads from the
> eastern to the western coast, the numbers of this singular animal will
> speedily diminish, extermination will have its full sway, and it will...be
> recorded as an animal of the past. (Qtd. in Paddle 223)[2]

The last known animal died in captivity, at the Hobart Zoo in Tasmania, on 7 September 1936.[3]

One of the earliest thylacine photographs known to exist, dating from 1869, is entitled "Mr. Weaver Bags a Tiger" (figure 8.1).[4] In stark contrast to the official Coat of Arms with its representation of proud, upright tigers supporting the state shield of Tasmania, the 1869 photograph shows a stiff, dead animal hanging upside down from an invisible ceiling beam or hook, its legs tightly trussed together with rope. Mr. Weaver, seated opposite the cadaver, gazes straight ahead, expressionless but presumably satisfied. He is dressed in full hunter's regalia with a long rifle resting against the arm closest to the camera. It is a classic "trophy shot" of a by-gone era.

The same image of Mr. Weaver and his kill features at the end of an incisive magazine article on the thylacine, Leigh Dayton's "Rough Justice," published in the May 2001 issue of New Scientist. It was while browsing through Atwood's extensive research files for *Oryx and Crake*,

Figure 8.1 "Mr. Weaver Bags a Tiger." Collection: Tasmanian Museum and Art Gallery.

located at the Thomas Fisher Rare Book Library in Toronto, that I came across Dayton's article inside a folder labeled "Threatened Species, 2000-2003."[5] In a statement reiterated in bold-caption lettering, Dayton remarks, "Native fauna was of little consequence to colonists who were bent on recreating England in the Antipodes" (Dayton 46). In this context, the word "bent" may have a double valence for the reader: in addition to the standard meanings of determined and resolved, it also suggests something warped or perverse. Since Atwood probably read "Rough Justice" before filing it away, the word "bent" may have been reapplied to the scientist, the one bent on retiring to Bermuda through the thylacine sale, in the final paragraph of "Thylacine Ragout." But whether or not her "bent" takes off from Dayton's, what his article does provide is another good reason for Mr. Weaver's satisfaction at bagging a tiger:

> For years Tasmania's thylacines thrived, safe on their island refuge. Then in 1830, six years after the arrival of the island's first sheep, things changed. A bounty was placed on the tiger, supposedly to protect flocks from hungry thylacines. Between 1888 and 1909, the Tasmanian government paid over two thousand bounties for thylacine scalps. (Dayton 46)

Selling out the thylacine was as openly lucrative in the late nineteenth century as it turned out to be for the "bent scientist" in Atwood's contemporary account.

It is apparently difficult to accept the fact that the unique Tasmanian tiger has gone the way of the mammoth and the dodo, an extinction predicted and preventable up to a point in time. This difficulty, as my further explorations showed, has had two creatively inventive—or, you might also say, hallucinatory—consequences. First, although following the death of the thylacine at the Hobart Zoo, no decisive evidence confirming the animal's continued existence has been found, reports of sightings persist to the present day. According to the Parks and Wildlife Service of Tasmania, "There have been hundreds of sightings since 1936…. Nonetheless, all sightings have remained inconclusive."[6] Put another way, the thylacine has entered into the annals of local folklore. There alone it continues to flourish. As Eric Guiler writes, "no other species in the Australian fauna…has aroused so many stories and even created its own legends in the short space of years since white settlement" (2).[7] In re-visioning the fate of the species in "Thylacine Ragout," Atwood may be said to carry on this tradition—but without a hope for actual recovery in her heart.

Second, whereas sightings are one mode of recreative effort motivated by a wish for the return of the dead, at the turn of the twenty-first century, Michael Archer, a professor of paleontology and then director of the Australian Museum in Sydney, made international headlines when he announced that the DNA extracted from a tiger pup sample preserved in ethanol was good enough to clone. Additional DNA from the specimens of two other tiger pups included bone, tooth, bone marrow and dried muscle. In May 2000, *News in Science* carried a report with the optimistic banner, "Bringing the Tasmanian Tiger Back to Life," that added a competitive edge to this bold venture: "'While there are similar extinct animal cloning projects elsewhere in the world,'" Archer was quoted as saying, "'the Australian Museum's project is the first to find good quality DNA'" (Salleh).

Work to recover DNA from museum specimens of the thylacine continued. Two years later, in May 2002, Archer was quoted in the Environment News Service describing these extractions as "an extremely critical step in producing sufficient amounts of Tasmanian tiger DNA to proceed with the research and extremely good news for future steps in accomplishing this project (Salleh). The Environment News Service also reported that "the story of the Museum's ongoing effort to clone an extinct species have been exclusively documented by the Discovery Channel in 'End of Extinction: Cloning the Tasmanian Tiger." The program, which was broadcast in 155 countries worldwide on July7, 2002, included "footage of the extraction of Tasmanian tiger tissue, the processing of the DNA and the next steps of genetic engineering which could make cloning the Tasmanian tiger a reality" (Anon.). Indeed, the "end of extinction" seemed to be in sight.

Simultaneously, doubts were being raised not only about the technical and financial feasibility of such projects but also about their ethical implications. In a folder marked "Cloning" in Atwood's research files for *Oryx and Crake*, I found a contemporaneous article by Arthur Caplan, a professor of bioethics and director of the Center for Bioethics at the University of Pennsylvania. Caplan's title, "Much Ado About Cloning: Why Two Is Not Better Than One," bespeaks his central argument:

> To date, the experience with cloning is best described as reproductive carnage…. Of those clones that have been created many are born dead, and many others are deformed and/or disabled…. Not only is old DNA damaged, but there are inherent "handshake" problems when the old DNA tries to talk to the egg where it is put. The egg is expecting to hear from new DNA and this is probably the reason why so many embryos either fail to grow or quickly abort. (Caplan)

Adjacent folders marked "Animals – Extinction" inside the same box of research files contain journal articles, newspaper clippings, booklets, and other items about species at risk in Canada and elsewhere. Hence the opening statements of Atwood's seemingly fanciful fiction, "They cloned the Thylacine. They got some DNA out of a bone and they emptied…the egg of a Tasmanian devil," not only draw closely on reality but also, by indirection, take sides in an ongoing debate—to clone or not to clone: "they implanted it, and it didn't work, and they did it again, again,

again…and they tweaked it this way and that" (73). And finally someone came along and ate it. By adopting the satiric stance of a fabulator, of a folkloristic commentator on human foibles, Atwood avoids explicit attitudes of moralizing, headshaking, or dire forewarning. "Thylacine Ragout," she may well assume, requires no epimythium or moral for its application to be understood.

Before turning to the Tasmanian devil, an update may be in order. Six years after the widely publicized attempt to clone the thylacine was launched, and a year after the first publication of "Thylacine Ragout" in *Bottle*, the February 2005 issue of *News in Science* carried a story whose headline unceremoniously announced: "Thylacine Cloning Project Dumped." The Australian Museum's new management team, appointed in 2004, reevaluated the ambitious project and decided not to proceed with it. "In fact," museum officials said, "further investigation has now revealed that the thylacine DNA is far too degraded to even construct a DNA library. Given this the project cannot proceed to the next stage" (Skatssoon).

The Devil's Story

Learning about the fate of the Tasmanian tiger clearly called for a search for the devil. Although it makes only the briefest appearance, a "minor" character in Atwood's just-so story of how the thylacine was cloned, the Tasmanian devil plays a vital role in this plot or process: the devil's egg, with its new DNA, "hosts" the old DNA taken from the thylacine bone. In case the reader wonders at this elaborate procedure— why is a devil required to reproduce a thylacine?—the explanation is twofold.

Atwood indirectly gives one reason for the devil's involvement. The end of her first paragraph begins on a note of confident, even triumphant assertion that rapidly changes to ontological (but not ethical) doubt about the results of the thylacine project and, then, to impatience with trivial objectors:

> It was a Thylacine all right, or it looked like one, or it looked like our idea
> of one, because it was an animal no one still alive had ever actually seen—
> anyway, what they got was close enough. Why quibble? (74)

The word "extinct" and its derivatives appear nowhere in Atwood's text. It is an avoidance that may be intended to reflect and mock the persistent refusal, in some parts, to recognize the annihilation of the species. The other reason for using a devil to make a tiger entails the kinship factor. Even though they do not look alike at all, both animals belong to the group known as marsupial mammals, a group including koalas, kangaroos, and wombats, whose young develop inside their mother's pouch--unless there is (and could be) no mother to offer the nurturing safety and warmth of her pouch to her newborn offspring.

In searching for the cloned thylacine's living parent, I returned to the Parks and Wildlife Service of Tasmania, which opens its website for the Tasmanian devil (*Sarcophilus harrisii*) with a dramatic, red-letter announcement: "A devastating disease is sweeping the Tasmania's devil population, killing more than 90% of adults in high density areas and 40-50% in medium-low density areas." Directly after this alarming update, the Parks and Wildlife Service explains how the devil got its bad name over two centuries ago:

> Its spine-chilling screeches, black colour, and reputed bad-temper, led the early European settlers to call it The Devil. Although only the size of a small dog, it can sound and look incredibly fierce. ("Tasmanian Devil")

The juxtaposition of these disparate pieces of information is, in all likelihood, coincidental; nonetheless, this opening already indicates that "The Devil" was never much loved. Its future was at risk from the early 1800s, when the European settlement of what was then called "Van Diemen's Land" began. In this respect and others, the stories of the tiger and the devil intersected long before the efforts to mix them in the same genetic soup, as it were, that is retold in Atwood's "fable" about species loss and belated mourning.

The facts are as follows: like the tiger, the devil once ranged throughout mainland Australia. However, its only habitat today is the island of Tasmania where it remains, for the moment, the world's largest surviving carnivorous marsupial. While protected by law from human depredation since 1941, the "Tasmanian devil is now listed as vulnerable," according to the web-page produced by the Department of Tourism and last updated on March 5, 2008. The reason given for the animal's "vulnerable" status (a classification to which I return at the end of this section) is the Devil Facial Tumour Disease. The virulent disease currently decimating the island's devil population was "first noticed in the north-east of Tasmania in the mid-1990s but has become more prevalent in recent times in other areas of the State" ("Tasmanian Devil").

No less significant than what the Parks and Wildlife Service website tells its visitors is what it elides or fails to disclose. Although the Devil Facial Tumour Disease (DFTD) was identified in 1995-1996, serious efforts to study this highly contagious type of cancer, with a 100% mortality rate within about six months of its manifestation, were begun only eight years later. Widespread publicity and conclusive statistics finally led the state government to acknowledge the gravity of the devil's plight and allocate funds for trying to save it from extinction.[8] Yet another omitted factoid is the probable cause of the fatal disease. In *Tasmanian Devil: A Unique and Threatened Animal* (2005), the first book devoted to this much-maligned marsupial, David Owen and David Pemberton write:

> [I]t may be that a combination of human-induced factors is fully or partly responsible for the outbreak of the devastating DFTD, from which the devil may not recover.... There is no historical account of a devil with gross external tumors, which indicates the DFTD could be a "new" disease and thus may be associated with human activity. (28)

More specifically, studies have suggested that the spraying of pesticides by the farming and forestry industries in Tasmania could have triggered the cancer or contributed to its rapid spread among the devil population. The highly toxic "1080 poison" (also known as sodium fluoroacetate and compound 1080), which is banned or tightly controlled in large parts of the world, is still widely used and even aerially dropped in order to kill targeted "pest" animals, such as possums and rabbits, thus making it also threatening to the devils of Tasmania.[9]

In 1986 the Tasmanian tiger, a prominent state symbol, was declared officially extinct, an incontrovertible outcome of the European colonization of the island. To reiterate Dayton's succinct comment: "Native fauna was of little consequence to colonists...in the Antipodes" (46). It is therefore not surprising that the Parks and Wildlife Service should attempt to counter such postcolonial perceptions by directing online visitors to an ancillary website entitled "Save the Tasmanian Devil." At this website they may learn that the devil itself—and who else?—is to blame for its own affliction:

> [I]t is the lack of genetic diversity among Tasmanian devils that is a key factor in the transmission of DFTD. Devils don't produce immune responses to DFTD because the diseased cells are too similar to their own cells. ("Save")

In other words, the manner of the devil's present-day downfall mirrors its very nature as perceived by European colonists in the early nineteenth century.

Moreover, as the virtual tourist soon discovers, in May 2008 Tasmania's *Threatened Species Protection Act 1995* reclassified the Tasmanian devil as an "endangered" species: "'The upgrading in status from vulnerable to endangered...reflect [sic] the reductions in the devil population, resulting from Devil Facial Tumour Disease,' said David Llewellyn, the Tasmanian minister for Primary Industries and Water" ("Save"). Could it still be that the less devils there are in Tasmania the better? Of course, the ministerial use of the word "upgrading" instead of, say, "change" to designate what is, in effect, a sharp decline or fall in the devil's fortunes may be deemed a technicality. Nevertheless, it does seem that the upgrading or promotion in status is inversely related to the rapid dwindling of the species. As previously noted, long before the outbreak of DFTD, the devil's standing was compromised by the colonial settlers of Van Diemen's Land.

It was while engaged in exploring how to "Save the Tasmanian Devil" that I found a sidebar-invitation to view a rubric entitled "Latest Research" and read the "full reports" of updated toxicological investigations:

> Independent assessments of toxicological data from healthy devils and devils suffering from Tasmanian Devil Facial Tumour Disease found that a chemical cause of the disease is unlikely. ("Savet")

May it all be true and the devil get well soon. After the obliteration of the Tasmanian tiger by poison, entrapment, and bounty-hunting throughout the nineteenth and early twentieth centuries, it is indeed unlikely, and intolerable, to allow that the Tasmanian devil may also become extinct during the twenty-first century due to further human interference with the native fauna of the island.

Trugannini's Story

"There is no frigate like a book" wrote my second-grade teacher on the blackboard early one morning in Hartford, Connecticut. (It was many years before I learned that the line belonged to a famously reclusive, white-clad lady of New England.) The unknown word "frigate" fired my seven-year-old imagination and, in the mysterious way poetry sometimes works, may have set me in the direction of my professional formation. In any case, although Atwood's text now led me to venture down under and far out, I did avoid seeking Trugannini for a time. "Thylacine Ragout," whatever its generic category, provides a clear-enough indication of what such a voyage into darkness would entail.

Atwood distills Trugannini's history into a single, convoluted sentence that reports the verifiable events as exactly as possible, and yet also evokes the many versions (and distortions) of the life and times of her subject:

> Anyway, they named it [the thylacine clone] Trugannini, after the last fully Aboriginal inhabitant of that island, who was raped, or that is the story, whose sisters were killed, or that is the story, whose mother was killed, whose husband was killed in front of her eyes, whose father died of grief, who lived in solitude, solitude of a kind that would kill most people, whose bones were dug up and put on display for a hundred years, against her will, but she was dead so what will did she have, what right do the dead have to a will, they are dead after all, they are not present except in bone form, in a glass case, for people to stare at. (74)

Almost as an afterthought, Atwood adds a sentence fragment in the form of a simile—"Like the Thylacine bones, the ones that were stared at for years, the ones they raided for the DNA to make the Thylacine clone" (74-75)—and thus concludes the second paragraph of her narrative. But the allusion to the glass-encased display of human and animal remains is no metaphor or figurative comparison. The woman variously called Trugannini (also spelled Truganinni), Truganina, Trucanini, Trugernanna, and Lalla Rookh was dehumanized in her death as in her life.

The name "Trugannini" may have entered into the pseudo-fabled annals of "Thylacine Ragout" in the following manner: in March 2001, while Atwood was on a book tour in Australia, she visited several cave complexes where, as she later wrote, "Aboriginal people had lived continuously, in harmony with their environment, for tens of thousands of years" ("Writing" 284). It does not take long, however, to find more direct connections. Trugannini once inhabited the same geographic circumference as the tiger and the devil. The presence of an indigenous people, known as the Tasmanian Aborigines on the island of Tasmania dates back about 35,000 years. In 1803, at the time of the British colonization, they were estimated at between 4,000-10,000 people. By 1833, only a generation later, as a result of disease, persecution, and other ravages of their colonial encounter, their numbers were reduced to 300. When Trugannini (born in 1803 or 1812) passed away without leaving any children in 1876, she was indeed pronounced "the last fully Aboriginal inhabitant" of Tasmania ("Thylacine Ragout" 74). Thus the state government made it understood that the native problem was solved. The occasion of Trugannini's death was used to declare the extinction of her race. This extinction was taught as a fact in schools and widely accepted in

Tasmania as elsewhere, even though other Tasmanian Aborigines outlived Trugannini and their descendants survive to the present day.[10]

The anthropologist Clive Turnbull begins his 1948 study, *Black War: The Extermination of the Tasmanian Aborigines*, with an elegiac, albeit outraged, reassertion of this alleged fact. I quote the passage at length because of the tragic social history it evokess:

> Not, perhaps before has a race of men been utterly destroyed within seventy-five years. This is the story of a race which was so destroyed, that of the aborigines of Tasmania—destroyed not only by a different manner of life but by the ill-will of the usurpers of the race's land. When that ill-will was active it found expression in brutality. When passive it deplored extermination while condoning, and participating in the rewards of, a system which made extermination inevitable. In this remote island was the opportunity for the indulgence of those passions upon which an organized society imposes its most severe restraints. With no defenses but cunning and the most primitive weapons, the natives were no match for the sophisticated individualists of knife and gun. By 1876 the last of them was dead. So perished a whole people. (Turnbull 1)

Since the mid-1970s, the notion of the "extermination" or extinction of the indigenous population of Tasmania has been seriously challenged. Despite the contemporary dispute within the Tasmanian Aboriginal community over what constitutes Aboriginal descent, there are an estimated 150,000 people who claim to be descendants of "full-blood" women, many of whom were abducted, raped, and bore the children of their persecutors during the nineteenth century.[11]

Atwood retells a segment of one woman's story. It was told by Trugannini herself to a member of the white community of Tasmania after she had learned English:

> Her mother was stabbed to death by a European. Her sister was carried off by sealers. In her girlhood, accompanied by her intended husband, Paraweena, and another native man, she was once on the mainland of Van Diemen's Land. (Turnbull 100)

Two convict woodcutters agreed to row the party of three to the nearby settlement on Bruny Island where natives were expected to take up permanent, isolated residence:

> In mid-channel the white men threw the [male] natives overboard. As they struggled to the boat and grasped the gunwale Lowe and Newell chopped off their hands with hatchets. The mutilated aborigines were left to drown

and the Europeans were free to do as they pleased with the girl. (Turnbull 100)

Trugannini was captured in a variety of ways. Photography was introduced into Tasmania in 1858, and as a well-known figure in the colonial community, a kind of local curio, Trugannini was a sought after object. James Bonwick, a fellow of the London Anthropological Institute, visited the island state when Trugannini was "much over fifty years of age" and wrote in 1884: "Thirty years before, she would have been captivating to men of her colour, and not by any means an uninteresting object to those of whiter skins" (185, 140). After describing the demeanor of Trugannini, "this sylvan goddess of Tasmania," Bonwick underscores the prevailing view: "'She is the last of the race'" (186). A relic of a disappearing past, Trugannini's image, if not her people, was worth salvaging for white posterity. The photograph titled "John Woodcock Graves the younger [with] Truganinni," whose creator and exact date are unknown, was taken during the last years of her life (figure 8.2). In this sepia-toned photograph Trugannini appears older than in the more frequently reproduced albumen print, dated circa 1866, taken by Charles Alfred Woolley (1834-1922), a Hobart photographer. I will not attempt to describe the expression on her face—viewers may try to read or reflect (on) it as they choose—but, rather, will focus on the external appearance and position of the two subjects.

Graves (1829-1876), a Tasmanian lawyer about a generation younger than Trugannini, probably commissioned this portrait of himself with the woman perceived to be a historical artifact in her own lifetime. He stands looking down on her, arms akimbo, a properly suited, vested, and cravated Victorian gentleman. The partial view of a pedestal on the left indicates the studio locale. Trugannini is dressed in a thick woolen-looking garment, with a fringed wool scarf instead of a shell necklace around her neck, and a kerchief bound around her head.[13] According to eyewitness accounts, early drawings, and other evidence, prior to the colonial occupation of Tasmania, Trugannini and her people wore nothing more than a single kangaroo pelt and a covering on their skin of a combination of animal fat and ash to ward off the cold. Showing her thus clad, seated and submitted to the gaze of John Woodcock Graves and the camera, is intended to demonstrate not only the social status of Mr. Graves. It also shows that the natives of Tasmania have been civilized and Christianized—shortly before their anticipated extinction. "John Woodcock Graves the younger [with] Truganinni" emblematizes the divinely-ordained progress and triumph of British civilization.

Figure 8.2 "John Woodcock Graves the younger [with] Truganinni." Collection: Allport Library and Museum of Fine Arts, State Library of Tasmania.

The ordeals of Trugannini did not end with her life. As Atwood's text synoptically indicates, the despoliation even intensified after her death in 1876. Although different accounts have been composed, with varying degrees of reliability, it is indisputable that Trugannini had good reason to fear what would be done with her remains after she died. The gruesome desecration of her native compatriot, William Lanney, because of rivalry between the Royal College of Surgeons in England and the Royal Society in Tasmania over the possession of his corpse apparently gave rise to her urgent last wishes.[14] She asked to be wrapped in a rock-weighted bag and dropped into the D'Entrecasteaux Channel, according to one report, or to be buried behind the mountains, according to another. What happened next, just as "Thylacine Ragout" records, confirmed Trugannini's worst fears. Disregarding her dying request, the Tasmanian government arranged for Trugannini to be interred, within easy reach, in a vault of the chapel that was part of the Hobart Penitentiary. Andrys Onsman sums up the ascertainable events:

> In 1878 she was exhumed and what was left of the flesh on her bones was removed, so that they could be boiled clean.... Some time later the bones were strung together and mounted in a glass case and put on display. In 1947 public sentiment caused the Museum to take her skeleton down and store it in the basement, where it stayed until 1976, a century after her death. (Onsman)

The Tasmanian Museum and Art Gallery finally returned the skeleton to the Aboriginal community in 1976 and, later the same year, her bones were cremated and the ashes scattered on the D'Entrecasteaux Channel. After one hundred years, it seemed that the rites of mourning were accomplished and Trugannini laid to rest at last. In 2001, however, the British College of Surgeons revealed that it held samples of Trugannini's skin and hair in its collection of Aboriginal specimens for study. These remains have now been repatriated and given back to the Aboriginal community of Tasmania. As Onsman writes in his 2004 essay on Trugannini's burial, "She had the longest funeral in the history of the world."

The story of Trugannini may seem far removed from the districts that Atwood usually inhabits in her fiction. But it has an analogue in the history of the First Nations of Canada. Atwood's critical engagement with the indigenous peoples of her birth country is already evident in her second novel, *Surfacing* (1972), long before post-colonialism became an academic buzz word. The central protagonist, a woman in her late twenties, and her friends visit an island in northern Ontario where blueberry bushes are abundant. Blueberry picking evokes her childhood memory of "the others who used to come" to this island. This excerpt may serve as an early gloss on the concerns reiterated over thirty years later in "Thylacine Ragout":

> There weren't many of them on the lake even then, the government had put them somewhere else, corralled them, but there was one family left. Every year they would appear on the lake in blueberry season and visit the good places the same way we did, condensing as though from the air, five or six of them in a weatherbeaten canoe…. faces neutral and distanced, but when they saw that we were picking they would move on, gliding unhurried…and then disappearing around a point or into a bay as though they had never been there…. It never occurred to me till now that they must have hated us. (*Surfacing* 36)

Final Impressions, or Bushmeat

But you may say, half-hopefully, at least the last part about some kinky rich person eating the thylacine is wholly fabricated. Surely that surprise twist ("He ate it in the form of a ragout. He had a yen for the unique…") is a figment of Atwood's playful, and occasionally mordant, literary imagination. The closing paragraph may be deemed a modern-day folktale.

I thought so, too, until I was better or, rather, worse informed. In April 2008 I returned to the Thomas Fisher Rare Book Library at the University of Toronto in order to check out something else. Looking again through the folder labeled "Threatened Species, 2000-2003" in Atwood's research files, I now noticed an article clipped from *Scientific American*—Atwood is a frequent reader of that journal—dated June 2001 and just preceding Dayton's "Rough Justice," with the memorable image of Mr. Weber and the trussed-up thylacine.[15] Josephine Hearn's article, "Unfair Game: The Bushmeat Trade Is Wiping out Large African Mammals," begins with a vignette from Bioko Island, off the coast of Cameroon:

> "How would you like it if I cooked porcupine tonight?" our cook asks hopefully. After four weeks in Central Africa, I had become accustomed to eyebrow-raising questions. "How about fish?' I suggest". (24D)

Hearn goes on to report that all across tropical Africa, "where timeless village ways are meeting the cash economy," the trade in bushmeat is threatening, and even eradicating, wildlife populations "According to the Convention on International Trade in Endangered Species (CITES), the practice affects 30 endangered species—among them gorillas, chimpanzees, elephants, duikers…and monkey" (24D, 26). On Bioko, Hearn writes, there are seven species of monkeys, of which five are classified as endangered, and yet these animals are "heavily hunted for bushmeat and then marketed at prices only the upper classes can afford" (26).

The surprise at the end of Atwood's what-to-call-it is a spin-off of this unfair game. That is, the last paragraph of "Thylacine Ragout," like everything else in it, meticulously draws on contemporary reality. It tells the scarcely credible tale of how so-called humankind is using up and wasting the resources of this once good earth. Now it's still here. Soon it'll be over and done. Like the true stories of the tiger, the devil, and Trugannini.

Notes

[1] For the fantastic yet actual account of how a multinational U.S.-based company came to "own" this iconic marsupial of Tasmania, see Owen and Pemberton, *Tasmanian Devil*, 145-69. Warner Bros. has trademarked the character of Taz, registered "Tasmanian Devil" as a brand name for goods, and zealously polices the copyright: "Wigston's Lures, a small Hobart fishing lure company, spent eight years battling for the right to use the name Tasmanian Devil for one of its lures" and eventually reached a "one-off agreement" with the entertainment conglomerate (Owen and Pemberton 162).

[2] Qtd. also in "Thylacine, or Tasmanian tiger," *Wildlife of Tasmania: Tasmanian Mammals.*

[3] Chapter eight of Paddle's *The Last Tasmanian Tiger* gives a detailed, harrowing account of the fate of the last tiger and other animals at the Hobart Zoo:

> It could easily have lived much longer, but it did not, and the reason for its failure to survive lies in a series of insensitive and offensive administrative decisions made by a bureaucratic management structure with no representation from keeper or curatorial staff. (184)

Among the offensive decisions referred to here was the refusal to allow Alison Reid, the daughter of the zoo's curator and an animal expert in her own right, to carry on caring for the animals after her father's death:

> Despite the fact that…Alison Reid had been effectively acting as curator for the previous twelve months, the Reserves Department would not countenance the idea of appointing a female, even in an acting capacity, to the vacant curatorial post. (189)

Locked out of their sheltered sleeping quarters at night, left on open display twenty-four hours a day in extreme temperatures, and indifferently fed, the animals at the zoo died off one by one. Paddle's account concludes, "Thus, unprotected and exposed, the last known thylacine whimpered away during the night of 7

September 1936 (Reserves Committee [records], 16/9/1936), as much a victim of sexual as species chauvinism" (195).

[4] See also "Image One—*Weaver*," in Campbell, "Additional Topics: Persecution," *The Thylacine Museum*, accessible at <http://www.naturalworlds.org/thylacine/additional/persecution/image_1.htm>.

[5] Atwood, *Oryx and Crake* research files, Ms. Coll. 335, Box 115. . I am indebted to the staff at the Thomas Fisher Rare Book Library for their generous assistance.

[6] See the section on Sightings and Searches, in "Thylacine, or Tasmanian tiger," at *Wildlife of Tasmania: Tasmanian Mammals*.

[7] For a modern-day example of a thylacine story thematically linked to Atwood's concerns, see the Australian author Julia Leigh's novel *The Hunter* (2000), whose central protagonist sets out in search for what may be the only remaining thylacine in Tasmania in order to harvest its genetic material for biotechnical research.

[8] Analogously, although the cartoon series *Taz of Taz-Mania!* has earned millions of dollars for Warner Bros., which has expressed occasional concern about the real-life creature's survival, until recently the company has given no assistance to efforts to save the devil. As reported in a June 2006 article in *The Independent*,

> Now, after three years of pressure, Warner Bros [sic] has finally agreed to contribute hard cash to help save the Tasmanian devil. The company will permit Taz to feature in a nationwide television campaign aimed at raising funds for scientific research. (Marks).

[9] For the effects of this lethal compound, see the Australian Humane Society International (HSI) website for "1080 poison," which is part of an effort to promote conservation and challenge Australia's over-reliance on pesticides:

> Death by 1080 poison is one of the most cruel and inhumane ways in which an animal can die. Consumption through ingestion results in a painfully slow death over several hours from convulsions, cardiac arrest, failure of the central nervous system and respiratory arrest.

Cf. the Tasmanian Department of Primary Industries and Water's online information about "1080 Poison": "The 1080 Code of Practice has recently been revised to ensure that it meets community expectations that 1080 is used only as a last resort for the control of browsing animals."

[10] For further details of this history, see especially the entry for "Tasmanian Aborigines," *Wikipedia* and Onsman, "Truganini's Funeral."

[11] See "Tasmanian Aborigines," *Wikipedia* and also Rashidi's "Postscript," a revision dated August 2002, to his 1998 lecture notes on "Black War: The Destruction of the Tasmanian Aborigines."

[12] On shell necklace making and wearing within the Aboriginal community, see Hawkins. Although focusing on the history of necklace production, Hawkins also presents a detailed account of the impact of Europeans on the indigenous population, and especially on the women, of Tasmania.

[13] For an account of the mutilation of Lanney's body after his death, see Turnball, *Black War*, 234-36.

[14] See Atwood, Ms. Coll. 335, Box 115.

Works Cited

Aesop. "The Lion, the Bear, and the Fox." 1947. In *Aesop's Fables*, n. ed., 110. Kingsport, Tenn.: Grosset & Dunlap.

Anon. "Cloning May Bring Extinct Tasmanian Tiger to Life." Environment News Service 28 May 2002. *International Daily Newswire*. 8 June 2008
<http://wwwns-newswire.com/ens/ may2002/2002-05-28-03.asp>.

Atwood, Margaret. Atwood Papers, Manuscript Collection 335. Thomas Fisher Rare Book Library. University of Toronto. Ontario, Canada.

—. *Bottle*. Hay, 2004. UK: Hay Festival Press.

—. *Oryx and Crake*. 2003. London: Bloomsbury.

—. *Surfacing*. 1972. Toronto: McClelland & Stewart.

—. "Thylacine Ragout." 2006. In *The Tent*, 73-75. Toronto: McClelland & Stewart.

—. "Writing Oryx and Crake." 2005. In *Writing with Intent: Essays, Reviews, Personal Prose: 1983-2005*, 284-86. New York: Carroll and Graf.

Bonwick, James. "The Lost Tasmanian Race." 1970. London: Sampson Low, Marston, Searle, and Rivington, 1884. Rptd. in *Landmarks in Anthropology*. Series ed. Weston La Barre. New York: Johnson Reprint Corporation.

Campbell, Cameron R. "The Thylacine Museum: A Natural History of the Tasmanian Tiger." 2006. *C. Campbell's Natural Worlds*.
<http:// www.naturalworlds.org/ thylacine/>.

Caplan, Arthur. "Much Ado About Cloning: Why Two Is Not Better Than One." 2001. *World Link* 14, no. 5. 22-25.

Dayton, Leigh. "Rough Justice." 19 May 2001. *New Scientist* 2291. 46-47.

"Fable." *Wikipedia*. 2 June 2008. Wikimedia Foundation.
<http://en.wikipedia.org/wiki/Fable>.

Guiler, Eric. *Thylacine: The Tragedy of the Tasmanian Tiger*. 1985. Melbourne: Oxford University Press.

Hawkins, John. "A Suggested History of Tasmanian Aboriginal Kangaroo Skin or Sinew, Human Bone or Skin, Shell, Feather, Apple Seed and Wombat Claw Necklaces." Feb. 2008. *Australiana*. 21-35. 22 June 2008
<http://www.jbhawkinsantiques.com/articles/documents/TasmanianAppleseed Necklaces.pdf>.

Hearn, Josephine. "Unfair Game: The Bushmeat Trade Is Wiping out Large African Mammals." June 1991. *Scientific American*. 24D, 26.

Leigh, Julia. *The Hunter*. 2000. New York: Four Walls Eight Windows.

Marks, Kathy. "Taz: How a Cartoon Character Has Come to the Rescue of a Threatened Species. The Plight of the Tasmanian Devil." 27 June 2006. *The Independent*.
<http://www.independent.co.uk/news/world/australasia/taz-how-a-cartoon-character-has-come-to-the-rescue-of-a-threatened-species-405664.html>.

Onsman, Andrys. "Truganini's Funeral." Autumn 2004. *Island* 96.
<http:// www.islandmag.com/96/article.html>.

Owen, David and David Pemberton. *Tasmanian Devil: A Unique and Threatened Animal*. 2005. London: Natural History Museum.

Paddle, Robert. *The Last Tasmanian Tiger: The History and Extinction of the Thylacine*. 2000. Cambridge, UK: Cambridge University Press.

Rashidi, Runoko. "Postscript: Indigineous Tasmanians Today." 1 Aug. 2002. "Black War: The Destruction of the Tasmanian Aborigines." 1998. In *The Global African Community: Lecture Notes*.
<http://www.cwo.com/~lucumi/tasmania.html>.

Salleh, Anna. "Bringing the Tasmanian Tiger Back to Life." News in Science 5 May 2000. Science News Archives. *ABC Science Online*.
<http://www.abc.net.au/science/news/stories/s123723.htm>.

"Save the Tasmanian Devil." 6 May 2008. *Department of Primary Industries and Water*.
<http://www.tassiedevil.com.au/disease.htm>.

Skatssoon, Judy. "Thylacine Cloning Project Dumped." News in Science 15 Feb. 2005. Science News Archives. . *ABC Science Online*.
<http://www.abc.net.au/science/news/stories/s1302459.htm>.

"Tasmanian Aborigines." *Wikipedia*. 2 June 2008. Wikimedia Foundation.
<http://en.wikipedia.org/wiki/Tasmanian_Aborigines >.

"Tasmanian Devil." In *Wildlife of Tasmania: Tasmanian Mammals. Parks and Wildlife Service, Tasmania*. 5 Mar. 2008. Department of Tourism, Arts and the Environment.
<http://www.parks.tas.gov.au/wildlife/mammals/devil.html >.

"Thylacine, or Tasmanian Tiger." In *Wildlife of Tasmania: Tasmanian Mammals. Parks and Wildlife Service, Tasmania*. 5 Mar. 2008. Department of Tourism, Arts and the Environment.
<http://www.parks.tas.gov.au/wildlife/mammals/thylacin.html>.

Turnbull, Clive. *Black War: The Extermination of the Tasmanian Aborigines*. 1948. Melbourne and London: F. W. Cheshire.

"1080 Poison." *Australian Humane Society International (HSI)*. 11 June 2008
<20Habitats%20and%20Threats/Threats_Wildlife_and_habitats/1080.htm>.

"1080 Poison." Food and Agriculture: Tasmanian Department of Primary Industries and Water. 8 May 2008. *Tasmania Online | Service Tasmania.* 10 June 2008
<http://www.dpiw.tas.gov.au/inter.nsf/ topics/cart-63s826?open>.

CHAPTER NINE

ATWOOD'S FEMALE CRUCIFIXION: "HALF-HANGED MARY"

KATHRYN VANSPANCKEREN

"Half-Hanged Mary" is the remarkable poem Atwood devoted to her ancestor, Mary Webster. In the epigraph to the poem, Atwood writes that

> Half-Hanged Mary was accused of witch-craft in the 1680s in a Puritan town in Massachusetts and hanged from a tree – where, according to one of the several surviving accounts, she was left all night. It is known that when she was cut down she was still alive, since she lived for another 14 years (*Morning in the Burned House* 58).[1]

Atwood has told several versions of this story. In the poem, Mary is hanged in Massachusetts, but in a 1980 address Atwood said she was hanged in Connecticut. In the poem, published in *Morning in the Burned House* (1995), Mary is hanged for any of several possible reasons, but in the earlier account she was hanged "for 'causing an old man to become extremely valetudinarious.'" In the poem, she survives by drawing on her psychic strength as a woman and refusing to give in; in the address Atwood puns that Mary survived because she had a "stiff neck ("Witches" 331). In yet another account, Atwood offers a scientific reason for Mary's strange survival — the hanging occurred "before they invented the drop and therefore her neck was not broken" ("Witch Craft" 28). While Atwood's early accounts focus on legal and scientific aspects, the poem teases out the feminist dimensions. The story's outlines remain, but the interpretation has evolved. The present essay explores this evolution.

From an early age Atwood was aware that one of her ancestors was associated with witchcraft and rare powers of survival. Mary Webster became a transgressive role model and Atwood's favorite ancestor, beating out "privateers and massacred French Protestants" ("Witches" 331).

Mary's story may have influenced her early reading: she loved witches and scary stories as a child, and had read all of Poe by 6th grade, as well as the entire unexpurgated Grimm's ("Margaret Atwood: Queen of Canlit"). Such a family legend helps us understand the importance of witches and uncanny women in Atwood's writing.

In the brilliant satirical *Lady Oracle*, Atwood produces Gothic conventions like candy from a Halloween bag: haunted dwelling, intricate maze, mysterious stranger, endangered heroine. The Bluebeard figure's late wives provide Joan Foster with lurid examples of what happens to women who aren't uncannily clever. In *Surfacing* the unnamed narrator had drawn talismanic pictures or magical beings as a child; Native American pictographs help her recover her identity, and she engineers a liaison with Joe under the moon where she may conceive a child with magical powers. Offred in *The Handmaid's Tale* is a walking Scarlet Letter, "some fairytale figure in a red cloak, descending towards a moment of carelessness that is the same as danger. A sister, dipped in blood" (19). In Atwood's fiction, seemingly normal women harbor eerie powers. They dominate *The Robber Bride*, *Alias Grace* and *Oryx and Crake*. Such a woman appears as an artist in *Cat's Eye*, and as a writer who weaves family stories in *The Blind Assassin*. *Good Bones and Simple Murders* offers a gallery of mystic women. In her poetry Atwood is even more in tune with magic. Circe is Atwood's mouthpiece in her long sequence in *You Are Happy*. The "Snake Poems" from *Interlunar* revision the Christian view of woman and serpent, while *Morning in the Burned House* is structured around a female descent myth with roots in ancient ritual (VanSpanckeren, "Atwood's Space Crone"). Atwood's recent works continue the theme of women with special knowledge, which often entails suffering. Penelope prevails but grieves, even in the underworld, over her hanged maids in *The Penelopiad* (2005), while the short shorts of *The Tent* (2006) concern spirits, gods, and unearthly figures. The autobiographical stories of *Moral Disorder* (2006) begin with omens and barbarians clamoring at the gates, and end with a mysterious stranger vanishing among trees.

The present paper focuses on a single poem that is central to Atwood's writing and her feminist vision. This poem draws together crucial recurring themes——uncanny women, patriarchal violence against females, female struggles for survival and autonomous identity—to construct a mythical paradigm for women that may subtly interrogate the traditional Christian message of sacrifice and forgiveness epitomized by Christ's passion and crucifixion. The poem suggests that Christ's story of faith, submission and forgiveness is a gendered account that may not work for women. The poem recounts Mary's passion, as it were, phase by phase, each set at an hour of the evening; as the night wears on, her questioning of Christian doctrine becomes more pronounced. After the decisive hour of midnight, when she wrestles with death, she develops a heretical and pagan sensibility and in the end she becomes a witch, imbued with an inhuman consciousness linked with nature.

The phases of this ritualistic poem begin with the witch-hunt due to "rumors" against her at 7 p.m., her stringing up on a tree at 8 p.m., the gathering of a fearful and ineffectual, largely female audience at 9 p.m., and her debate with God about free will at 10 p.m. Twelve midnight brings death's visitation in the shape of a crow or judge, with his insinuating seductive whisper: "*trust me*, he says, caressing/ me. *Why suffer?*"(63).[1] Yet Mary refuses

> to give up my own words for myself,
> my own refusals.
> To give up knowing,
> To give up pain.
> To let go (63).

At 2 a.m. Mary hears a "thin gnawing sound" coming out of her strangling neck and questions prayer: "maybe it's/ a gasp for air" (63-4). At 3 a.m. she loses normal consciousness and begins to merge into the leaves and wind, yet thinks "this is/ a crime I will not/ acknowledge...I will not give in" (65). By 6 a.m. dawn her lonely vigil drifting in space "listening to the gospel/ of the red-hot stars" provides an alternative vision: "Most "will have only one death/ I will have two" (66). At 8 a.m. she is cut down and cannot be re-hanged due to double jeopardy, and this is ironic: before "I was not a witch./ But now I am one" (67). In the last section, "Later," she assumes uncanny powers and merges with nature.

Nowhere in this poem is Jesus explicitly mentioned, yet the setting, imagery, theme of witch-hanging, and religious debates common to the Calvinism practiced in Massachusetts Bay Colony in early Colonial times remind readers forcefully of the Christian background. Mary's story is not an exact parallel, but rather a counterpoint. Both live twice, as it were. Yet she does not die, to be reborn later—she survives. Both are crucified (crucifixion was a term formerly used for hanging, "to put to death by suspension of the neck" ("Hanging," *Oxford English Dictionary*). Mary, however, in the poem is accorded no trial—rumor alone is enough to provoke the witch hunt. Both endure a dark night of body and soul, but unlike Jesus, Mary suffers alone. Where Jesus forgives and rests his faith in God, Mary refuses to acknowledge authority in her case and is forced to rely on herself. She prevails, but at a high cost: she becomes (like) the witch figure that the men had feared and projected onto her.

The present essay considers Atwood's poem as a feminist expression of myth, beginning with its specific contexts, especially the place of the poem in the volume in which it appeared. The body of the essay consists of a close analysis of the drafts, which reveal Atwood's artistry and continual elaboration of a feminist mythic vision. The story's historical sources are then considered, and the poem is set in the larger context of ongoing feminist calls for a revisioning of myth. The poem is postmodern and open to several differing interpretations: Mary may represent a triumph over the patriarchy, another story of victimization, a disturbingly unstable post feminist Gothic witch tale interweaving both meanings, or more.

"Half-Hanged Mary" appears exactly in the middle of Atwood's *Morning in the Burned House*, between the striking dramatic monologues of women from myth and pop culture—Sekhmet, the Helen of Troy who does Counter Dancing, Ava Gardner, Manet's Olympia—and the moving elegiac sequence recording her father's passing. In the final organization (which Atwood labored over) the sassy public figures balance the inwardness of the dying father. It is not an accident that "Half-Hanged Mary" occurs at the fulcrum of the book. Like a hinge, this poem is the no-woman's-land where personal and impersonal realms meet. Mary Webster is a private woman thrust into history and legend. Possibly the poem expresses the writer's unconscious and vain hope that the father might not die, but miraculously survive death's visitation, as Mary Webster had done some 300 years earlier.

Insofar as Atwood experienced the creative process of writing as "negotiating with the dead," she was familiar with entering uncanny states. As she tells us in *Negotiating with the Dead* (2002), the artistic self is far from the ordinary self who gets up and eats asparagus and remembers babysitting as a child in part one of *Mornings in the Burned House*. Bearing this distinction in mind, it is possible to see "Half-Hanged Mary" as a quasi-autobiographical poem suggesting, in a distanced way made possible by the change of time and place—Massachusetts 300 years ago—the forging of Atwood the artist. Mary was (like the young Atwood) an ordinary woman whose gender exposed her to victimization (marriage or life in a boring job) by pre-feminist social structures; to preserve her autonomy she was forced to access new sources of strength (in Atwood's case, writing). In the end, suffering forged a woman with exceptional powers where none had been before. The patriarchy had created the uncanny "other" it hated and feared. The role of artist is not easy: Mary's lonely vigil is a crucifixion told in hours of the night, like sections of a mass or stations of the cross.

The poem's tone is complex, supple, and uncompromising; wit flickers like white lightning around the dark and painful core of the subject. On one level this is an anti-elegy, a death-poem by someone who did not die, a ritual crucifixion as spoken by the survivor. Yet the poem records terrible loneliness and agony. Such a poem is not easy to write. There is a satisfaction in reflecting that this poem speaks for thousands of women wrongly hanged and otherwise executed as witches, and that an ancestral woman has been given voice by a female descendent. The witch-hunt is a subject ripe for treatment that has commanded the attention of post feminist critics.

First Draft: Witch as Woman Transformed

There are three rough drafts of "Half-Hanged Mary" in the Atwood Papers at the Thomas Fisher Rare Book Library of the University of Toronto.[2] In the following discussion, words and letters in parentheses were crossed out; words underlined were added from the margins or above the lines. Words originally underlined in the draft are italicized, as they are in the final published book form (if Atwood retained them). Illegible words are noted as such, with questionable readings marked with a question mark.

The first rough draft consists of seven handwritten pages without page numbers; its first four pages—the original heart of the poem—are in ink on unlined paper, and appear in sections under centered hour headings beginning with 7 p.m. The hour headings were probably revised right after Atwood wrote the first four pages (the ink and handwriting, which can vary with mood, materials, speed, etc., are all of a piece). Originally the poem began at 7 pm and ended at midnight, but revisions show that Atwood quickly spotted the possibilities if she were to expand the poem by adding sections. In the first four pages of ink manuscript, the most important action occurs: Mary is accused, hanged, almost dies, miraculously survives, and assumes mystic powers. This dynamic paradox—that persecution can be transformative—is the crux that inspired Atwood to write the poem. The next three pages are additional scenes or passages she could insert, written on lined paper—the first two pages in pencil, and the final page in ink. This seven-page draft has itself been revised at least twice; ink corrections were made on pencil on page 5, and pencil is used to correct the ink draft on page 1. Most likely the draft was done in two or perhaps three sittings.

The first ink draft originally lacked a title; a provisional one was added, probably not long after, in ink. Since there was no space to center it, it appears at the upper right of the page: "(Twice) Half-Hanged Mary." Why did she imagine Mary as *twice* hanged? Was she thinking of her as reborn at the end, and hence living twice? Possibly "witch" was the original working title, since in the first line of the poem—"The word witch was loose in the air —Atwood underlined "witch." The importance of the word "witch" is seen in the fact that this beginning line—"The word *witch* was loose in the air"—continues throughout all three rough drafts, even though there are many important changes made in the poem. The idea of "witch" was the nucleus of this poem, present at its creation.

The final printed poem changes the first line to read "Rumour was loose in the air,/ hunting for some neck to land on." This change—from "witch" to "rumor"—is important; Atwood clung to "witch," only relinquishing it at the very end of the revision process, after the third rough draft, right before publication. Clearly she liked the implication that Mary was a bit of a witch; that had been her idea of Mary since childhood. Nevertheless, mention of "witch" in the first line implies that Mary originally had special powers. These powers detract from the dynamic transformation of the finished poem in which an ordinary woman actually becomes a witch (as it were). In the final poem, cruel, inhuman authorities create the very thing that they fear. This insight and its feminist ramifications ultimately outweighed Mary's bona fides as a witch. The draft reveals a tension or confusion in the original idea of the poem: was Mary a witch or an ordinary woman who turned into one? The first draft has it both ways. On page four, after she survives, Mary sounds like a witch, exulting:

> I dance afterwards in moonlight
> valid as the just-born
> (words) the words boil out of me
> coil after coil of sinuous possibility
>   the cosmos unravels from my mouth
> all fullness (&), all vacancy
> my body of skin waxes and wanes
> around my true body
> (I mean) inner nimbus

The first four pages of rough draft dramatically recreate the urgency, inhumanity, and suffering of Mary, and highlight her strong-willed refusal to give in. Death visits but she says "NO" in this first draft. This image of an ancestress speaking truth to power is what may have inspired the young

Atwood as a writer. Even though her "throat is taut against the rope" Mary realizes "it's the words they wanted to choke off/ the words bulging like blood in my skull…" and she draws on language, her true power:

> I call on the words to save me.
> to shape my refusal
> all my muscles (struggle) are locked
> in struggle until the (insidious) angel
> birdheaded, (feathers), insidious, in his glossy feathers
> who whispers to me to let go.
> In silence/ I say NO.

Mary's strength is emphasized throughout. Here is the second line of the original ink draft, showing changes: "(search) and (looking) searching for some (place no) neck to land on." Mary's stiff neck is the mark of her strength. It is, as it were, her strong backbone, which a truth-telling writer like Atwood needs. The rumors could not land just any place: they had to land on her neck, which becomes elided with her throat and mouth, the living apparatus of the singer, linked by the end of the poem with the muse, nature, and the cosmos. When the cord most threatens to choke her breath and song, the crucifixion is closest to completion—but where Christ returned violence with questions ("wherefore hast thou forsaken me") and forgiveness of those "who know not what they do," Atwood's not-quite-crucified Mary turns the evil intent of her tormentors back on themselves and refuses to admit guilt.

The first draft's lined paper pages, though afterthoughts compared to the first four inked pages written all in one burst of inspiration, offer insight into Atwood's creative intentions. The first page, only about half full of writing, contains a grotesque passage that Atwood did not use in the final poem:

> over there by the skyline, there's (?) thunder
> beginning to push itself out
> Lightning slow as asparagus   nothing to do with god/or with me either/just
> an occurrence
> the thick shoot the delicate branching
> (fine in my) <u>small</u> veins or eyelids
> (this could take all night) <u>or cracks in blank marble</u>
> (the) each (flash) <u>jissim</u> lasts an hour,
> <u>because</u> time (slows) shuts down when you're dying.
> Then a long jumble of stone boulders of air
> high tension down
> I think, how full is this tree

(I think, are these my father?) I think, I am not god's fuse
I think, Don't let it hit me!

  I think this between one torn
last breath & another

The passage looks backward to the humorous "Asparagus" from section one of *Morning in the Burned House* in which Atwood lunches with a much younger man and thinks "I could wrinkle up my eyelids,/ look wise. I could get a pet lizard." It also looks forward to poems in part four about Atwood's father such as "Lear in Respite Care" where the confused father faces mortality alone, as Mary does. The linkage of lightning to the spurts of a male god's sexuality (a Zeus/Jupiter given to abducting and raping women) works intellectually, but associations with classical myth are out of character for the speaker, a relatively uneducated Puritan woman.

The second and third lined pages consist of monologues addressed to God. The second lined page closely resembles the 10 p.m. section of the final printed version, and deals with free will and the problem of evil (how a good god could create pain, suffering, and death). Atwood's revisions give the passage a feminist slant: Mary's "tasks" carried on "at the hen level" are changed to "fingerwork" and "legwork," explicit, ribald words carrying sexual innuendo. This sort of "work" has left Mary, like most women, no time to address such philosophical problems. Ironically, the hanging gives Mary time to think philosophically. The passage interrogates the idea that nature reveals god's intentions. Mary's phrasings ("If Nature is your alphabet") challenge not just the men who hang her, but the Puritan's legacy of optimistic Emersonian transcendentalism. Mary also reinterprets the "*cogito ergo sum* of Rene Descartes (1596-1650). The passage reads:"

  Well, God, now that I'm up here
  with maybe some time to spare
  away from the daily
  (tasks) fingerwork, legwork, work
  at the hen level,
  we can continue our quarrel.
  the one about free will.

  Is it (be) my choice that I'm dangling
  like a (drawn) (semi-naked) turkey from this
  more than indifferent tree?
  (Or did you select the rope?)

If Nature is your alphabet
what letter is the rope?
Does my twisting body spell out grace?
(Is the blank of the sky your face?)
I hurt, therefore I am.
Faith & charity & Hope
are three dead angels
falling like burnt (?) <u>crows</u> across the
profound (sky) blank sky of your face.

The third page, on lined paper in darker and thicker ink than that of the first four pages, takes up a new theme, the nature of prayer and divine visitation. Mary begins to speak, not in prayer but impelled by terror and agony. The imagery recalls Pentecostal manifestations — tongues of fire and speaking in tongues.[3] Mary imagines these as horrible tortures similar to her hanging. The section is a gothic parody of Puritan grace and election, where crows substitute for angels. The section closely resembles the 2 a.m. section of the final printed version:

out of my mouth is coming, at some
(surreal senses?) <u>distance</u> from me, a thin gnawing sound
which you might think is praying, except that
praying is not constrained.
                    or is it, Lord?
maybe its more like (strangling) being strangled
than I once thought. Maybe it's
a gasp for air, prayer.
did those men at Pentecost ask
for flames to shoot out of their heads?
Did they ask to (roll on) be tossed (on the ground)
on the ground, eye(s)<u>balls</u> bulging?

they aren't so far apart, (fea) grace
and terror

as mine are, as mine are.
there is only one prayer; it is not <u>knees in the clean nightgown on the prim</u>
<u>hooked rug</u>
I want this, I want that. Oh far beyond.
Call it <u>please</u>. Call it <u>mercy</u>.
Call it not yet, not yet
As Heaven threatens to explode
<u>inwards</u> in fire and shredded flesh, and the angels caw.

The Second Draft: Gendered Resistance

This draft consists of four typed, numbered pages, and two additional unnumbered pages in ink on lined paper. The first section, entitled "7 p.m.," shows Atwood shaping the raw material by reinforcing Mary's gender through tactile adjectives. The word "witch" now lands on Mary "like a <u>soft</u> bullet" though she does not feel it penetrate her newly "<u>smashed</u>" flesh. The diction suggests stealth and rape. Now that she has amplified the scene with more detail (and length) Atwood divides the first section's original two stanzas into three – typical of her process of revision. The second stanza lists reasons she was hanged: "having blue eyes/ and a dark skin, tattered skirts/and an infallible cure for warts;/ for living alone/ and for giving advice to the lovelorn"). The next stanza on breasts begins "Oh yes, and breasts" — the separate stanza and new stanza break imply that gender is the real bedrock reason she was fingered as a witch.

The second section, in which Mary is hauled up "like a windfall in reverse,/ a blackened apple stuck back onto the tree," is entitled "9 p.m." The tree recalls Eden and the cross, termed a rood or tree in medieval English. Mary imagines herself as a flag saluting the moon, "old bone-faced goddess, old original,/ who once took blood in return for food." The section is identical to the second section in the final printed version, there entitled "8 p.m."

The third section is entitled "10 p.m." here as in the first draft; in the final printed version it appears as "12 midnight." Midnight is a time of reversals, of the welling-up of the uncanny, associated with the witches' Sabbath. Atwood worked hard on this key section in which Mary confronts death. Usually she writes fluently, her revisions confined to reordering sections of poems and changes and amplifications in diction. Here she shows uncertainty, adding words and phrases to the first draft version only to omit them later. An example is the comparison of death to "a judge, like a refusal,/ an incarnation of the word NO." Atwood flirts with this comparison, which nicely links patriarchal judgment to a negating and death-dealing male authority, but finally decides against it. In the final printed version, gender is again emphasized, and death is made to be driven by sex, hypocritical "like a judge/muttering about sluts and punishment/and licking his lips." One reason for not having the judge say no, of course, is that Mary is the central figure, the one finally who is given the chance to reject gendered injustice and victimization. The final stanza reads "I call on the words to save me" and ends "I say

NO." Perhaps Atwood did not want Christian readers to be thinking of the Last Judgment. In any event, after much effort, this stanza has been crossed out and Mary's refusal is made more subtle (her defiant utterance "I say NO" appears nowhere in the final version). The original Mary had been overtly strong: "I am reduced to muscle." The Mary of the final version has a different, more internal strength. She has to fight not a male judge, but her conditioning as a woman; she must fight the insidious urge to give up her identity and will. She triumphs over death not like a Christ who forgives, but as a survivor who resists the act of "letting go" of the self. Atwood gives a feminist reworking of "the fall" that Hester Prynne would recognize:

A temptation, to sink down
into these definitions.
To become a martyr in reverse,
or food, or trash.

To give up my own words for myself,
my own refusals.
To give up knowing.
To give up pain.
To let go.

The next section of the second draft, entitled "12 Midnight," appears in the first handwritten draft, but there a large arrow suggests Atwood had cut it. It reappears, typed, in the second draft, so I discuss it here. It appears in the third draft also, but is missing from the final poem. Atwood may have wanted to keep it for its mysteriously rhyming, Frost-like ending: "don't provoke the tree./ Imitate ice/ in complete lucidity." However appealing they are in themselves, these lines depict a passive Mary. Elsewhere Mary rages and questions, so the section is out of character. Atwood "kills her darlings" in the parlance of MFA programs. This section presents Mary as pretending to hang quietly to "counterfeit death," "a limp silhouette, hardly worth spitting at./ A woman in poor clothing/depending by the neck from a tree." The section emphasizes Mary's lower-class origins, and as scholars such as Steve Nissenbaum and Paul Boyer (*Salem Possessed*) have shown, poor and marginalized women were most likely to be accused as witches, though Carol Karlsen (*Devil in the Shape of a Woman*) argues persuasively that women with inheritances were especially at risk for witchcraft accusations. Atwood may have cut the section because she wanted the poem to apply equally to all women.

The second draft is incomplete; the fourth typed page ends with a title, "6 a.m." but no subsequent typed 6 a.m. section. Instead we have two handwritten pages of different, untitled material. The first of these is a draft of the wry "bonnets" passage in which the fearful Puritan women stare at Mary—depicted here as a midwife and healer—as she hangs. Additions in the margins of the three draft stanzas result in the five-stanza final published version, made more vivid through added detail and imagery. The draft is enlivened by a small sketch of a plump, bundled-up Puritan woman, nostrils flaring, craning her head to look up at the speaker. This tiny Puritan woman is placed to the right of "You were my friend, you too." One senses how closely Atwood identified with Mary, not only as ancestress with uncanny verbal powers, but perhaps also as someone lonely and singular though "looked up to."

> The bonnets came to stare,
> the (shawls) skirts also
> the upturned faces in between, mouths closed so tight they're lipless.
> I can see down into their (nostrils) eyelashes
> and nostrils, I can see their fear:
>
> You were my friend, you too.
> I cured your baby, Mrs.,
> and (dug) flushed yours out of you,
> Non-wife, to save your life.
>
> Help me down? You don't dare.
> (Some of) I might rub off on you
> like soot or gossip. Birds
> of a feather burn together,
> (and ravens) though as a rule ravens are singular.
>
> In a gathering like this one
> the safe place is the background,
> pointing your finger.
> You can't spare anything, a word, a slice of bread, a shawl
> against the cold,
> a good word. Lord
> knows there isn't much. You need it all.

This section is important because it complicates gender relations and conveys the ambivalent relationship of Mary to the other women, for whom her hanging is a warning. It shows women internalizing their roles as victims and collaborating with their repressive society, as in *The Handmaid's Tale*, for which the story of Mary was one inspiration.

The second handwritten page, entitled "6 a.m.," contains the original draft of the "6 a.m."section in the final, printed version (like the "bonnets" section, it appears nowhere in the first draft). The revisions, as usual, organize the draft into short stanzas while improving diction, particularly in the beginning—the opening line "sun comes up, huge and blaring" was moved from near the end of the draft. This section, like the previous one, injects welcome notes of humor ("I'm about three inches taller") to counterbalance the philosophical sections in which Mary addresses God.

> 6 a.m.
> the moon goes down, the sun
> rustles the morning birds before (light)
> (it's true) time is relative, let me tell you
> I have lived a millennium (in a night)
> of moonlight. I would like to say my hair
> turned white, but this is not true.
> It was my ordinary heart (bleached
> that) bleached out.
> (Don't ask me any more
> for dainty feelings.
> No more tears in these)
> like meat in water. Also
> I'm about 3 inches taller.
> This happens to you when you drift
> in infinite space.
> Listening to the gospel
> of emptiness.
> What I heard there is burned
> into my (eyes, like some) skull, pinpoints
> (pinpoints) of hot blue light riddle my brain
> a revelation of (silence) deafness.
> Sun comes up, a (blinding song) huge and blaring
> song of mechanical grace which (deafens) flattens my eyes.
> At the end of my rope
> (I melt like thaw like a glacier)
> I testify to silence.
> Don't say I'm not grateful
> Most have only one death.
> I will have 2.

The last page of the second draft ends with a short section entitled "8 a.m." in which Mary is cut down. Atwood writes the section in a ghastly nursery-rhyme fashion reminiscent of Plath, and allows Mary the last word, "double jeopardy." In the final version, this material appears as the

first half of the "8 a.m." section, which goes on to describe her actual fall
(into clover), her grinning at the captors, and the fact that the Puritan men
"see their own ill will/ staring them in the forehead/ and turn tail." It ends
with the transformation: "Before, I was not a witch./ But now I am one."
Atwood's revisions add wit and irony. She strengthens the first line,
highlighting death and rebirth. For "double jeopardy" she adopts the frothy
diction and domestic imagery of cooking, a gendered and devalued
occupation:

> When they came (to cut me down/ my body /corpse) <u>harvest my corpse</u>
> open your mouth, close your eyes
> cut my body from the rope
> surprise surprise
> I was still alive.
>
> <u>Double jeopardy</u>
> it sounds like a (fancy dessert) company
> dessert, (all) <u>whipped cream</u> and (chocolate) gelatin
>
> Tough luck folks
> I know the law:
> you can't (kill) execute me twice
> for the same thing. How nice

The Third Draft: Moving Beyond Time
into Transformation

The third draft consists of eight typed and numbered pages. Most of
the pages are the same as in the second draft, but here Atwood is working
on the end of the poem. She lengthens the chronology to span a much
longer period, from 7 p.m the first day, through midnight and 8 a.m. when
they took Mary down, to new sections entitled "7 p.m." and "Midnight" of
the second day. This draft encompasses 29 hours. Evidently, after Atwood
had balanced the contemplative, philosophical sections with the comic
sections, her next concern was to deepen the characterization as Mary
transitions from ordinary woman to witch. She may have been exploring
parallels with Christ's resurrection; a period of mysterious absence occurs
after his crucifixion on the cross. In *The Man Who Died*, D. H. Lawrence
allows for some time to pass before Jesus gathers his faculties. Atwood's
impulse was similarly novelistic – to use more time and space.

The first of the two new sections was destined to be omitted from the final printed version. In it Mary imagines her trying to go back to her former life:

I am a practical person
I use the rope for a belt.
I milk the cow.
I have an infallible cure for warts
and for love too if you want one.

There are few buyers.
They fear whatever malice
got seeded in me
by spending twelve hours
as a flesh decoration strung on a tree.

Rumour has it
I've got the town penises
threaded on a leather thong
I wear as a necklace.
I could, if I wanted.

But revenge doesn't interest me.
I have other things to do,
the crops and stars to attend to.

This section might work in a novel such as *Alias Grace*, to give a sense of alternative outcomes for a person accused of a crime that has not been proven, but it is not dramatically satisfying in the poem. Despite bold imagery—the penis necklace—Mary seems unchanged here. The last line mentioning "crops and stars to attend to" is not enough to suggest new-found powers.

The second section, entitled "Midnight" in this draft, begins with lines imported from the first draft; it appears (with minor revisions) as the ending of the published version, where it is simply entitled "Later." In the final published version, Atwood condensed the third draft's 29 hours back to a little more than 13 hours; that final ending establishes that Mary has indeed been permanently altered by her experience. The transition from chronological time to relative or mythic time ("later") reinforces her transformation into witch and leaves open the question of whether she has suffered possible brain damage as well as traumatic stress. The ending describes a woman beyond binaries, for whom flowers and dung are "two forms of the same thing." She could be mad, but also possibly a seer, or

both, when she asserts in the words that reflexively end the poem, "the
cosmos unravels from my mouth,/ all fullness, all vacancy."

Final Print Version: What Stays Unchanged,
or the Making of the Goddess

As mentioned before, the poem's nucleus came to Atwood early on, in
the first four pages of the first draft. The basic character of Mary, and
sequential shape of the poem, divided into hours (later expanded to
resemble Stations of the Cross, or sections of a church service or mass)
appear in this draft. So also does the movement from innocence to
experience, from ordinary woman to witch. The opening remains
throughout all drafts, as does the section about the rope and the men who
hanged her and for whom she wears their own evil "inside out." Following
this are further sections about the torment of hanging, the rope around her
throat, Mary's belief that words will save her, her lapse into semi-
consciousness, and her final triumph.

One section that appears almost unchanged from all drafts through the
final printed version is "3 a.m." (in the first draft, originally entitled
"midnight"), which begins "wind seethes in the leaves around/ me the
trees exude night" and dramatizes Mary's near-blackout by means of brief,
rapid, strongly enjambed lines. The stream of consciousness (reminiscent
of visionary passages near the end of *Surfacing*) evokes Mary's vision and
strength, perhaps unknown up to that time even by her since it is
unconscious, felt as a wind: "the wind seethes/in my body tattering/the
words I clench/ my fists hold No/ talisman or silver disc my lungs/
flail…"(64-5). This part of the poem may hint that nature, imagined as
wind (like the breath of the Creator in Genesis), can have a beneficent and
even magical power. Many times in the Bible wind signals divine
appearances (Miller 362). The section ends:

> I call
> on you as witness I did
> no crime I was born I have borne I
> bear I will be born this is
> a crime I will not
> acknowledge leaves and wind
> hold on to me
> I will not give in (65)

The power of this section lies partly in the subtle ways in which Mary
is aligned with forces of life and nature. Like all living things, animals as

well as plants such as the tree she hangs from, she resists death and fights for life. In this section Mary becomes like the older Susanna Moodie; she merges into the land, beyond human conditioning or victimization — a lessen Atwood spells out in *Survival*. Mark Bruhn has noted Wordsworth's influence on Atwood, especially in his "Lucy" poems, which merge a female figure into a numinous landscape. Atwood's Mary Webster is lustier than Wordsworth's dying young Lucy, and more like the daring Lucy of Atwood's open-ended story "Death by Landscape." Mary Webster, like the Lucy of that story, is a rebellious and active agent, full of lust for life.

Divine imagery sheds scalding radiance in this section. When she is being drawn aloft, Mary recalls that the ancient moon goddess had exacted blood sacrifices. In the conclusion, Mary becomes nature's oracle or perhaps a caricature of this, "mumbling to myself like crazy,/ mouth full of juicy adjectives/ and purple berries." Mary imagines herself as moon goddess: "My body of skin waxes and wanes/ around my true body,/ a tender nimbus…". The word "nimbus," suggestive of the halo around saints' heads, reappears in the next stanza, where her newfound power is attributed to her death: "My first death orbits my head,/ an ambiguous nimbus/ medallion of my ordeal." The result is a magic circle around her body, such as sorcerers drew to call up spirits: the stanza concludes "No one crosses that circle." Death gives her verbal power: "Having been hanged for something/ I never said, I can now say anything I can say." Words have lost their meanings: blasphemies "gleam and burst in my wake/ like lovely bubbles." "I speak in tongues/ my audience is owls" (67-69).

By owls, Mary means witches. Owls, who can see in the darkness, are associated with the moon; the Greek moon goddess Selene shared attributes with Hekate, the wise crone of the ghost world (Larrington 85). In the next poem in *Morning in the Burned House*, "Owl Burning," a witch is burned alive. The man doing the burning explains that times are hard: "Why should an old woman suck up the space,/ the black roots, red juice that should be going/ instead into the children?" (70) Graphic details—dense smoke from "thick fat on fire," "grey screams," the cutting off of body parts — remind us that witchcraft was no mere philosophical debate. The speaker points out "the fingers, those are the wings./ We watched her smoulder and got drunk after." His rationale is a favorite of vigilantes: "Her heart was the ember/ we used to relight our stoves. This is our culture." As for those who disapprove, it's "no business of yours," "You don't know what it's like,/ so close to bedrock" (70-71).

To continue, the last section of "Half-Hanged Mary" characterizes Mary as a crazy woman who is also something of a seer, much like Yeats' late Crazy Jane. Mary's crazy words weave a tapestry of humor and philosophy, which were kept separate until the end of the poem, two sections of each having been added to the original draft. In the end, Mary scrambles humor and philosophy. Her diction is filled with puns in which the profane and sacred are mixed: "My audience is God,/ because who the hell else could understand me?" Having returned from death, she speaks nature's inhuman truth. Words "boil" out of her in "coil after coil of sinuous possibility"—coils recalling Atwood's snake poem sequence, and the great goddess's affinity for serpents as symbols of life and secret knowledge. The poem ends with a time travel vision of creation. She becomes a creator (and if so, perhaps she may create her own salvation): "the cosmos unravels from my mouth,/ all fullness, all vacancy."

Evolution from History to Personal Narrative

Mary Webster's story was well known during her time, and it features in two important Puritan histories. The indefatigable Cotton Mather devotes a one-page chapter (VII) of Book VI of his remarkable 800-page *Magnalia Christi Americana* (1702) to Mary Webster's case.4 The wise and moderate Massachusetts Bay Colony Governor Thomas Hutchinson, a descendent of Anne Hutchinson who had the unenviable job of governor of Massachusetts from 1771-1774, on the eve of the American Revolution, also discusses her in The History of the Colony and Province of Massachusetts-Bay "(chapter one, Volume II). From at least 1980, when she borrows his odd word "valetudinarious" in her address to Radcliffe students, Atwood knew Cotton Mather's account, and she was no doubt aware of Thomas Hutchinson's as well.5 "The epigraph of "Half-Hanged Mary" quoted at the beginning of this essay mentions "several surviving accounts."

Atwood took three courses on early American Literature with influential teachers at Harvard – The American Puritans and The American Revolutionary Period with Alan Heimert, and The American Romantics with Perry Miller (Cooke 92). Miller breathed fresh life into American literary studies by exploring Puritan literary genres—histories, sermons, meditations—and world view, demonstrating the depth and influence of Puritan thought in subsequent American literature. Miller's course on Hawthorne, Melville, Poe and the Transcendentalists stressed their historical foundations and links with Puritan writing. Atwood was impressed enough with Miller to dedicate *The Handmaid's Tale* to him, along with Mary Webster. Having studied the origins of American culture at Harvard enabled her to kick start Canadian cultural awareness in *Survival*—on one level, she was importing an American Studies approach to Canadian literature.

In any event the Puritan obsession with witches would have fascinated and disturbed this descendent of Mary Webster. She probably looked up the sources of Mary's stories at Widener Library when she was a graduate student at Harvard in the mid 1960s (in her Radcliffe address, she mentions spending time in the bowels of Widener and comments dryly that Lamont Library was still off- limits to women students) ("Witches" 329).

Mather and Hutchinson's accounts are complimentary. A local history, Sylvester Judd's *History of Hadley* (1905), quotes both of them and offers passages from court transcripts as well as details of local geography. Bridget Marshall, a scholar on New England witch trials, has condensed them and noted current scholarship; her account is accessible on the internet. According to Judd and Marshall, the historical Mary (Reeve) Webster lived in a small house on the main road out of the village. She had married William Webster, age 53, when she was probably somewhat younger. They had become very poor, and she grew resentful and bitter. She was abused by neighbors, and retaliated with her spiteful tongue; eventually, stories that she was a witch began to circulate. She was said to bewitch horses and cattle so that the beasts would refuse to pass by her house until the drivers beat her. Once she was present in a house when a hen fell down the chimney into a pot of boiling water; her scald-marks were said to be like those of the hen, whose shape she was evidently imagined to have assumed. The accusations were considered by a court at Northampton in 1683, which sent the case to the Boston court. The Boston grand jury indicted her "for that she...being instigated by the devil, hath entered into covenant and had familiarity with him in the shape of a warraneage [fisher or wild black cat of the woods] and had his imps sucking her...." She pleaded not guilty. At length the Boston court, under Governor Bradstreet, found her not guilty.

Sent back to Hadley, Mary ran afoul of one Lieutenant Philip Smith, whom Mather identifies as an upstanding citizen and deacon of about 50. Mather writes, "About the beginning of January, 1684-5, he began to be very valetudinarious," and he blamed Mary Webster. Mather paints him as a paragon of "devotion, sanctity, gravity and all that was honest" and enumerates the ghostly shapes, strange fires, scratchings, and moving objects that haunted the sickroom, and the sensation of pins and needles Smith suffered. Witch-beating was a common practice (described in the

Salem witch trials, for example), and Mather writes that Smith only found relief from suffering when men from the town went to "disturb" Mary. Mather goes into detail about strange wounds on Smith's corpse, wounds that may have inspired "Owl Burning." Interestingly, Mather's account ends with Smith's body remaining fresh and warm from his death on Saturday morning till "Sabbath-day in the Afternoon" – this delayed time taken in transit from life to death may have remained submerged in Atwood's memory, prompting her to play with extending the time of Mary's transformation in the third draft (70).

"Writing generations later, Hutchinson – no believer in witches, and admittedly an American apologist – explains the Massachusetts witch trials as a contagious panic, and puts them in perspective. He notes that more people were executed "in a single county in England in a short space of time, than have suffered in all New England until the present" (16). While Mather's lurid discussion blames the supposed witches, Hutchinson, a man of the Enlightenment, sees them as unfortunate victims. Like Mather, Hutchinson does not mention Mary Webster by name, focusing on the man. Hutchinson describes Smith as a judge, military officer, and town representative and "an hypocondriack person" who "fancied himself under an evil hand" (18). Hutchinson's account provides detail about the "disturbing" of Mary: "a number of brisk lads tried an experiment upon the old woman. Having dragged her out of the house, they hung her up until she was dead, let her roll down, rolled her sometime in the snow [this was in early January] and at last buried her in it, and there left her; but it happened that she survived, and the melancholy man died" (Hutchinson II,18, Mayo II 14). She lived for another eleven years and was around seventy when she died peacefully in 1696, having come unscathed through the tumultuous Salem Witch Trials of 1692 (Marshall 1-6).

Evolution from Personal Narrative to Mythic Revisioning

Atwood's narrative of Mary Webster evolved over time, and she emphasizes one or another aspect of the story responding to differing audiences and changing conditions. In her address delivered at Radcliffe in 1980 Atwood says Mary was hanged for "causing an old man to become extremely "valetudinarious," echoing Cotton Mather (70). She does not stop to rehearse Mather's benighted and longwinded account, however. Shaping her story to the needs of her audience of young Radcliffe women, Atwood cautions that even after ten years of the Women's Movement, men fear powerful females and project their fear onto women. This,

Atwood warns, makes men dangerous and aggressive to women, especially smart women and women writers. While male writers are seen as good craftsmen, a woman writer is thought to be frightening and unnatural. After all, Atwood continues, writing itself "is uncanny: it uses words for evocation rather than denotation: it is spell-making" ("Witches" 331).

In a 1989 interview for *Mother Jones*, whose audience tended to be more interested in social history than in belles letters, Atwood offers a historical reason for Mary's survival—the hanging occurred "before they invented the drop and therefore her neck was not broken" ("Witch Craft" 28). The "drop" involved dropping the victim from some height, so gravity would snap the victim's neck (though this did not always occur). The drop was an improvement over the earlier method of simply slinging a rope over a tree limb and hauling the person up, or pushing them horizontally from a cart (as was used for the thirteen women hanged as witches in Salem). Without a drop, victims were likely to strangle slowly, in agony ("Hanging"). In *The Handmaid's Tale* (1985) Atwood depicts a Salvaging (public hanging) of three women involving overturned stools and shoes dancing in air. Like most hangings this one is meant to intimidate and deter; Handmaids and Wives are made to touch the rope. By the time of the *Mother Jones* interview Atwood must have known that public hanging had long been the most common method of execution, and that it was widely practiced up to the 1890s in Western countries including the U.S. (in fact hanging is still legal in Washington State and New Hampshire) ("Hanging"). The repugnant hangings in the novel and the poem constitute an implicit indictment of capital punishment.

Atwood could hardly find a more patriarchal account than Cotton Mather's to transform. However, in the poem the female "witch," the threat of death, and the successful struggle for survival through language rise into the realm of myth. Atwood's creative processes through the various drafts reveal techniques of deep imagination. She remembers the story and gives it personal meaning for herself; the dramatic monologue in Mary's voice is as disturbing and vivid as watching a hanging. The reader is turned into something of a witness. Atwood re-visions history, bringing out feminist and mythic dimensions–the moon, the debates with God, the lapse into semi-consciousness, the transformation. The four-page heart of the first draft gives Mary's personal story; additions to it bring in dialogues with God. The second draft develops other people in the story–the judge and the audience. What would become the "midnight" section presents the threatening and negating male judge, and Mary's survival of the dark night of the soul by resisting "letting go." The "bonnets" section reveals the fear of the women who watch, and implicates the reader in this near-execution of everywoman. The third draft expands the story to two days in almost novelistic fashion, giving alternative lives for Mary. In one, she goes back home and resumes her life (Atwood rejected this idea), in the other, which Atwood kept, she becomes a (possibly crazy) witch-like seer. In the final version, we find the most complete and uncompromising depiction, a fierce feminist gothic version of crucifixion.

Usually scholarly approaches to myth involve discussions of archetypes in terms of long narratives, but when literary sources, drafts and revisions are available, a fine-grained approach may shed light on the myth-making imagination. It is likely that Mary Webster's hanging came to have the force of a vivid, recurring dream for Atwood. Jung has demonstrated the riches of stories and myths that may be activated in a person's imaginative life, whether in fantasy, dream, or art. In cases where an archetypal figure is activated, such as a witch, great power may be released. Jung worked with over 80,000 dreams, and developed a nuanced method of staying focused on the content of the dream; he used "direct association" or amplification to assist the dreamer to explore all associations with particular images of the dream, returning to the image repeatedly (Craze 50-1). The image of Mary Webster as she hangs from the tree was something that Atwood returned to over and over in her rough drafts, in which she amplifies details and explores associations. Critics have noted Atwood's method of accretion which, like Jung's dream-work, gives us images and hints from the unconscious, the ultimate ground of subjectivity. Isabel Carrara Suarez describes Atwood's "gradual amplifications of the subject, a self which survives (and communicates) against all theoretical odds, against fragmentation, gaps and deconstruction" (230) while Sherrill Grace stresses Atwood's very gradual creation of an increasingly strong "autobiographical 'I'" out of multiplicity (202). Gradually these associations led her to produce a poem that has the force of a feminist archetype or myth.

Assuming it is artistically realized, an archetypal work of art usually makes a strong impact on audiences, and "Half-Hanged Mary" has done this. Like a rumor or witch, it has flown like an arrow into the wide-open and echoing spaces of popular culture, and has taken new forms unimagined by the author. Some readers respond to the political dimension and see the poem as a parallel to Arthur Miller's *Crucible*, possibly like that drama encoding a critique of U.S.-sponsored torture under George W. Bush. An example is the chamber opera by Seattle composer and musician Tom Baker entitled *The Gospel of the Red-Hot Stars*, which was composed in 1999 and performed by the Seattle Experimental Opera

(SEXO) in 2006. Its libretto features sections from Atwood's poem, interspersed with passages from the sermons and letters of Cotton Mather and *The Book of Psalms* (1612) compiled by Henry Ainsworth. This experimental yet melodic work is for clarinet, percussion, piano, violin, viola and cello, as well as a soprano (Mary), baritone (Mather), and chorus of Puritans. A CD was released in 2008, with clips available on the internet. On his website Baker points to the archetypal nature of the piece: "This opera explores the idea of the witch hunt...a topic that is as relevant to us today as it was to Mary in 1680" ("Tom Baker").

For other readers, it is not the witch hunt but the witch that has inspired passion – one feature of archetypal works is that they support different and even contradictory meanings. Mary has been embraced by Wiccans, neopagans, and those interested in the occult, who have posted "Half-Hanged Mary" on various websites. For example, Rosie Weaver reproduces it on a site called the "Lyceum of the Sacred Mother Isis" and recommends it for use at Samhain (Samhain). The traditional Gaelic festival of Samhain, celebrated at end of harvest around Halloween, was dedicated to the dead; it is now celebrated as one of four major Wiccan festivals.

Atwood is well aware of the explosive and mythological content of her daring poem, in which a hanged witch is elided with Jesus on the cross. Revisioning of myth has long been a central project for feminist writers and literary scholars, and Atwood's poem may be seen in this larger context. Landmarks in Anglo-American scholarship include Atwood's own 1972 *Survival*, which calls for a "jailbreak...and a "recreation," a new "way of seeing, experiencing, and imaging – or imagining – which we ourselves have helped to shape" (246). Carol Christ and Judith Plaskow's *Womanspirit Rising* (1979) takes as a premise that "the traditional religions of the West have betrayed women" (1) and warns against the dualistic thinking of the patriarchy. The authors call for "new feminist spiritual visions" and remind us that "the real danger lies not in deriving insight from the past but in dealing with the past on *its* terms" (11). In her essay "When We Dead Awaken–Writing as Re-vision" from her 1980 volume *On Lies, Secrets and Silence* Adrienne Rich finds "revision–the act of looking back" crucial for women's survival (35). Alicia Ostriker invites female personal revisioning of public myth as a way of reframing cultural and gender discourse in her influential 1981 essay, "The Thieves of Language–Female Poets and Revisionist Mythmaking" (316-7) reprinted in *The New Feminist Criticism* edited by Elaine Showalter (1985). Annis Pratt's *Archetypal Patterns in Women's Fiction* (1981) makes a similar point, with its sections leading like Diotima's ladder from

Self, through Society, then Love, Rebirth and Transformation. Pratt concludes that women's novels perform a transformative role similar to the Eleusinian, dying-god, and witchcraft rituals–"a restoration through remembering, crucial to our survival" (176) but male readers do not see this: "the new space indicated in women's fiction describes a world so alien to the patriarchy as to be invisible" and silent (177). In 1992 *The Feminist Companion to Mythology* edited by Carolyne Larrington offered feminist revisionings of religions in history and from cultures around the world.

Recent scholarship has identified the figure of the witch as a "crucial metaphor," a second-wave construct formed to "break through the silence and invisibility of female history and to elevate the notion of female alterity" in Justyna Sempruch's words. Charlotte Beyer has singled out Atwood's "Half-Hanged Mary" as a clear example of feminist revisionist mythology, while Colette Tennant has shown how Atwood has transformed the Gothic novel, with its abject female victim, to "free and empower" her readers ("Introduction 1-3). "Half-Hanged Mary" provides a similar, terrifying transformation that seems to turn the Christian crucifixion on its head; what Mary represents and will do after her ordeal remains open to question. Mary may be seen as an unstable, transgressive, postfeminist Gothic figure, like Zenia in Atwood's *The Robber Bride*, who raises questions about postfeminism as a reactionary backlash against feminism, and/or a new liberal politics (Tolan).

Mary Webster looked in vain for support from the women in her community, but feminist scholars since Ellen Moers have reaffirmed the importance of community for literary women. It is fitting to recognize a source for "Half-Hanged Mary" in Atwood's earliest community, her family. Most often, as in Atwood's family, the storytellers are older women. If a story has potential to cast a shadow over the family they may feel compelled to tell it selectively, perhaps suggesting that it's not true. This was the case with Atwood's maternal grandmother Killam, who told the story–including whether or not she was related to Mary—differently according to her moods (Sullivan 52). Yet is to her that we are indebted for telling Atwood about Mary Webster.

A handed-down story may allow individual family members to form an identity around the story as a construct, like crystals forming from a matrix, and a family legend may play a part in preserving a family's identity over generations. A strong role model such as Mary Webster may have inspired Atwood's mother's family of independent Killam women that included formidable Grandmother Killam, in addition to a writer and biographer, two academics, and Atwood's remarkable mother, bush homemaker extraordinaire. As Cooke comments, "Atwood has come by her disregard for gender roles honestly. It is in her blood (Cooke 47-9).

Notes

The author wishes to thank the University of Tampa for Dana and Delo grants that supported research, as well as Margaret Atwood for permission to quote from the drafts, and the helpful staff of the Thomas Fisher Library.

[1] This and subsequent references to "Half-Hanged Mary" are taken from Margaret Atwood's *Morning in the Burned House* (Boston and New York: Houghton Mifflin, 1995) pp. 58-69.

[2] The drafts in the Thomas Fisher Rare Book Library are from MS Coll 200, Box 163, Folder 8.

[3] Pentecost was a holy Jewish mid-summer harvest festival. After Jesus ascends to heaven, Peter and the other disciples return to Jerusalem. Devout Jewish pilgrims from many nations have come to the city to celebrate Pentecost. Acts 2:2-4 describes "cloven tongues like as of fire" that sat on each disciple as, "filled with the Holy Ghost," they begin to "speak in tongues," preaching in the languages of these Jews, languages they themselves do not know (Holy Bible. King James Version). Over 3,000 converts are made, and this episode begins the Christian movement according to Stephen M. Miller 363.

[4] Cotton Mather's Book VI, entitled "Thaumatographia Pneumatica: Relating the Wonders of the Invisible World in Preternatural Occurrences," consists of fourteen "examples" of witchcraft, culminating in the Salem witch trials. Mary Webster, whose name Mather omits, is marginalized in this account, which Mather presents as a story of the torments of witchcraft visited on the male victim. This is his usual practice in this account of the colony, which includes biographies of notable figures, most all of them male. No doubt he also did not want to reward witches by naming them and thereby conferring fame on them. Cotton Mather, *Magnalia Christi Americana* Book VI, Chapter VII. [No place: no date] 1702, p. 70 [pagination is irregular, and book pagination is not continuous; VI begins at page one]. Facsimile of 1702 volume is available online through books.google.com.

[5] The best source for Hutchinson's history is the scholarly Arno Press facsimile edition of 1972, clearly organized by date and preserving the original spelling and diction. The Mayo edition, while more accessible and modernized, lacks the flavor and omits some passages.

Works Cited

Acts. *Holy Bible*, King James Version. 1611. London.
Atwood, Margaret. *Alias Grace*. 1996. New York: Bantam.
—. *The Blind Assassin*. 2000. New York: Anchor.
—. *Cat's Eye*. 1988. Toronto: McClelland and Stewart.

—. "Circe/Mud Poems." *You Are Happy*. 1974. New York: Harper and Row. 45-70.

—. "Death by Landscape." 1991. *Wilderness Tips*. New York: Anchor.

—. *Good Bones and Simple Murders*. 1994. New York: Doubleday.

—. "Half-Hanged Mary." *Morning in the Burned House*. 1995. Boston: Houghton Mifflin. 58-69.

—. *The Handmaid's Tale*. 1985. Toronto: McClelland and Stewart.

—. *Interlunar*. 1984. Toronto: Oxford UP.

—. *Lady Oracle*. 1976. New York: Simon and Schuster.

—. Margaret Atwood Papers. MS Collection 200. "Half-Hanged Mary" Drafts: Box 163, Folder 8. Thomas Fisher Rare Book Library, University of Toronto Libraries, Toronto, Canada.

—. *Moral Disorder*. 2006. New York: Doubleday.

—. *Morning in the Burned House*. 1995. Boston: Houghton Mifflin.

—. *Negotiating with the Dead: A Writer on Writing*. 2002. New York: Anchor.

—. *Oryx and Crake*. 2003. New York: Doubleday.

—. *The Penelopiad*. 2005. Edinburgh, Scotland: Canongate.

—. *The Robber Bride*. 1993. Toronto: McClelland & Stewart.

—. *Surfacing*. New York: Popular Library, 1972.

—. *Survival: A Thematic Guide to Canadian Literature*. 1972. Toronto: Anansi.

—. *The Tent*. New York: Anchor/Random House, 2006.

—. "Witch Craft." Interview with Camille Peri, April 1989. *Mother Jones*. 28-33.

—. "Witches." *Second Words: Selected Critical Prose*. Toronto: Anansi, 1982. 329-333.

Baker, Tom. *The Gospel of the Red-Hot Stars*. 1999. Chamber Opera. Perf. Seattle Experimental Opera (SEXO), Seattle, April 2006.

Baker, Tom. *The Gospel of the Red-Hot Stars*. CD. Present Sounds Recordings (www.presentsounds.com) PS0801, 2008. Clips at: http://www.tombakercomposer.com/gospel.pdf.

Beyer, Charlotte. "Feminist Revisionist Mythology and Female Identity in Margaret Atwood's Recent Poetry. Sept 2000. *Literature & Theology* 14.3. 276-298.

Boyer, Paul and Stephen Nissenbaum. *Salem Possessed: The Social Origins of Witchcraft*. 1997. Cambridge, MA: Harvard UP.

Bruhn, Mark J. "Margaret Atwood's Lucy Poem: The Postmodern Art of Otherness in 'Death by Landscape'" Sept. 2004. *European Romantic Review* 15.3 449-461.

Carrara Suarez, Isabel. "'Yet I Speak, Yet I Exist': Affirmations of the Subject in Atwood's Short Stories." 1994. *Margaret Atwood: Writing and Subjectivity*. Ed. Colin Nicholson. New York: St. Martins P. 189-203. Quoted in Bruhn 451.

Christ, Carol P. and Judith Plaskow, eds. *Womanspirit Rising: A Feminist Reader in Religion*. 1979. San Francisco: HarperSanFrancisco.

Cooke, Nathalie. *Margaret Atwood: A Biography*. 1998. Toronto: ECW Press.

Craze, Richard. *The Dictionary of Dreams and Their Meanings*. 2003. London: Hermes House-Anness Publishing, 2008.

Grace, Sherrill. "Gender as Genre: Atwood's Autobiographical 'I'." 1994. Colin Nicholson, ed. *Margaret Atwood: Writing and Subjectivity*. NY: St. Martins P. 189-203.

"Hanging" Discovery Communications. *How Stuff Works*. http://people.howstuffworks.com/death-by-hanging.htm. retrieved July 15, 2008.

"Hanging," *Oxford English Dictionary* (O.E.D.) http://dictionary.oed.com/cgi/entry/50102310?querytype=word&query word=hang&first. Retrieved July 10, 2008.

Holy Bible. King James Version. London: 1611. Cleveland (OH): The World Publishing Company, n.d.

Hutchinson, Thomas. *The History of the Colony of Massachusets-Bay*. 1764, 1767, 1828. New York: Arno P (facsimile, Research Library of Colonial Americana): 1972.

Judd, Sylvester. *History of Hadley*. 1905. Springfield (MA): H. R. Hunting.

Karlsen, Carol F. *The Devil in the Shape of a Woman*. 1987. NY: Vintage.

Larrington, Cartolyne (Ed.). *The Feminist Companion to Mythology*. 1992. London: Pandora-HarperCollins.

Lawrence, D. H. *The Man Who Died*. 1929. NY: Vintage.

"Margaret Atwood: Queen of Canlit" 4 Nov. 1975. Radio interview no. 1 ("A Precocious and Creative Child") with Jody La Marsh. Audiorecording, Canadian Broadcasting Corporation (CBC) Digital Archives. archives.cbc.ca/arts_entertainment/literature/topics/1494

Marshall, Bridget M. "Mary (Reeve) Webster, the 'Witch' of Hadley." Lecture, Massachusetts Center for Renaissance Studies, Amherst, MA. May 2003. http://faculty.uml.edu/bmarshall/Mary520Webster.htm.

Mather, Cotton. *Magnalia Christi Americana*. n.d.:n.p., [1702.] pagination irregular [Book VI begins with page 1]. books.google.com. Rpt. NY: Russell & Russell. 1967.

Mayo, L.S. [Ed.] *The History of the Colony and Province of Massachusetts* 3 Vols. 1936. Cambridge, MA: Harvard UP. *Thomas Hutchinson, History of the Colony of Massachusetts Bay. 1764, 1767* and 1828.

Miller, Stephen M. *The Complete Guide to the Bible*. 2007. Uhrichsville (OH): Barbour Publishing.

Moers, Ellen. *Literary Women: The Great Writers*. 1963. New York: Doubleday Anchor.

Ostriker, Alicia. "The Thieves of Language–Female Poets and Revisionist Mythmaking." 1985. *The New Feminist Criticism*. Ed. Elaine Showalter. New York: Pantheon. 314-338.

Pratt, Annis. *Archetypal Patterns in Women's Fiction*. 1981. Bloomington: U Indiana P.

Rich, Adrienne. "When We Dead Awaken." 1980. *On Lies, Secrets and Silence*. New York: Norton.

"Samhain." Rosie Weaver, "Lyceum of the Sacred Mother Isis." Yahoo! 360blog360.yahoo.com/blog-7sv5090jdLu1vQ9uziVvhmzx2HM-?cq=1&tag=Samhain. Retrieved July 15, 2008.

Sempruch, Justyna. "Feminist Constructions of the "Witch" as a Fantasmatic Other." 2004. *Body & Society* 10.4. 113-133.

Tennant, Colette. *Reading the Gothic in Margaret Atwood's Novels*. 2003. Lewiston, NY; Queenston, Ontario; Lampeter, Ceredigion, Wales: The Edward Mellen Press.

Tolan, Fiona. "Sucking the Blood Out of Second Wave Feminism: Postfeminist Vampirism in Margaret Atwood's *The Robber Bride*." Nov. 2007. *Gothic Studies* 9.2. 45-57.

"Tom Baker" A/T Artist Trust. 2005 GAP Recipient Profiles. www.artisttrust.org/grants/recipient_profiles/GAP.

VanSpanckeren, Kathryn. "Atwood's Space Crone: Alchemical Vision and Revision in *Morning in the Burned House*. 2007. *Adventures of the Spirit*. Ed. Phyllis Perrakis. Columbus, OH: Ohio State UP.

CONTRIBUTORS

SARAH A. APPLETON has taught seminars on Margaret Atwood and other women writers. She is the author of *The Bitch Is Back: Wicked Women in Literature* (SIU, 2000) and, with Mica Howe, co-editor of *He Said, She Says: An RSVP to the Male Text* (Farleigh-Dickinson, 2000). Professor Appleton has also published essays on Margaret Atwood and many others in such journals as *Margaret Atwood Studies* and *African-American Review*. She is currently writing one book on the fates of male and female narcissists in literature and editing another collection of essays. She is currently teaching Literature at Old Dominion University.

SHULI BARZILAI teaches in the English Department of the Hebrew University of Jerusalem. Her fields of specialization include literary theory, psychoanalytic criticism, folktales and fairy tales, and contemporary women's writing. She is the author of *Lacan and the Matter of Origins*, co-editor of *Rereading Texts/Rethinking Critical Presuppositions*, and has published many articles in leading journals: *Canadian Literature, Marvels and Tales: Journal of Fairy-Tale Studies, New Literary History, PMLA, The Psychoanalytic Review, The Psychoanalytic Study of the Child, Signs: Journal of Women in Culture and Society*, and others. Professor Barzilai has been the recipient of the Canadian Government Faculty Research Award for her monograph on "Emily Carr, Margaret Atwood, and Landscape as Archive" (in *Word & Image*, Spring 2007) and of the Canadian Government Faculty Enrichment Award for her course on "Margaret Atwood: Literature and Ideology." She has twice won the annual Atwood Society Award for the best essay published on Atwood's writings. Among her administrative activities at the Hebrew University, she has served as chairperson of the English Department (1996-1998) and associate dean of the Faculty of Humanities (2002-2004).

SHANNON HENGEN teaches an undergraduate Margaret Atwood seminar and has co-published, most recently, a comprehensive bibliography of works by and about the author, with Ashley Thomson. She also teaches and publishes on theatre in Canada and the US, especially aboriginal, feminist, and testimonial. With a colleague in the English Department at

Laurentian University in Sudbury, Ontario, Canada, where she is a Professor, she initiated the annual Margaret Atwood Fundraising Dinner, a birthday party for the author whose proceeds fund local Atwood-worthy projects.

CORAL ANN HOWELLS is Professor Emerita of English and Canadian Literature, University of Reading, England, and Senior Tutor on MA in postcolonial studies at Institute of English Studies, University of London. She has lectured and published extensively on contemporary Canadian women's fiction in English. Her books include *Private and Fictional Words* (1987), *Margaret Atwood* (1997) *2nd edition* (2005), *Alice Munro* (1998) and *Contemporary Canadian Women's Fiction: Refiguring Identities* (2003). She is editor of the *Cambridge Companion to Margaret Atwood* (2006) and co-editor with Eva-Marie Kroller of the *Cambridge History of Canadian Literature* (forthcoming). She is a former President of the British Association of Canadian Studies and former associate editor of the *International Journal of Canadian Studies.*

CAROL OSBORNE, an Associate Professor in the English Department at Coastal Carolina University, received her Ph.D. from the University of Virginia in 1998. She has published articles on the recovery narrative (*Signs*), cultural studies (*Bridges* and *Popular Culture Review*), pedagogy (*Teacher Education Journal of South Carolina, Kentucky English Bulletin*, and *Arizona English Bulletin*), Virginia Woolf (forthcoming in *The CEA Critic*) and Margaret Atwood (*Frontiers* and *LIT: Literature, Interpretation, Theory*). In addition to teaching courses in Media and Culture and Popular Fiction, she is beginning a larger project on the images of teachers in contemporary film and literature. This spring, she was elected as chair of the College English Association's Women's Connection.

KAREN F. STEIN, Professor of English and Women's Studies at the University of Rhode Island, served as Director of the Women's Studies Program from 2004-2008. She was chosen as a Woman of the Year, 2007, by the Rhode Island Commission on Women. She has published articles about Margaret Atwood, Margaret Laurence, Adrienne Rich, Sylvia Plath, Alice Walker, and other North American women writers. She is the author of Margaret Atwood Revisited (Twayne 1999), and is currently writing a book on Toni Morrison. She is a Humanities Faculty Fellow at URI in 2008-2009.

THEODORE F. SHECKELS is Professor of English and Communication at Randolph-Macon College, Ashland, Virginia. He is the editor of *Margaret Atwood Studies*, and he is the author of *The Island Motif in the Fiction of L. M. Montgomery, Margaret Laurence, Margaret Atwood, and Other Canadian Women Novelists*, as well as book-length studies of South African literature, Australian film, and several political communication topics. He has published articles on Atwood and Montgomery in *The American Review of Canadian Studies* and in several collections. He has also published articles on political communication topics in journals such as *Communication Quarterly* and *Rhetoric & Public Affairs* and on Australian film and fiction in *Antipodes* and several collections. He is currently President of the American Association of Australian Literary Studies and is working on a book-length study of the political dimensions of Atwood's fiction.

KATHRYN VANSPANCKEREN has published widely on Atwood, and co-edited the first scholarly volume on her, *Margaret Atwood: Vision and Forms* (1988). She writes literary history (*Outline History of American Literature*, in print and online, 2006) as well as literary criticism (with a focus on oral tradition and mythology) and poetry, and has worked extensively abroad, especially in Asia. She is Professor of English at the University of Tampa.

SHARON R. WILSON is Professor of English and Women's Studies and teaches twentieth-century literature and other English, MIND, and Women's Studies classes at the University of Northern Colorado. She haspublished two books: *Margaret Atwood's Fairy-Tale Sexual Politics* (Jackson and Toronto: U Press of Mississippi and ECW, 1993) and *Myths and Fairy Tales in Contemporary Women's Fiction* (NY: Palgrave Macmillan, 2008) and edited two books: *Margaret Atwood's Textual Assassinations* (Columbus: Ohio SUP, 2003) and, with Thomas B. Friedman and Shannon Hengen, *Approaches to Teaching Atwood's* The Handmaid's Tale *and Other Works* (NY: MLA, 1996). .She has also published articles and book chapters, on Margaret Atwood, Doris Lessing, Rosario Ferre, Jean Rhys, Samuel Beckett, E.R. Eddison, and the film Citizen Kane. She was Founding President of the Margaret Atwood Society and is currently President of the Doris Lessing Society.

INDEX